ARTHRITIC JAPAN

EDWARD J. LINCOLN

ARTHRITIC JAPAN

The Slow Pace
of Economic Reform

BROOKINGS INSTITUTION PRESS
Washington, D.C.

Library of Congress Cataloging-in-Publication data

Lincoln, Edward J.
  Arthritic Japan : the slow pace of economic reform / Edward J. Lincoln
  p.   cm.
Includes bibliographical references and index.
  ISBN 0-8157-0074-1 (cloth) — ISBN 0-8157-0073-3 (pbk.)
  1. Japan—Economic conditions—1989- 2. Japan—Economic policy—1989- I. Title.
HC462.95 .L56 2001
338.951—dc21   2001004200

9 8 7 6 5 4 3 2 1

The paper used in this publication meets minimum requirements of the
American National Standard for Information Sciences—Permanence of Paper for
Printed Library Materials: ANSI Z39.48-1992.

Typeset in Minion

Composition by Oakland Street Publishing
Arlington, Virginia

Printed by R. R. Donnelley and Sons
Harrisonburg, Virginia

Foreword

A s ambassador to Japan at the end of the 1980s, I was involved in a dialogue between the United States and the Japanese government about structural economic reform. The Structural Impediments Initiative (SII), which was primarily concerned with features of the domestic economic system that impeded imports and led to Japan's chronic large current-account surplus, achieved some success on this issue. More broadly, however, the economic reform movement in Japan has accomplished relatively little in the decade since. Indeed, in many ways these years have been troubling, characterized by economic stagnation, a very large and growing nonperforming loan problem in the banking sector, and little positive outcome from expansionary fiscal policies and low interest rates.

Reform and change are difficult undertakings in any nation, but Americans have been puzzled by how slowly Japan has addressed its serious domestic economic problems. In *Arthritic Japan,* Lincoln examines this slowness and explains why the road toward reform will continue to be difficult.

In spring 2001 Morihiro Koizumi was elected prime minister of Japan on the basis of his outspoken emphasis of the need for economic reform, ranging from resolving the enormous bad loans of the banking system to reducing wasteful public works spending and making labor markets more flexible. Prime Minister Koizumi and the public enthusiasm for his message raise the hope that Japan will finally dig itself out of the economic slump of the 1990s. This book is therefore all the more timely and important. *Arthritic Japan* shows why, despite the encouraging rhetoric and the favorable opinion polls, Prime Minister Koizumi still faces a very tough job.

As outsiders, it is easy for Americans to think that the Japanese should or will make institutional changes that will lead their economic system toward convergence with that of the United States—lessening the role of government and making freely operating markets more robust. Lincoln argues, however, that the relatively weak economic growth of the past decade has not entirely erased Japanese people's belief in the virtues of their own variety of capitalism. Moreover, Lincoln describes the many vested interests with substantial stakes in the current system. Overcoming these interests was a daunting task during the SII talks, and it remains so today.

Lincoln also discusses the compatibility of the economic system and norms of social behavior in Japan. My own thirty-five years of involvement with Japan have taught me that while Americans and Japanese share many values and goals, they go about social and economic interaction in very different ways. This observation should be commonplace but it is worth repeating, given current American hubris in thinking that Japan must or will adopt American economic practices. Meaningful reforms are vitally necessary to underwrite Japan's economic recovery, but it is fully to be expected that the Japanese economic system will remain distinctive.

Arthritic Japan will be of great importance to American policymakers. Japan is the United States' largest economic partner and our key friend and ally in the Pacific. Japan's economic health matters both to our own economic welfare and to our efforts to maintain peace around the Pacific. Some Americans may take smug pleasure in seeing Japan stumble after having been worried about Japanese economic ascendancy through the 1980s. Such attitudes are wrong. A sputtering Japanese economy hurts the United States economically and complicates U.S. efforts to forge a true partnership on security issues. Therefore Lincoln argues that the U.S. government should continue discussions on the model of the SII talks, while cautioning that its leverage will be modest. At least the new Japanese mood of reform provides some hope that the hurdles analyzed in this book might be overcome to restore Japan to a path of healthy economic growth.

The author is grateful to Robert Angel, Richard Samuels, and Michael Smitka for many helpful comments on the first draft of this study. Excellent research support was provided by Kaori Lindeman, Mica Kreutz, and Angela Stavropoulos. Todd DeLelle verified the factual content. At the Brookings Institution Press, Janet Walker guided the publication process, Deborah Styles edited the manuscript, Joanne Lockard proofread the pages, and Enid Zafran compiled the index.

Funding was provided by the Japan-United States Friendship Commission, the Smith Richardson Foundation, the Freeman Foundation, the Henry Luce Foundation, the Carnegie Corporation of New York, and the Starr Foundation.

The views expressed in this book are solely those of the author and should not be ascribed to any of the persons or organizations acknowledged above, or to the trustees, officers, or other staff members of the Brookings Institution.

MICHAEL H. ARMACOST
President

August 2001
Washington, D.C.

Contents

1

Introduction

At the turn of the millennium, the Japanese economy remained mired in a pattern of stagnation that had continued since the early 1990s. As this disappointing condition dragged on, some in Japan called for systemic reform as a central part of policies to restore economic health. Beginning in 1994, the government formally pursued an agenda of broad economic deregulation, a specific package of deregulation measures for financial markets, and administrative reform. The private sector, prompted by substantial excess capacity in some industries, has also carried out some restructuring. The casual outside observer might easily infer that substantial—and beneficial—systemic change was well under way by 2001. Having recognized their problems, the Japanese appeared on the surface to be charging forward to embrace practical market-oriented solutions.

That appearance is deceiving. The central conclusion of this study is that fundamental aspects of the economic system are not changing very much. Like a person with arthritis, the existing Japanese economic system has lost much of its nimbleness; its joints have become creaky and painful. Japan has been taking aspirin for its arthritis—partially alleviating the pain temporarily. Something more radical—like hip replacement—would restore some mobility on a long-term basis, but so far this is not happening. As is the case with arthritis, surgery and more powerful medicine will not return Japan to its youth; Japan is a mature industrial economy with a diminishing population of working age, so even reform will not restore the high growth pattern of the past. Nevertheless, more radical treatment would produce better economic performance than in the past decade.

To be sure, the formal policy of deregulation has been proceeding since 1994 and has increased competition in some markets. However, the nature of corporate governance, corporate finance, labor markets, and the role of government in the economy continue without much alteration. This conclusion will elicit some protest among readers. As reform was getting under way in 1997, *Wall Street Journal* editor Paul Gigot opined that the Japanese economic system had failed, proving that the American style of capitalism is superior and that Japan would now reform to be more like the United States.[1] Then–prime minister Keizo Obuchi published an op-ed in the *New York Times* in 1999 stating that his nation recognized the need for extensive reform and was pushing boldly ahead.[2] Even some outside observers believe that radical changes are under way that will propel the economy back on to a stronger growth path.[3] Careful analysis, however, leads to the conclusion that such views are incorrect and provide misleading expectations for American businesses and policy makers.

This conclusion has important implications. The economic stagnation of the 1990s was largely macroeconomic in origin, stemming from the rise and collapse of real estate and stock prices. Such asset bubbles can occur—and have—in any economy. However, the macroeconomic origin of the problems obscures the fact that structural flaws in the existing system contributed to the creation of the asset bubble. Furthermore, the failure to reform through most of the 1990s complicated and delayed the recovery of the economy. Therefore, robust economic recovery depends on further systemic reform and not just macroeconomic fixes. Cyclical macroeconomic developments and simple downsizing in the corporate sector should produce an upturn in growth over the next few years. However, Japan's moving to a sustained higher growth path and avoiding renewed recession or financial crisis over the next decade requires more substantial reform. Given the nation's grim demographics—decreasing population and a rapid increase of retirees relative to workers—acceleration of economic and productivity growth is crucial. Without reform, the economy will not achieve this acceleration.

Failure to change will result in a stumbling economy bedeviled by recession and financial crisis, a scenario that would be worrisome for Japanese society, the rest of the region, and the United States. Should the economy sink into recession and crisis—a distinct possibility—Japanese households will obviously suffer. In a larger perspective, Japan will not contribute much to global growth by sucking in more imports and investment. Furthermore, the politics of a disgruntled population could easily lead toward a more nationalistic stance in foreign policy.

None of this need happen. More extensive reforms that enhance reliance on freely operating and transparent markets for goods, services, and finance, with a concomitant decline in interference by the government, would underwrite a brighter future. Economic growth under the best of circumstances will not be high, given the decline in the working age population and the financial burden of handling the exploding share of retirees. A more vibrant economy is crucial to surviving these problems without incurring a decline in standards of living. With reform Japan might manage a growth rate of two to two-and-a-half percent annually in the next decade; without reform annual growth of one percent or less will be Japan's fate.

The record of the past 130 years in Japan since modernization began is one of a pragmatic people who dramatically and successfully transformed their nation into one of the leading industrial nations of the world. That record does not guarantee success this time. The obstacles to reform have been formidable, and success itself may have made society less flexible.

Background

All across the globe nations have been getting government out of the market place over the past quarter century. The United States began a process of deregulation during the Carter administration in the 1970s, and the process continues today. In Britain, Prime Minister Margaret Thatcher presided over the privatization of nationalized industries during the 1980s. China has permitted private corporations and markets to operate. Experiments with communism, socialism, and regulation, undertaken in many countries in the name of fairness and promotion of economic growth, failed to meet expectations, leading to this massive reversal in policy. Behind the reversal lay a strong intellectual movement based on theory and on empirical research concerning the inefficiency and failures of government when it meddles excessively with markets.[4]

On the surface, Japan would appear to conform to this broad global trend, as deregulation, administrative reform, and industrial restructuring have been the hot topics of discussion for most of the past decade. The 1990s were certainly a troubling decade for Japanese society. After a half century of rapid economic growth and successful transformation to an advanced industrial nation, the economy stagnated and a mountain of bad debt weighed down the financial sector. Economic growth in the eight years from 1992 (when the slowdown began in earnest) through 1999 averaged a relatively weak annual rate of 1.0 percent.[5] The general stagnation was accompanied by the first real recessions since 1974, with negative growth in calendar 1998 and in two consecutive negative quarters in the second half of 1999. This economic performance was hardly the disaster that it might have seemed from the exaggerated adjectives used to describe it in the media; Japan remains one of the most affluent nations of the world, and unemployment remains modest. Nevertheless, after such a long period of unusually successful economic performance, stagnation and bad debts left many Japanese dismayed and bewildered by their problems.

The proximate cause of this poor economic performance lay in the speculative asset price bubble in the stock market and real estate market during the second half of the 1980s. In five years both equity prices and urban real estate tripled in value. When a worried government finally raised interest rates to constrain this situation, the party came to an end. The collapse of asset prices from the beginning of the 1990s, wiping out all the price gains since 1985, had a serious negative effect on the economy, as it would on any economy. Banks were also left with massive amounts of nonperforming loans, secured by real estate collateral that was shrinking in value. Both poor macroeconomic performance and the bad debt problem were exacerbated by poor decisions within the Japanese government. Fiscal stimulus was an on-again, off-again affair for much of the 1990s, while the bad debt problem was allowed to fester unchecked until near the end of the decade.

Arguably, any market economy could encounter the problems Japan experienced in the 1990s. Speculative bubbles, driven by excessively positive expectations about the future, can occur anywhere. Collapse of asset prices of the magnitude experienced in Japan would have a negative macroeconomic effect in any economy and would produce massive amounts of bad debt in the banking sector. The record of policy on the nonperforming loans of the savings and loan industry in the United States during the 1980s amply demonstrates that poor policymaking is certainly not unique to Japan.

Even though the problems of the 1990s can be traced directly to the rise and fall of asset prices, the problems lay deeper. Why did the speculative bubble occur? Why did the bad debt problem fester so long without any serious effort at resolution? Why did low interest rates in the 1990s fail to encourage new business investment? Answers to these questions lay in structural flaws in the organization and operation of the economy rather than in just an unfortunate but understandable speculative mistake in asset markets. The existing Japanese economic system is a modification of capitalism involving, among other things, a strong indirect government intervention in markets that may have been well suited to the needs of a rapidly industrializing nation. The problems of the 1990s, however, demonstrated that this model did not suit the needs of an advanced industrial nation.

Poor economic performance in the 1990s, therefore, sparked a vigorous domestic debate over the need for government administrative reform, economic deregulation, new accounting rules, and other changes to spur more efficient corporate behavior. Beginning in 1993, all of these topics gained serious attention in government and the private sector. Over the course of the rest of the decade, government moved forward with a plan for general economic deregulation, a "big bang" deregulation of the financial sector, and government administrative reform. Corporations also began to cope with their own problems—bad debts, excess labor, and excess facilities—by late in the decade. By 2001, talk of change was very much in the air.

Is Japan really forging ahead with major economic restructuring, institutional reform, and deregulation? This study argues that the surface image of change is misleading. That "something" is changing cannot be denied, and the pace of change has clearly increased from the stasis of the preceding two decades. Nevertheless, a number of important and interrelated factors impede the reform process, and the result will be an economy that continues to differ in organization and behavior from that of the United States and most other industrial nations. The government will remain more intrusive in the economy than is the case in the United States or some other nations that have been deregulating. Mistrust of markets will continue, leading to constraints on the scope of their function. Corporate governance will not change to put shareholders in the driver's seat, and corporations will temper their drive for efficiency by other social considerations. Corporations might succeed in raising their return on investment relative to the dismal performance of the 1990s, but remain less profitable than their western counterparts.

All economies change over time. Economic institutions, the laws enabling those institutions, and regulations affecting economic behavior are all artificial constructs created by political systems and can be changed at any time. New technologies, experience gained concerning the success or failure of existing institutions and rules, shifts in macroeconomic variables (such as private-sector savings and investment), as well as shifts among growing and shrinking sectors all produce changes in laws, regulations, institutions, and economic behavior. In this basic sense, Japan is no different from other countries. Many changes have occurred in the past fifty years; new industries have been created, and some sectors have been deregulated.

What other kinds of changes have occurred? In just the past decade the number of franchise outlets (an American corporate organizational innovation of the 1950s) has increased four-fold, with convenience stores and fast food outlets popping up everywhere.[6] Franchised convenience stores have morphed into a distinctly Japanese format, providing a set of goods and services quite different from their American counterparts. Cellular telephones have come into widespread use since substantial deregulation occurred in 1994; the number of cellular telephone subscribers rose explosively from 2.1 million to 60 million in the seven years from 1993 to 2000.[7]

These rather dramatic changes in the context of a largely stagnant economy certainly suggest that economic vitality was not entirely lost. However, such examples do not offset the harsh reality of a stagnant economy and the need for broader reform. The fact is, Japan does not have enough examples of such successes to drive the economy back to health and needs further systemic change to provide a more receptive environment for them.

The Japanese are well aware of the trends in the rest of the world. They have been deeply interested in deregulation in the United States and in changes in other countries that have reduced the role of government in the economy. Much of the call for change at home has been driven by knowledge of these trends abroad. The continuing revolution in information technology and its explosive deployment in the United States have attracted particular attention. In many aspects of information technology the Japanese economy lags behind that of the United States, but it is moving forward quite rapidly (and leads in some areas, such as wireless communication). Japanese society is rich in technical expertise and generally has a pragmatic approach to new industries and technologies that will enable the economy to adjust reasonably quickly to the information revolution. Concern over lagging behind the Americans provides a powerful incentive to both corporations and government to push development of this sector of the economy.

However, this technical strength and the ability to respond to foreign trends should be kept in perspective. The Japanese economy has coped quite successfully in the past century with a constantly changing economic *structure*. Industries have emerged, grown, and died. A massive movement of people out of agriculture into modern industry occurred in the past century, and it was accompanied by a wholesale relocation of population from rural to urban areas. The textile industry, once a dominant exporter, has shrunk to insignificance. Much of the current news in Japan relates to restructuring—bloated corporations shedding capital and workers, banks recouping from disastrous amounts of nonperforming loans, and new industries taking off. *Structural* change is quite different from *systemic* change, however, and the big question is not restructuring, but systemic change. Are the basic rules and practices that constitute the architecture for economic behavior in Japan undergoing major reform? No. Is the economy moving toward greater reliance on freely operating markets for goods, services, labor, and corporate control? Not much. Will the Japanese economic system continue to appear distinctive when compared with that of the United States or other advanced industrial economies? Yes.

A decade from now the Japanese economic model or system will not have converged on the practices of the United States or other industrial nations. Why Japan will not adopt radical reforms and embrace a more market-oriented economic architecture is the central topic of this study. Japan's economic system will be somewhat *different* a decade from now, but it will remain *distinctive*. Government will remain intrusive in a number of areas of the economy, driven by a continuing belief that its guidance remains necessary for prosperity and to ensure the competitiveness of Japanese firms vis-à-vis their American and European competitors. Financial markets, labor markets, and corporate governance will experience some reform, without converging on American practices. Deregulation will unleash new competition in some markets, to the benefit of consumers, but the tendency even in those markets to temper competition with informal cartel arrangements will remain strong.

The terms American model and American standards have become quite faddish and are thrown around loosely in Japan. One could argue that Japan is not so different from European countries, but when people discuss reform that would move the Japanese economy to greater reliance on markets, it is the contemporary American system that they usually have in mind as a model. This study does not attempt to define an American economic model; it is, therefore, occasionally guilty of using the term rather loosely as shorthand for a system that relies heavily on markets for goods, services, and corporate control. Keep in mind that American institutions and behavior have also changed considerably in the past several decades, and they continue to change. Economic regulation in the United States has lessened or been eliminated in some industries, including transportation and telecommunications, but the economy is hardly a completely unregulated laissez-faire model today. American venture capital, and equity markets in general, play a larger role today than they did three or four decades ago. Shareholders— especially mutual funds and pension funds—exercise strong roles in corporate governance, representing another change from the past. Government plays less of a role than in the past in overt economic regulation, but retains a critical function in establishing ground rules for markets and monitoring them to combat fraudulent or other undesirable behavior. In summary, though, the contemporary American economic model relies more on markets with relatively freely determined interaction of demand and supply for exchanging goods, services, labor, corporate finance, and corporate control than is the case in Japan or even in most other advanced industrial nations.

The Japanese economy will not come to resemble the more market-dominated American model over the next decade. The comforting notion that it might, as expressed by Paul Gigot or Prime Minister Obuchi, is a misinterpretation of what is occurring in Japan. Despite the evident need for systemic reform, a set of powerful interconnected factors implies that change will not produce a clone of the American economy. The five main inhibiting factors emphasized in this study are:

—belief in the value of the existing system, which has been shaken but hardly destroyed by the events of the 1990s;

—the interconnected nature of the distinctive features of the existing system, implying that tampering with a few pieces of the system is not sufficient to change the whole;

—strong vested interests in the current system that may include a majority of the population;

—conformity of the system to broader social norms and expectations, representing values that society is loath to lose; and

—a weak process of deregulation and administrative reform, driven by the bureaucracy itself rather than by broad political pressures from voters, coupled with a corporate restructuring that emphasizes downsizing more than reforming the nature of the corporation.

These five factors are mutually reinforcing, and together they will shape the nature of change. A decade from now, the organization and behavior of the Japanese economy will certainly be different from that of today; as formidable as they may appear, these factors will not totally block systemic change. The resulting economic framework will still look quite distinctive from an American viewpoint, however.

The nature of change matters, for both Japan and the United States. For Japan, if the restraining factors identified here are too powerful, then very little systemic change will occur, and the economy will perform poorly for many more years. Renewed recession, dangerously rising levels of government debt, and generalized failure to meet the financial needs of a burgeoning retired population are clear possibilities. The Japanese public will be less well off than they could be.

This outcome matters to the United States and the rest of the world. With the Japanese economy just muddling through, it will not contribute much to regional or global growth, and U.S. officials will have to cope with the international consequences of recurring financial problems in Japan. Meanwhile, Japan is unlikely to adopt a more liberal stance on bilateral or multilateral trade negotiations because weakness at home will result in a continued defensive trade posture. Even security policy could be affected, including both the specifics of the bilateral alliance and Japan's broader participation in regional or global security issues. Self-absorption with domestic economic problems will leave Japan in a marginal role in security discussions among the major powers. In general, Japan's failure to produce more vigorous economic reform creates a series of challenges and problems for American policy.

Outline

Chapter 2 begins this study by defining the starting point: what distinguishes the organization and behavior of the Japanese economy from that of the United States or other industrial nations? Over the past half century, Japan adopted neither the American pattern of extensive use of independent regulatory agencies nor the European pattern of nationalized industries and extensive welfare. What Japan did adopt was:

—reliance on banking (rather than stock or bond markets) to move funds between savers and investors and, as a corollary, broad collections of firms (horizontal *keiretsu*) associated with the major banks from which they borrowed;

—a system of corporate governance that downgraded the role of shareholders in favor of banks and other stakeholders;

—long-term contracting in the corporate sector (vertical *keiretsu*);

—reduced price competition in the marketplace; and

—a heavy dose of indirect government interference in the operation of the economy (often called industrial policy).

When this system was working well—as it did during the first four decades after the Second World War—people felt strongly that they had created a kinder and gentler version of capitalism than that preached by neoclassical economists or practiced in the United States. Economic growth was high, unemployment was low, and rapid gains in personal income were broadly distributed through society.

Chapter 2 also articulates the first two problems for systemic reform. First, the Japanese have been proud of their system for the past several decades. Why tamper with a system that provided high growth, rising incomes, and low unemployment? The economic malaise of the 1990s certainly shook belief in the efficacy of the system, but hardly destroyed it. Many also see other benefits that they believe flow from their system—relatively low income disparities between rich and poor (in comparison with the United States) and lower crime levels than in other countries. Some in society believe the system is truly broken and must be radically reformed. Most in society, though, seem to be far less certain that the system is broken and are reluctant to abandon a model they firmly believed superior to their perception of American capitalism.

Second, the distinctive economic system involves a set of interlocking features. Changing or tinkering with one individual feature of the system without simultaneously addressing most or all of the others is not likely to be successful. At best, the piecemeal approach takes time, as alteration of one feature of the economy creates incompatibilities elsewhere, leading to further changes. At worst, the incompatibility that would result from tinkering with one piece of the economy would cause the proposed changes to be watered down or the resulting effect of the change to be minimized.

Chapter 3 explores why pressures have mounted for change and why reform should occur. As noted above, the main source of pressure for reform in the 1990s was the collapse of the asset bubble and the ensuing economic stagnation and nonperforming loan problems. In addition, evidence mounted concerning inefficiency or failure in some aspects of the economic system. Why, for example, has Japan needed the highest ratio of investment to gross domestic product (GDP) among OECD nations to sustain a virtually stagnant economy? Some flaw in the system led to continued high levels of investment in both private and public capital despite low rates of return or lack of social need.

Chapter 4 considers vested interests. Many groups in Japan have benefited from the existing configuration of the economic system and are very reluctant to embrace change. Farmers and those living in rural areas more generally, workers with lifetime employee guarantees, bureaucrats, construction firms and their employees, workers in small firms, and homeowners all benefit from the current system. Although each of these groups is a minority of society, and each feels particularly protective about only those parts of the system that benefits itself, in total these groups represent a majority of the population. The extensive nature of vested interests provides much of the explanation of why the democratic political process has not driven economic reform more vigorously.

Chapter 5 explores the compatibility of the economic system with broader social norms. Japanese society differs in many respects from that of the United States or the West more generally. It would be surprising if those differences did *not* affect economic institutions and behavior. In broad terms, those differences include a strong group orientation, a sense of hierarchy, reliance on personal relationships, avoidance of uncertainty, emphasis on facades, and preference for indirectness. The features of society are compatible with—and have helped shape—all of the distinctive aspects of the economic system. Change in social behavioral norms certainly occurs over time, and Japanese society today is rather different in some respects from fifty years ago. These changes generally occur slowly, however. As long as Japanese social behavior is visibly different from that in the United States, convergence on an American economic model is unlikely. Alteration of the existing overarching architecture for the economy is certainly possible, but whatever those changes might be, they must also be broadly consistent with social expectations.

Chapter 6 concludes the discussion of why reform will remain relatively weak by looking at the process of reform itself. At the governmental level, deregulation and administrative reform have been squarely in the hands of the bureaucracy itself. Unlike the United States or other countries where political dissatisfaction led to electoral outcomes that brought deregulation and a reduction in the economic function of government, in Japan the bureaucrats themselves have been granted the mandate for change. This is a rather weak means to achieve real reform. Deregulation has involved a bean-counting game, with bureaucrats emphasizing the number of regulations that have been eliminated or altered. Little attention has been given to reshaping the overall regulatory framework for particular industries. Meanwhile, administrative reform yielded a major reshuffling of the bureaucracy—moving pieces of various ministries around within the ministerial structure—without addressing the larger issue of the role of government in the economy. While the government has been touting deregulation and administrative reform, its involvement in the economy has actually expanded, and its schemes to promote various industries continue unabated.

In the private sector, structural change has been driven by stark necessity. Banks were burdened by massive amounts of bad debt, life insurance companies failed to earn promised returns for their policy holders, foreign financial institutions injected new patterns of behavior into the market, and many nonfinancial corporations experienced financial losses and increasingly stiff global competition. In the 1980s the high-flying economy caused some outside observers to believe that Japanese firms could defy normal economic rules—since they aggressively expanded market share without regard to profits. In any economic system, though, the bottom line matters. Japanese firms could get away with low profits for years, but a firm hemorrhaging money eventually either restructures or goes out of business. By the late 1990s parts of the private sector faced this dire constraint, and some restructuring was moving forward. The resulting restructuring has focused on the immediate causes of poor financial performance, however, without much alteration of fundamental aspects of corporate governance. Cutting employment through attrition and early retirements, for example, does not alter the underlying practice of lifetime employment. Nor have firms exhibited much alteration in the relationship between managers and shareholders. This approach should not be a surprise. The kind of financial pressures faced by Japanese firms lead necessarily to the restructuring that is occurring; any firm that wants to survive must cut costs. These pressures do not, however, lead logically to fundamental reform of corporate governance. What is occurring is more of a one-time slimming of bloated corporate structure, a delayed but normal response to stagnation and recession.

Thus neither government nor the private sector is embracing fundamental reform as enthusiastically as is commonly portrayed in the press. Unless or until the public exerts its democratic voice, more radical changes are unlikely. Optimists can point to the increasing integration of Japanese financial markets with the outside world, brought about by the recent inroads made by American financial institutions in Japan. Bringing with them western assumptions about corporate governance, these institutions are not shy about pressing firms in which they invest for changes in corporate behavior. Nevertheless, it remains unlikely that foreign financial institutions will be sufficiently powerful within the domestic Japanese market to bring about major change in corporate governance.

Chapter 7 concludes the study by asking what the weak process of reform means for bilateral relations. The starting point is simply to recognize that reform is not proceeding vigorously, that the organization of Japan's economy will remain distinctive, and that economic performance is likely to be disappointing. American government and corporate planning should begin from this premise. Adversity actually creates opportunities for some foreign firms, but for government the implications are more sobering.

To begin with, is there anything the U.S. government can do to nudge Japan toward reform and a return to economic health? American interests clearly lie with a healthy, growing Japanese economy. Bilateral discussion of how to restore health and growth should certainly be on the U.S. government's agenda, even though American options in encouraging a reform process that underwrites a healthy economic recovery are actually quite limited. Because Japan has a very large economy and is a large net creditor, opportunities to nudge it in desired directions are few. Discussion and advice are always desirable and should be pursued, but there is no guarantee that advice will be heeded. No official should enter into this process with unrealistic expectations about what American government policy can do to help fix the Japanese economic system.

On systemic economic reform issues, American trade policy will play a useful if modest role. Deregulation is central to many trade issues. Because foreign firms play a larger role in the Japanese economy as the result of negotiations that make the market more open, they can promote systemic reform from within. Foreign financial institutions, for example, have brought with them important financial innovations that help change broader corporate behavior. Even this possibility, however, should be kept in perspective. Foreign financial institutions play a larger role than they used to, but they are not important enough to bring major change on their own in either the nature of financial markets or broader corporate behavior. They will have an effect at the margin, but not much more. Still financial institutions and other foreign firms will have an increasing presence, which will help the reform process along, and that prospect should persuade the U.S. government to continue pursuing an active trade agenda with Japan.

More broadly, the Japanese will make economic reform decisions on their own, and U.S. government input will have relatively little influence. Americans are constantly asked for advice about what Japan should do, and supplying verbal pressure (known as *gaiatsu*, or outside pressure) has been a staple of bilateral relations since the time of Commodore Perry. In some cases, there may be opportunities, through government or even nongovernment settings, to supply *gaiatsu* that feeds into existing domestic pressures for change. However, most of Japan's economic problems are internal and for the most part will be worked out internally, without reliance on American or other foreign input. Japanese officials may seek advice and then ignore it. They may even choose to avoid bilateral arrangements in which the U.S. government can apply pressure; *gaiatsu* has become a pejorative term for many younger Japanese government officials who resent

American interference in what they deem to be domestic issues. There is no harm in seeking ways to advise Japan on what to do, but U.S. government policy must recognize that these issues are domestic, and that American influence will be small.

Even though *gaiatsu* may have little impact in general, times of approaching crisis (as when the Japanese banking industry was sliding toward wholesale collapse in 1998) justify strong pressure because of the potential international consequences of real economic crisis in Japan. Stronger public statements by senior administration officials at least get high visibility in the Japanese media, providing some input into policymaking. When necessary, that less diplomatic public pressure should be applied. American government officials should be aware that such crises will remain likely, given the weakness of reform, and they should monitor Japanese developments closely for warning of approaching problems.

The conclusion of this study is that Japan is unlikely to do more than muddle through even with American advice and occasional stronger pressure. Reform will probably be sufficient to prevent a serious collapse of the economy, but the most probable outcome is a weak growth rate, of zero to one percent, with recurring financial problems. In this scenario, the Japanese polity will remain absorbed with its domestic economic dilemmas for some time to come. Rather than thinking expansively about leadership on a global stage, Japanese political and bureaucratic leaders will focus heavily on domestic problems, and their behavior on international issues will reflect their domestic orientation. On economic issues, for example, the Japanese government will not be a progressive force within the World Trade Organization (WTO) and will work to undercut market-oriented policy proposals at the International Monetary Fund (IMF). The nation's relatively weak economic performance and bungling of reforms undermines the confidence of Japanese leaders on the global stage, and it undercuts the willingness of other nations to consider seriously international policy proposals from Japan. Even if American pressure were to lead to formal relaxation of the strict constraints on Japanese participation in peace-keeping operations (to include, for example, armed participation in collective security actions like the Gulf War), this lack of confidence and the predominance of domestic self-absorption would be likely to leave Japan a relatively passive actor in multilateral deliberations during security crises and a reluctant participant in policies that have been determined by others.

Continued weak economic performance could also affect the bilateral security relationship. A government concerned about the size of its rising debt levels will be less willing to increase budget expenditures related to American military bases. Furthermore, a Japan that feels less certain about its own economic performance could possibly adopt a more nationalistic approach to the rest of the world. Unable or unwilling to conform more closely to an American-style, market-based economic model, Japanese leaders might feel the time has come to distance the nation in other ways as well, pursuing a more independent or Asia-centric diplomatic and defense posture. Nationalistic attitudes and a desire for greater distance from the United States would be exacerbated should limited reform lead to a stumbling economy and financial crises that increase resentment of a more successful U.S. economy.

Could all of these predictions turn out to be wrong? One certainly hopes so. However, the probability of accelerated and more thorough economic reform that revitalizes the economy and yields a more confident global player is small. In fact, the downside risk—in which failure to reform creates worse problems—is higher than this upside possibility. While one may hope for a more optimistic outcome and for direct American policy encouraging Japan to move in that direction, the presumption should be that Japan's performance will be disappointing.

2

The Postwar Economic System

Japan is a capitalist nation in the most basic sense of the word. That is, the means of production for goods and services are largely in the hands of the private sector rather than the government, and economic transactions take place mainly through private markets and contracts rather than through the government. In many important ways, however, the organization and operation of the economy differs from that of the United States. This observation should not be controversial since European and other capitalist countries all have distinctive features that affect economic structure and behavior. Japan never moved as far as European countries toward nationalizing industry, imposing outright price controls (except in wartime and during the immediate postwar period), or creating a generous social welfare net. Nevertheless, the overall architecture of the economic system—rules, regulations, basic corporate governance, corporate behavior patterns, and the role of the government—differs rather significantly from that of the United States.

Whether these distinctive features of the economy caused high economic growth in the first forty years after the Second World War is a more difficult question, since the counterfactual experiment is not possible (that is, what would economic growth have been had the institutional setting been different). Nevertheless, a reasonable case can be made that the institutional, regulatory, and behavioral characteristics of the economy were at least consistent with high growth. Since the economy grew, obviously this basic framework did not seriously inhibit growth and industrialization (and it is difficult to imagine Japan growing even faster than it did). This record of past success

Table 2-1. *Distinctive Elements of the Japanese Economic Model*

Feature	Presumed advantage
Bank-centered financial system	Permits a longer-term corporate planning horizon (in contrast to the short-term view of American corporations influenced by impatient shareholders)
Corporate governance with weak shareholders and boards; strong managerial control and bank oversight	Places corporate control in hands of expert managers rather than nonexpert, impatient shareholders; bank oversight substitutes for shareholders
Vertical *keiretsu*	Cost benefits flow from long-term contracting, better quality control, and smaller inventories
Reduced price competition	Increases profits and reduces their fluctuation over the business cycle; reduces corporate failure and the attendant waste of investment resources
Internal labor markets and "lifetime employment"	Enhances productivity through greater employee loyalty and longer-term development of firm-specific skills
Industrial policy	Produces greater efficiency and higher economic growth as government guides the allocation of resources to the best use and reduces duplicate or excess investment

actually becomes one of the inhibiting factors in reform—why change a system that many felt was instrumental in producing affluence? What matters for this study, though, is not the impact of those features in the past but their existence as a distinctive set that has become the focal point of debate over reform in the past decade.

This chapter elucidates the principal features of the economy that have differed substantially from the U.S. economic example. These features are:

—a strong bias toward banking in the financial system and the associated groups of firms centered on particular banks known as horizontal *keiretsu*;

—the nature of corporate governance;

—the prevalence of long-term contracting among firms, popularly known as vertical *keiretsu*;

—limited price competition among firms;

—labor market practices; and

—a strong role for government in influencing the allocation of resources in the economy (known as industrial policy). Taken together, these features of the Japanese economy have created a system whose operation is quite different from the U.S. model. Furthermore, they operate in an interlocking or mutually dependent manner. Table 2-1 catalogs these distinctive features, with brief comments on the supposed advantages accruing from each.

The elements evolved over time, mostly from the early 1930s through the early to mid-1950s. They are not the result of a coordinated or comprehensive plan to deliberately create a specific economic architecture in the postwar period, as Great Britain did. The government pushed a number of changes as part of the emerging war effort in the 1930s, when centralization, government control, and forced harmonization in the economy were strong themes. The overall notion of strong government intervention in a managed economy had intellectual support from influential economists like Hiromi Arisawa, a leading academic economist and an active participant in government policy planning from the 1930s through the 1940s. The postwar system evolved well beyond wartime controls, dismantling some controls and modifying others. Themes such as state intervention, priority sectors, and managed capitalism (with their intellectual lineage from Arisawa and others) pervaded the postwar system, but the overall nature of the economic system resulted from vigorous debates among competing ideologies, individual government policy decisions, and some reforms imposed by the Allied Occupation. By the mid-1950s this stream of independent policy developments had modified the wartime economic system into what people think of as the "Japanese economic model."[1]

Further changes have occurred since the 1950s; the system has been evolving slowly. Many of the formal or explicit tools available to government to pursue industrial policy were dismantled in the decade following the mid-1960s. Relations between banks and nonfinancial corporations weakened as the capital shortages of the earlier postwar years eased in the 1970s. Slow financial deregulation beginning in the 1970s enabled firms to pursue other sources of funding.

Even with evolution, a number of the basic features of the system remained largely intact going into the 1990s. The overall architecture of the economic system remained quite distinctive in comparison with that of the United States or other mature industrial economies. Labor practices such as lifetime employment remained different from those in the United States or Europe. Financial resources continued to be mediated through the banking system more than in the United States. Shareholders continued to have a very weak voice in corporate governance. Long-term subcontracting ties remained a core part of corporate behavior. Informal cartels and other anti-competitive behavior remained endemic. While government lost some of its explicit tools for industrial policy, it certainly continued to pursue an active role in guiding the economy.

Understanding this set of distinctive features is the starting point for analyzing the pressures for change in the 1990s and beyond. Debate and action on structural reform in the 1990s has been about how to modify or even jettison these distinctive features of the economy. This chapter sets the stage for evaluating change by establishing the base line—the nature of the distinctive features of the economy and their status in the 1990s. This base line provides two important keys to understanding why reform has not proceeded more vigorously. Each of these features evolved because of a belief among government officials or corporate executives that it would be beneficial to the economy. Getting people to shed their beliefs or commitment to these aspects of the system is not an easy task after decades of believing in their efficacy. Second, the interlocking nature of the distinctive features of the economy implies that piecemeal tinkering with a subset of the system will not result in effective reform.

Banking Bias and Horizontal *Keiretsu*

Normally a financial system comprises a variety of direct and indirect methods of connecting savers to those engaged in real investment—banking, stock markets, bond markets, and other forms of corporate financial paper. Because of variations in risk and expected return, a robust economic system involves a mixture of all of these financing methods. In Japan, however, from the early 1950s through the 1980s, the government deliberately skewed the system heavily toward banking (and secondarily toward insurance companies).

Banking

The emphasis on banking was perceived as having several benefits for the Japanese economy. Japanese have often looked askance at the stock market–dominated system of the United States, believing that it has forced American firms into an excessively short-term focus in order to satisfy shareholders. Banks were presumed to provide Japanese firms with more patient capital; as long as a firm could service its loans, banks were content even if investments required a long time to become profitable. The recent American willingness to pour equity capital into start-up Internet firms that have shown consistent losses might turn this argument on its head, but for decades in the past the advantages of patient bank capital were a staple in Japanese arguments in favor of their system.

Banking provided another critically important advantage in the earlier postwar period—enhancing government influence in the economy. Financial markets can be a problem for a government desiring to guide industrialization. In bond and stock markets, private institutions make decisions on creditworthiness in deciding to underwrite bond or stock issues, and myriads of individual actors then determine the price of those instruments in the market based on their individual assessment of probable returns and risk. The large numbers of these investors and their constant demand for believable assessments from issuing corporations, investment banks, and rating agencies make bond and stock markets difficult for government to manipulate. In contrast, banking and insurance are much easier for government to influence because the number of major institutions is relatively small and transactions with borrowers nontransparent. The Japanese government, therefore, deliberately chose to emasculate the stock and bond markets to favor intermediation through banks and insurance companies.

Establishing very stiff eligibility requirements for issuing corporate bonds and granting discretionary authority for approval of such issues to the Ministry of Finance (MOF) easily suppressed the bond market. Thus the private market model for determining eligibility and interest rates for bonds that exists in the United States was replaced with an explicitly government-dominated model. Until the 1980s this effectively permitted the MOF to allow only a handful of favored large corporations, with the government-owned telephone company, Nippon Telegraph and Telephone (NTT), principal among them, to issue bonds. Financial deregulation from the mid-1970s through the 1990s presumably opened new opportunities for corporations to raise funds through bond markets, but relatively little shift in that direction occurred.

The stock market was trivialized by the elimination of its role as a mechanism of corporate control. The evolution of rules and custom (such as mutual long-term holding of shares and issuance of new shares to existing shareholders at a low par value) that separated stock ownership from contestable corporate control reduced the stock market to a purely speculative game. Corporate managers were not influenced by movements in share prices since a falling price did not expose firms to takeover bids or pressure from existing shareholders. Shareholders could not express discontent through the board of directors since these comprised mainly the firm's managers, nor was executive compensation tied to stock performance. The stock market was further controlled by a tax on transactions and MOF approval of high, fixed commissions by stockbrokers.

Banking and insurance were controlled through a regulatory game.[2] Because it completely controlled interest rates for both deposits and loans, design and pricing of insurance products, and entry into both industries, the Ministry of Finance was in a position to virtually guarantee profits for banks and insurance companies. Banks were sorted by the government into narrow niches—short-term lending versus long-term, nationwide banks versus regionally and locally constrained banks, and banks lending to large corporations versus those for small business. Insurance firms were separated into discrete life and nonlife (property and casualty) categories. New entry into banking and insurance was nonexistent in the postwar period. In exchange for protected and profitable market niches, banks and insurance companies generally heeded formal and informal signals from the government about the allocation of credit.

This structure gave government a strong but indirect role in credit allocation. Control was weaker than in socialist countries, where government ministries or government-run financial institutions allocate credit (although the Japanese government does have some financial institutions of its own whose behavior has been part of the signaling process). Nonetheless, the emasculation of market-determined finance and the protection—through regulation—of cartel behavior in banking and insurance certainly gave government a far larger voice in influencing credit allocation than is the case in the United States.

This stylistic picture is undoubtedly overdrawn; banks certainly made their own decisions on many loans and did not always slavishly follow advice or signals. Banks could also cheat on loan interest rate limits by requiring borrowers to make compensating deposits, but government tolerance of this practice only increased the profits of the banks by widening the spread between low deposit rates and loan rates. Certainly the MOF had regulatory goals other than guiding the economy, including preventing a repetition of the extensive bank failures that occurred in the 1920s. Nevertheless, there can be no doubt that the government manipulated a highly regulated and profitable banking and insurance sector in order to influence the allocation of credit.

A principal feature of households' savings behavior, as a consequence of the government's emphasis on banks, has been to rely on demand and savings deposits. Households can save in a variety of ways—by holding cash, demand and savings deposits at banks, equity shares, bonds, or insurance policies and pension reserves. American and Japanese household financial portfolios differ substantially, as shown in table 2-2.

Table 2-2. *Household Financial Portfolios, Japan and the United States, Selected Years, 1962–2000*[a]

Percent

Category	Japan[b]					United States		
	1962	1977	1989	1996	2000	1970	1990	1997
Bank total	66.4	73.51	56.1	61.8	56.6	28.5	31.7	14.2
Currency and demand deposits	(20.3)	(15.6)	(10.3)	(10.0)	(11.5)	(6.6)	(5.4)	(1.9)
Time and saving deposits	(46.1)	(57.9)	(45.8)	(51.8)	(45.1)	(21.9)	(26.3)	(12.3)
Insurance and pension reserves	10.1	13.2	21.5	25.4	28.5	19.5	35.9	36.0
Stocks and bonds	23.4	13.3	22.4	12.8	15.0	52.0	32.4	49.8

Sources: Japanese data—1962 data, Bank of Japan, *Economic Statistics Annual* 1963, pp. 17–18; 1977 and 1996 data from Edward J. Lincoln, "Japan's Financial Problems," *Brookings Papers on Economic Activity* 1998:2, p. 30; 1989 data, Bank of Japan, *Economic Statistics Annual* 1990, pp. 209–10; 2000 data are from "Flow of Funds Account of 1st Quarter 2000," www.boj.or.jp/en/siryo/siryo_f.htm; zip file sj0003.zip. U.S. data—U.S. Census Bureau, *Statistical Abstract of the United States: 1998*, p. 513.

a. Based on flow-of-funds accounts for each country. U.S. data include one item not found in the Japanese data—proprietors' equity, excluded from this table for the sake of comparison.

b. Japanese data for 1962 are end of December; all others for Japan are end of March.

These wide differences have persisted despite some change in household behavior over time in both societies. In 1962 Japanese households held 66 percent of their financial portfolios in the form of currency and bank deposits, a ratio that actually rose to 74 percent by 1977 before slowly dropping to 57 percent by 2000. Offsetting this gradual decline, life insurance and pension reserves have increased as part of household savings, reflecting the aging of the baby boom generation as well as the creation and expansion of funded pension plans at Japanese corporations. Corporate pension plans were virtually nonexistent before 1980; companies instead provided lump-sum retirement bonuses out of current operating expenses.

The most interesting aspect of Japanese portfolios is the role of stocks and bonds. In 1962 Japanese households had 23 percent of their financial assets in the form of equities and bonds, but this portion fell to 13 percent by 1977. The rise of the stock market in the second half of the 1980s brought this ratio back up to 22 percent, but it had subsided once again to just under 13 percent by 1996. Low interest rates on bank deposits in the late 1990s and the advent of new mutual funds offered by both foreign and Japanese investment banks made securities investments more attractive, but by the end of

Figure 2-1. *Corporate Financing, United States (1975) and Japan (1976)*

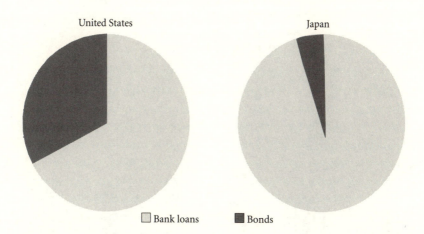

Source: Bank of Japan, *Economic Statistics Annual 1997*, pp. 23–24; U.S. Census Bureau, *Statistical Abstract of the United States: 1976*, p. 177.

March 2000 the share of equities in household financial portfolios had risen only marginally, to 15 percent.

The contrast between Japanese and American household portfolio behavior is stark. Americans held 29 percent of their assets in the form of cash and bank deposits in 1970, and that share fell precipitously in the 1990s to only 14 percent by 1997. Similar to the Japanese case, part of the offset has been a substantial rise, from 20 percent to 36 percent, in insurance and pension reserves. However, Americans have also held a far higher share of their portfolios in stocks and bonds—52 percent of their assets in 1970, dipping to 32 percent in 1990, then returning to 50 percent by 1997. These data confirm the enormous relative preference of Japanese households for bank accounts over stocks and bonds. Even when Americans had moved away from equity markets in the 1980s, the share of American portfolios in stocks and bonds was still more than double the share for Japanese households in 1999.

The counterpart to households' putting savings into banks has been the dependency of the corporate sector on bank loans. Figure 2-1 shows the relative shares of bond and bank debt for American and Japanese corporations in the mid-1970s. While bonds were only 5 percent of Japanese corporate debt (exclusive of trade credit, which is important in Japan, but not a net source of funds for the corporate sector), they represented 33 percent of American corporate borrowing.

Figure 2-2. *Bank Loans as a Percentage of GDP, 1980–99*

Percent of GDP

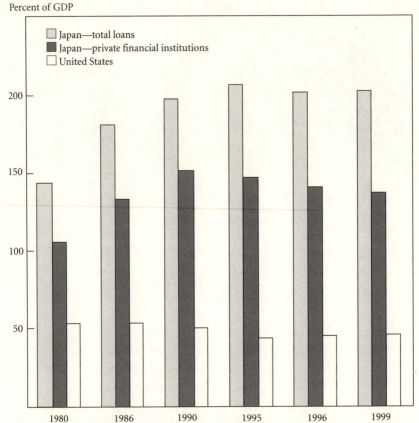

Source: Japan GDP data are from Japan Economic and Social Research Institute, www.esri.cao.go.jp/jp/
sna/qe004-2/gaku-mcy0042.csv (May 3, 2001); loan data for Japan are from flow-of-funds data, Bank of Japan, *Economic Statistics Annual 1981*, pp. 31–32; 1987, p. 220; 1991, p. 210; 1996, p. 267; 1997, p. 267; and Bank of Japan web
site, www.boj.or.jp/en/down/siryo/dsiryo_f.htm for 1999 data. U.S. data are from U.S. Census Bureau, *Statistical
Abstract of the United States: 1999*, pp. 459, 521, 524; 1988, p. 477.

Another way to visualize the difference between American and Japanese
financing patterns is in the value of outstanding loans to gross domestic
product (GDP). Not only have Japanese firms relied on bank loans more
than on bonds, but they have also relied more heavily on external borrowing
than have American firms. The result is that the ratio of bank loans to GDP
has been much higher in Japan than in the United States, as shown in figure
2-2. While outstanding bank loans (commercial banks plus savings institutions) have been roughly 50 percent of GDP in the United States (declining

slowly over time), they have composed a greater—and sharply rising—percentage in Japan. From 143 percent of GDP in 1980, total loans rose to 206 percent in 1995 before declining slightly, to 202 percent, in 1999. This ratio includes loans by government lending institutions; private-sector institutions alone had outstanding loans totaling 105 percent of GDP in 1980, increasing to 147 percent in 1995 and 137 percent in 1999. These flow-of-funds data include loans by all financial institutions; other data for outstanding loans by central government–licensed banks show a somewhat lower ratio of loans to GDP, 96 percent in 1996.[3] This smaller amount of lending is commonly used by the press in reporting the relative size of the bad loan problem, but it omits agricultural cooperatives and other local financial institutions that do not fall under the jurisdiction of the Ministry of Finance.

These data underscore the wide differences between Japanese and American financial behavior. The dominance of banking in Japan is truly stunning, and it has persisted until the present. The question with which Japanese society is now grappling is whether this system—with its low returns for households, opaque transactions between banks and borrowers, and indirect government influence—remains appropriate for the nation.

Keiretsu

A corollary to dependence on bank loans is the existence of broad groups of corporations known as horizontal *keiretsu*. These groups are technically leaderless, but one of their distinguishing characteristics is that the member firms have their largest loans from the group bank, and the bank generally has equity ownership in member firms at or close to the 5 percent maximum holding legally permitted for banks.

These *keiretsu* groups evolved out of the prewar family-controlled conglomerates known as *zaibatsu*. The *zaibatsu* were broken up during the Occupation. The families were removed from ownership; the holding companies that coordinated the operating firms were eliminated (and holding companies remained illegal until 1999), and shares in the constituent operating firms were sold broadly to the public.[4]

After the Occupation these groups reassembled into the looser *keiretsu* groupings. Six of these groups have predominated—Mitsui, Mitsubishi, Sumitomo, Fuyo, Sanwa, and Dai-Ichi. Other banks have also had sets of companies associated with them, though without prewar *zaibatsu* antecedents. Without dominant family ownership or holding companies, what has provided the sense of identity for these groups? First, members of a group have their largest bank loans from the group banks (usually a commercial bank and a trust bank). Second, mutual shareholding among the members of the group represents a substantial minority—not enough for control, but enough to demonstrate some preference. In 1978 the range of mutual shareholding varied from 27.2 percent in the Sumitomo group to 14.4 percent in the Dai-Ichi group (see figure 6-6a, in the discussion of the evolution of these ties in the 1990s). Third, the chief executive officers (CEOs) of the principal member firms meet once or twice a month informally.

Why these distinctive horizontal groups have persisted has been a puzzle. On average, group firms have had somewhat lower reported profits than other firms, suggesting that the trading of information within the group does not confer competitive advantages.[5] However, participation in such groups may be a form of risk-sharing—reducing the variability of profits over the business cycle and enhancing employment security for managers, who might otherwise be vulnerable to hostile shareholder pressures (as discussed later in this chapter). Some analysts see the *keiretsu* as having been a positive element of the postwar high-growth era, with the risk-sharing features enhancing flexible, economic adjustment in the face of external shocks such as the oil price shocks of the 1970s. Perceptions of reduced risk may also have encouraged high levels of investment, thereby contributing to the high economic growth rates from the 1950s to the 1970s.[6]

Some change has occurred in these groups over time. At the margins, some firms have entered or left group affiliation. Group membership may have conferred more important benefits during the years of capital shortage in the 1950s and 1960s when identification with a leading bank may have eased access to capital. Nevertheless, the existence and prominence of these groups continued into the 1990s. By 2000, however, some mergers were occurring across group lines that blurred the meaning of group identity—a topic explored further in chapter 6.

Corporate Governance

Accompanying the very different flow of financial funds has been a distinctive system of corporate governance. The common form of economic organization in capitalist economies is the limited liability stock corporation. In the United States, behavior of corporations is rooted in several interrelated concepts:

Corporations are owned by the shareholders. As owners, they bear the primary risk (limited to the extent of their share ownership) of the enterprise and share its profits. If the company fails, the owners lose their investment, but if it succeeds, they receive its profits. Because their money is at risk, the owners bear the primary responsibility of monitoring the behavior of the managers and employees of the firm, to ensure that their investment is run as efficiently as possible to produce profits.

Shareholders delegate oversight to a board of directors since stock ownership is often widely distributed among many stockholders. Shareholders select the members of the board, and they have the right to counter the board through a general vote of the shareholders. In the terminology of economics this is a "principal-agent" relationship, with the board acting as the agent for the shareholder principals. The board, in turn, is responsible for hiring management as its own "agent" to actually run the firm on a daily basis.

The corporation, and its constituent pieces (shares), can be bought or sold in a market for corporate ownership and control. As owners, shareholders may buy more shares or sell what they have. Should shareholders be dissatisfied with management and its performance, they may sell. Others who believe they can improve the corporation's performance may choose to buy shares and, with an increasing ownership share, force the board and management to behave differently. Management or some shareholders may contest shifting ownership control or "hostile" takeovers, but ultimately these battles are settled in the market. To enhance performance, the corporation may also split off pieces of its operations to sell to others or acquire control of other corporations or pieces of corporations. Thus a corporation represents a collection of assets (buildings, equipment, people, and intellectual property) that can be bought, sold, or repackaged in the equity market in the quest to enhance profits for the shareholders.

Other suppliers of financing—principally bondholders and bank lenders—bear less risk and have a lower expected rate of return from their investment. They have prior claim on the corporation's assets should it fail and hence bear a lower risk from corporate failure than shareholders, but in exchange they do not have primary responsibility for corporate governance. Obviously, purchasers in the bond market will assess the risk attached to management's behavior, causing the interest rate on bonds to rise or fall. Similarly, banks may choose to deny a loan or charge higher interest rates if the firm appears risky. However, neither bondholders nor bankers have any direct vote in the operation of the firm—they do not hire or fire management or approve strategic plans.

These are the basic or theoretical characteristics of the ideal of American corporate governance, from which actual practice deviates to some extent. The general ability and eagerness of shareholders to exercise corporate governance, for example, is stronger today than several decades ago because of the rise of large pension funds and mutual funds that use their role as major shareholders aggressively to press corporations for higher profits. However, corporate governance in Japan is very different in both theory and actual practice on all four of the basic features just described.[7]

In general, shareholders have little say in corporate governance. They are owners of the firm in only a very theoretical sense. If only a small number of shareholders (such as two or three other corporations) own the corporation, they may exercise real control. As a general proposition, however, the shareholders do not exercise much if any control over management even if they have fairly sizable minority ownership.

Rather than being chosen by the shareholders to represent their interests, the board of directors consists almost entirely of career managers of the corporation. A very small minority of the board may comprise individuals from major business partners (suppliers or buyers), financial institutions from which the corporation borrows, or the government. NEC Corporation (the large electrical equipment manufacturer), for example, has a board comprising forty-two members with only six outsiders. These outside board members include four retirees (one each from the Ministry of International Trade and Industry, NTT, the National Police Agency, and Sumitomo Bank) and two serving concurrently as managers in their organizations and on the board (one each from Sumitomo Bank and Sumitomo Life Insurance).[8] The outsiders may represent the interests of their employers (or former employers), but they do not necessarily represent broad shareholder interests. To diminish the ability of shareholders to exercise their prerogatives, most firms hold their annual shareholder meetings on the same day, and they have used the services of thugs (*sokaiya*) to prevent embarrassing questions from being asked at these typically very short meetings. The *sokaiya* eventually learned to collect bribes from companies in exchange for not asking embarrassing questions themselves. Thus the "principal-agent" relationship between owners, board, and managers does not pertain in Japan. Owners do not select or control the board, and the managers and board are largely the same group.

The corporation is more of an organic whole than an arbitrary collection of assets to be bought, sold, or rearranged in a market for corporate control for the sake of enhancing profits. Mergers and acquisitions do occur in Japan, but they are entirely friendly affairs often preceded by a lengthy courtship (or done at the behest of the government trying to arrange absorption of a failing firm by a healthy one). The corporation is certainly not subject to sale or purchase by shareholders acting independently of the wishes of current managers. Therefore, should the firm perform poorly and its share price fall, management need not fear that its shareholders will sell the firm to others who might force major changes in management.

Primary outside responsibility for corporate oversight generally rests with the banks from which the corporation borrows rather than with shareholders. The bank that supplies the largest amount of loans is designated the main bank for the corporation. On behalf of all the bank lenders, the main bank theoretically fulfills the primary role on corporate oversight. In addition to providing routine scrutiny, often a main bank will send its retiring officers to work at its borrowers (including, but not confined to, a member on the board of directors, as is the case with Sumitomo Bank's relationship with NEC). This person can convey additional inside information back to the bank about the corporation's performance. Should the borrower be in serious financial trouble, the main bank may dispatch other members of its senior management to occupy key management positions at the borrower. In a sense, such action is theoretically akin to a hostile takeover in the stock market since it involves at least some management turnover forced by the bank. The main bank bears responsibility to convene a meeting of all creditors to decide whether the company is beyond saving. The bank may also be a shareholder of the corporation, though banks are currently constrained to owning no more than 5 percent of the outstanding shares of another corporation (a level reduced from 10 percent in 1977). The theoretical importance of the main-bank system also explains why banks are generally considered the center of the horizontal *keiretsu*, since it serves as the main bank for *keiretsu* members.

In this model of corporate governance, large nonfinancial corporations may also provide primary corporate governance for smaller firms that act as suppliers of parts or services (in the vertical *keiretsu* relationships explored later in this chapter) regardless of the size of their ownership stake. Large corporations are in a strong position to provide such oversight because of their daily business contact with their suppliers. If Toyota, for example, is dissatisfied with the performance of one of its parts suppliers, it will react very quickly to work out the problems since the integrity of its own output may be threatened. Toyota may also dispatch its own retiring personnel to work at such suppliers or send its managers to take top management posts should the supplier be in serious trouble. Often such a major buyer may also have a strong minority equity stake in the corporation, but this is not necessary, nor does its influence over management depend on the size of its equity ownership stake.

As part of the effort to eviscerate the potential power of shareholders, companies preferred to exchange mutual holdings of shares with firms with which they conduct business; the shares were held on the mutual understanding that they were not to be traded. Preference for such mutual holdings increased in the late 1960s, when the Japanese government began to dismantle barriers on inward direct investment, as a means of thwarting possible takeover bids by foreign firms. Some 70 percent of outstanding corporate equity, according to estimates, has been held in such mutual long-term shareholding schemes, at least until recently. With only 30 percent of corporate equity available for trading on the stock exchange, the stock market has not been a viable venue for contesting corporate control. Keeping corporate control away from potentially hostile players in the stock market was a principal reason for the mutual shareholding within the horizontal *keiretsu*, though the phenomenon of cross-shareholding is far more pervasive than that within these groups.

Some have argued that the loose corporate governance provided by banks implies that Japanese corporate management has rather free rein. Banks are presumed to be rather patient and forgiving with their clients, unlike the supposedly relentless focus of American shareholders on the quarterly profit figures. As long as a corporation is paying the interest on its debt and is at least marginally profitable, the bank has little reason to scrutinize management closely. Unlike shareholders, management has no particular reason to pursue profit maximization; as long as the company maintains positive profits, management is more likely to focus on maintaining employment (especially management jobs) or pursuing increased market share (enhancing the corporate image for success to the detriment of profits). In the high-growth era the distinction between profit maximization and market share maximization was blurred. Profits that could be realized by combining foreign technology or imported capital equipment embodying that technology with inexpensive domestic labor were unusually high, and the economies of scale in production that were typical of these new technologies meant that a focus on market share would enable a firm to drive down unit costs and enhance profits. Since the economy matured in the 1970s, with slower growth and fewer economies of scale, the distinction between management objectives and shareholder desires for profits has mattered more.

As with the idealization of the American model, how closely Japanese behavior corresponded to the generalizations here is unclear. The notion of main banks' providing effective oversight of corporations, for example, has been vigorously challenged.[9] Indeed, the anecdotes about banks reneging on their supposed main bank responsibilities when faced with extensive problems among their borrowers, coupled with the scandals involving collusion between banks and borrowers to hide the borrower's financial difficulties, suggest strongly that the main-bank system never worked as advertised. If it did not, then managers appear to have had greater autonomy. What matters most, however, is that Japanese academics and government officials could theorize a system of main-bank oversight of corporations that they believed was equivalent or superior to the American model of shareholder governance through a principal-agent system.

For many years, the Japanese felt their version of corporate governance was superior to the American model.[10] Managers know the most about the technical details of their business and should not be subject to back-seat driving by ignorant stock market investors. The longer-term approach of bank lenders supposedly freed management from what it viewed as a destructive short-term American focus on quarterly profit reports. Rapid economic growth and growing global market shares grabbed by some leading manufacturing firms (particularly in steel, automobiles, and consumer electronics) fed the notion that the Japanese versions of corporate governance were superior. However, this aspect of the economic system is also being questioned as a result of the widespread problems in the corporate sector revealed in the 1990s.

Vertical *Keiretsu*

A corporation represents a collection of individual economic actions brought together within a single institutional housing for the sake of efficiency. One could manufacture a car by separating each individual part or assembly activity into separate corporations and have them buy and sell to one another. Alternatively, one could manufacture a car by placing all of those activities—from the manufacture of steel and rubber to final assembly and sale of finished vehicles—in a single corporate entity. The economic theory of the firm says that the boundary line of the corporation will be set at the break-even point where the internal cost of an activity equals the cost of purchase from outside.[11] The simple theory of the firm assumes a choice between internalization and purchase from other firms in a market.[12] In reality, however, many transactions occur between firms in the form of contracts that are rather different from simple market transactions. These transactional relationships in Japan have been quite different from those in the United States.

Large Japanese manufacturing firms have generally had a rather narrow boundary or scope, coupled with a high dependency on parts and services purchased from outside the firm. These outside relationships in Japan tend to be characterized by long-term contracts, producing a quasi-permanent vertical relationship known as vertical *keiretsu* (not to be confused with the horizontal *keiretsu* discussed earlier). Long-term contracting was by no means unknown in the West, but the aggressive Japanese development and use of it in the 1960s was distinctive and went far beyond western experience.[13]

Long-term contracting has important advantages over spot market purchases or short-term contracting for certain kinds of relationships in the manufacturing sector. One benefit is the simple reduction in transactions costs, since the act of bidding and contracting is not costless. More important, a long-term relationship enables the purchaser to draw the seller into the design phase of a new product. As a participant in the design process, parts suppliers may have valuable insights that lead to a higher quality design (in the sense of being less susceptible to breakdowns) and lower cost of production. A brake manufacturer, for example, might be able to suggest design modifications that enable it to offer a brake system that is less costly or that is less costly to install on the assembly line. Parts suppliers' involvement in the design process is feasible only if they know that their design effort will result in real sales once manufacturing is under way so that they can recoup their costs over the duration of the vehicle's production run.

Furthermore, long-term contracting enables close attention to quality. If a major manufacturer has committed itself to purchasing a particular part from a single source (or a limited set of two or three sources) through long-term contracting, then it must monitor the quality of supply closely and apply pressure when or if quality slips. In contrast, in a market or short-term contracting setting, the purchaser may be inclined to simply try another supplier rather than work with the existing supplier to fix problems. Japanese firms in the manufacturing sector have built elaborate monitoring and confidence-building exercises into their long-term contracting system to ensure that quality of incoming parts remains high and any slippage is quickly addressed. The common pattern has been for a firm to use two or three suppliers for most major parts, enabling some increase or decrease of purchases from them as a means of rewarding or punishing suppliers for their performance.

One consequence of this system has been the reliance of parts suppliers on sales to one large purchaser in many cases. A major manufacturer does not want a parts supplier who is privy to the design details of an upcoming product to be doing business with a competitor. Therefore, not only did the system produce long-term contracts, but it also increased dependency of parts suppliers on the major firm to which they had become attached. The Toyota *keiretsu*, for example, comprises Toyota Motor Corporation and the collection of parts suppliers that have been largely dependent on sales of parts and services to it.

One way to conceptualize these relationships is as being halfway between the bipolar choices of market transactions and internalization. The parts suppliers, with their output going largely to a single major manufacturer, are like internal corporate divisions, but operating as separate profit centers. Their independent management and financial responsibility may have advantages over the bureaucracy of internalization, and their closeness may have advantages in resolving problems quickly.

Long-term relationships that are presumably profitable come with a social cost. Parts suppliers dependent primarily on a single large purchaser are in a weak power position. Should they choose to break free of the contract, then they face a market with which they have little experience or that is populated with other major manufacturers who already have their own vertical *keiretsu* with other parts manufacturers. With strong dependency, the parts manufacturers have little choice but to submit to demands from their benefactors. Pressure to cut prices, speed up delivery schedules, and accept emergency changes in schedule can be brutal and provide emotional anecdotes that have formed the basis for a whole genre of Japanese novels in the postwar period.[14]

Such firms also become the repository for retired employees from the larger firm. Employees covered by lifetime employment at a large manufacturer often end up at the firm's parts manufacturers for their postretirement jobs, in a transfer arranged between the two firms (in which the parts manufacturer has little choice). Actions such as the transfer of employees can give these relationships a longevity that goes well beyond that envisioned by economists looking at the theoretical advantages of long-term contracting, a point that is pursued in chapter three.

The story of vertical *keiretsu* has been primarily one of major manufacturers and their parts subsidiaries. However, a similar story can be told of distributors, who are also often connected to a major manufacturer. In a few cases the connection extended as far as the retail level, especially in the well-known example of Matsushita Corporation (a major electrical appliance manufacturer) and its chain of "National" brand neighborhood retail stores across the nation, which handled only its own products. The economic case for efficiency in *keiretsu* relationships between manufacturers and distributors is weak, and the main motivation has been to gain control over the retail price of products.

Belief in the value of the vertical *keiretsu* system has been strong, bolstered by the major global market share gains of Japanese automobile and consumer electronics manufacturers against their U.S. competitors from the 1960s through the 1980s. Some Japanese manufacturers built their global success on the quality of their products, developing a reputation for durability and reliability at a competitive price. The perception of a quality difference between Japanese and American firms was the strongest in the automobile industry during the 1980s. The success of leading Japanese firms, such as Toyota, was believed to be intimately linked to the vertical *keiretsu* system.[15] The travails of Japanese corporations in the 1990s, however, have challenged even this core element of the Japanese economic model.

Restrained Price Competition

The Japanese market appears to be one of ferocious competition. If one firm creates a new product, its competitors will bring out similar ones with blinding speed. Advertising is certainly as prominent in the print media and television as it is in the United States, and the extensive advertising displays in commuter trains and subways can be rather overwhelming. Nevertheless, competition in Japan has focused more on product variation than on price, an outcome possible only in an environment of restrained competition.

Several features of economic organization point to reduced price competition. The first and most obvious has been the official sanctioning of some cartels and the widespread tolerance of others. Under the Japanese antitrust law, legal cartels may be formed under special circumstances, including as a defensive measure during recessions. This feature of the law was actively used in the 1950s and 1960s, and the number of government-sanctioned cartels peaked at 1,079 in 1971. Since that time the number has steadily declined, dipping to only twelve by 1997.[16] Virtual elimination of official cartels ought to imply a major change in the terms of competition in the economy, but the greater probability is that private restraint has replaced official restraint. In a recent study Mark Tilton amply documented the continuation of collusion in a variety of basic industries after the end of sanctioned cartels.[17]

In a few industries, price competition was officially constrained by legalized retail price maintenance. Government-authorized maintenance of fixed retail prices has also declined in scope over the past two decades, but it still exists. Printed materials (books, magazines, and newspapers), domestic sound recordings, some cosmetics (1,694 separate cosmetic products in 1996), and some pharmaceuticals (185 separate products in 1996) remain subject to retail price maintenance.[18]

Antitrust enforcement is provided by the Japan Fair Trade Commission (JFTC). For a variety of reasons, including the lack of treble damages and active discouragement by the government, virtually no private antitrust suits supplement its work. In 1997 the JFTC made formal decisions on only thirty cases. By contrast, the Antitrust Division of the U.S. Department of Justice completed fifty antitrust cases (fiscal year 1996).[19] The Federal Trade Commission, the other U.S. government antitrust agency, spends much of its energy on evaluating proposed mergers, but in the nonmerger area it pursued ten full-phase investigations and issued six consent agreements in 1996.[20] However, this federal government action is minor compared with private civil suits. In the five-year period from 1993 through 1997, federal district courts handled an average of 647 civil antitrust suits a year.[21] Furthermore, most government antitrust cases in Japan have involved small markets; nothing comparable to the American landmark cases involving leading corporations exists in Japan.

Given weak antitrust action, collusion is likely. Such a conclusion is enhanced by the strong behavior of trade associations in Japan. Government ministries regard trade associations as subsidiary organizations, which they use as part of their communications pipeline with industry. The Ministry of International Trade and Industry (MITI), for example, has a long list of trade associations in its annual personnel directory, ranging from the Japan Iron and Steel Federation to the Bowling Alley Association, all arranged by the division within MITI that has jurisdiction.[22] Trade associations exist in all industrial nations, and they have legitimate purposes unrelated to collusion. However, their function in Japan goes well beyond that permitted trade associations in the United States, and the presumption of many observers is that they often exceed the boundaries of what is legal and foster collusive behavior.[23]

With the drastic decline in authorized cartels and the low level of antitrust enforcement, the only choice is to infer their existence indirectly. One particularly striking piece of indirect evidence is prices. In freely functioning markets open to international trade, high prices should cause an inflow of less expensive products from abroad. This may not eliminate price differences, because of differences in purely local costs (such as rent for retail stores), but it should reduce the variation.[24] In Japan, collusion among domestic firms has often resulted in high prices relative to other markets, and market-entry bar-

Figure 2-3. *Comparative Price Levels, OECD Countries, December 1999*

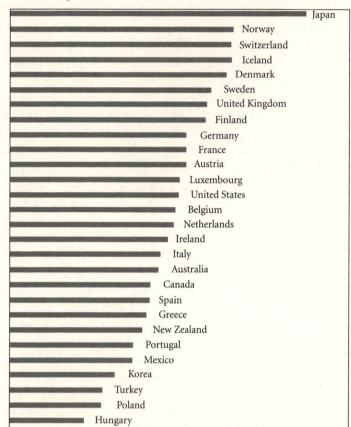

Price level (United States = 100)

Source: Organization of Economic Cooperation and Development, *Main Economic Indicators* (March 2000), p. 262.

riers have impeded foreign firms from undercutting the domestic arrangements. Progress in opening Japanese markets to international competition over the past two decades has resulted in some reduction in price differentials, but they persisted to some extent even at the end of the 1990s. Data from the Organization for Economic Cooperation and Development (OECD) presented in figure 2-3, for example, indicate that overall prices in Japan at the end of 1999 at prevailing exchange rates were 74 percent higher than those in the United States. With fluctuating exchange rates and imperfect global integration of global markets, some deviation of prices from the U.S. level is only to be expected; some OECD countries had lower prices at the end of 1999 (Greece, for example, had prices 19 percent below U.S. prices) and some higher. Overall prices are generally lower in less developed economies (such as Greece) because of the unavoidably labor-intensive nature of many service industries. Japan, however, was by far the outlier; the next most expensive country (Norway) had prices only 32 percent higher than those in the United States, and other developed European countries ranged from 11 percent below to 31 percent above U.S. prices. These data dramatically illustrate how collusion and obstructed market access can result in high prices.[25]

Some Japanese data confirm this picture. In 1998, for example, MITI found that the average price for industrial goods and services was 67 percent higher in Japan than in the United States (though manufactured goods were about equal, with the widest differences occurring in energy and services).[26] Some of these price differences are for services that are not generally traded internationally, such as electricity or domestic trucking. Even in these areas, however, collusion must exist. Japanese firms have access to the same technology as American or other firms for electric power generation, telecommunications, trucking, and other services. For Japanese prices for services to be so much higher relative to other countries of roughly similar economic development is difficult to explain unless collusion is part of the explanation. Obviously competition does exist in Japan, but the pattern has been for market competition to drift in the direction of collusion on prices, while permitting energetic competition on the basis of new products. The result is quite different from what prevails in the United States.

Reduced competition may seem a curious element of the Japanese economic system. Cartels and collusion lead to undesirable restraints on output and higher prices, to the detriment of economic welfare and efficient allocation of resources. However, the Japanese government believed that competition could be wasteful. In a high-growth environment, and dependent on finite amounts of domestic funding for investment, the government believed that the process of competition could lead to wasteful investment. That is, companies might invest too much relative to domestic demand for the resulting output (thereby putting an unnecessary strain on limited domestic funds for investment), or intense competition might leave profit levels too low for any firms to afford the investment in expanded plant and equipment that was so essential for rapid economic growth. Even economists admit that under certain circumstances in a high-growth environment, cartels might be economically rational at least on a temporary basis to enable viable but highly leveraged firms to survive short downturns in the economy.[27]

Even if there had been a rationale for cartels or collusion in a high-growth environment, that era was long gone by the 1990s. Collusion among firms, with official or implicit government sanction, had the same negative consequences as in any other economic system. Rather than working for the long-term benefit of economic growth and development, collusion raised prices to the detriment of consumers and restricted investment in industries below what would occur in an open competitive environment. Such costs were becoming evident to at least some in society by the end of the decade.

Labor Markets

Several interrelated aspects of the organization and operation of Japanese labor markets are quite distinctive. These include the practice known as life-time employment, the prevalence of a heavy seniority basis for wages and salaries, corporate reliance on internal labor markets for promotion rather than outside hiring, and a poorly developed market for midcareer job changing. Together they form a system that rests heavily on hiring workers as they graduate from school and that reduces the voluntary movement of workers from one firm to another during their working careers. While the differences in behavior between American and Japanese labor markets should not be exaggerated, real differences do exist in both actual behavior and the expectations of people in the labor force.

The stereotype of Japanese labor behavior is the system of lifetime employment.[28] The ideal pattern in lifetime employment is for a firm to hire both blue-collar and managerial workers directly out of school and keep them until a mandatory retirement age, at which time the firm will generally help them locate a postretirement job. The continued job assistance even at the time of retirement occurs because mandatory retirement is at a relatively young age (age fifty-five in the earlier postwar period, and age sixty at most companies now) and because retirement benefits have been generally inadequate. Hiring workers from school and promising to keep them until retirement implies that promotion occurs from within the firm. Firms practicing this system rarely hire outsiders at the midcareer level. No written contracts accompany this system—the guarantee of employment is implicit, and the employee can quit at any time.

The thin job market for midcareer moves provides one incentive for workers to stay, but the system is also accompanied by a seniority-based pay scale to provide the employee a monetary incentive not to quit. In the early years after joining a firm, workers are actually paid less than their marginal value, but steep seniority increases mean that in the later part of careers they receive pay greater than their marginal productivity—essentially a bonus or reward for longevity of service that workers should be loath to lose by quitting. The system also spawned a rather intense effort by firms to build loyalty through lengthy training programs emphasizing the firm's "culture," company songs, periodic employee retreats, corporate recreation facilities in the countryside, and other mechanisms that go well beyond the behavior patterns of American firms. This effort is aimed at reducing the probability that an employee will quit as well as combating the possible laziness that is inherent in a guaranteed tenure system.

For workers, such a system provides certainty of long-term employment, a goal that was especially important for workers in the early postwar years when the economy was in ruins and good jobs scarce. For firms the advantages are less obvious. A firm facing a business cycle needs to vary its costs; to fix labor costs by promising not to lay off workers would seem to be an undesirable move. However, Japanese firms were concerned in the earlier twentieth century with high turnover rates and, therefore, high training costs. Furthermore, they came to believe that the system led to more loyal and more productive employees. They also developed mechanisms other than laying off workers to inject some flexibility into their labor costs (discussed below).

The scope of this system should not be exaggerated. All analysts recognize that only a minority of employees work at firms practicing lifetime employment; estimates range from 20 to 30 percent of the labor force, mostly at large corporations. Women are generally not covered by this system; in theory they have been covered by a nondiscrimination law since 1986, but the law includes few penalties for violation.[29] As noted above, large firms often have some employees labeled temporary. In actuality, though, coverage may be somewhat broader, since workers at postretirement jobs in smaller companies should also be considered part of the system. Furthermore, for those firms not officially practicing lifetime employment, stability in job prospects accrues to those at smaller firms acting as subcontractors to large firms in vertical *keiretsu* relationships.

For those workers who do obtain jobs with firms practicing lifetime employment, some job changing also occurs. Young workers can leave the firm within a year or two if they are unhappy without incurring too much stigma or financial loss. Midcareer employees might be moved by the firm to newly created subsidiaries or joint ventures as the nature of the industry evolves. Others might be moved to subsidiaries over the course of the business cycle (such as shifting manufacturing employees to the firm's sales subsidiary). When a worker reaches the mandatory retirement age, the firm generally finds the employee a postretirement job with a parts supplier, distributor, or other related firm. Only a few brave employees quit on their own during their careers to pursue other opportunities.

The obvious effect of this system has been the existence of an entirely internal job market for the firm. Promotions are virtually always from within, and often across functional boundaries. Especially for managerial employees the result is broad experience in different departments of the firm. For a lucky few individuals, rotation and promotion lead to becoming CEO and then chairman of the board. However, in exchange for the promise of lifetime employment, the employee may be burdened with assignment to distant geographical locations or to departments outside the scope of his technical knowledge at the whim of the personnel department. Employees have essentially no veto power over personnel department decisions.

A major consequence of the preference for internal promotion has been the poorly developed state of employment agencies, classified job advertising, and other aspects of a market for people changing jobs. Any employee of a large firm thinking of quitting to seek better employment faces a market in which few firms are hiring from the outside and would suffer a loss of seniority pay at the new firm. This makes the market thin and discourages the development of the institutional support to run such a market. Recruit Corporation was formed in the 1960s to provide job information, but the fact that the company felt it necessary to bribe politicians in the 1980s to break through a tangle of regulatory impediments is indicative of the unfavorable environment for a job-changing market at the time.

Having promised at least a portion of their work force lifetime employment, firms still face the problem of coping with the business cycle and the need to vary their labor costs. This need led to a number of creative approaches, beyond hiring temporary employees and not extending lifetime employment guarantees to women. One approach has been the large amounts of overtime work for blue-collar workers, which can be adjusted up or down with the business cycle. Another solution has been either to move employees to other divisions of the firm or to send them to subsidiaries or affiliated firms when times are slack. In these ways, the firm can avoid a fixed labor cost, although the speed with which firms can adjust is slower than in American firms. Until the 1990s these mechanisms for adjusting labor costs appeared to be sufficient. More recently they have appeared less adequate, as considered in chapters 3 and 6.

Compared with the United States, average job tenure in Japan is longer and the seniority or age profile of wages steeper because of the existence of lifetime employment and its associated seniority-based pay scales. In the 1970s, for example, median job tenure at large firms (more than 1,000 employees) was twelve years in Japan compared with seven in the United States.[30] Although workers in both countries may have considerable loyalty to their employer, Japanese often identify themselves more closely with their employer than do Americans. In a sense, employment in a company is akin to being part of a family, a social phenomenon explored in chapter 5.

For years people have predicted the end of lifetime employment. When decades of rapid growth yielded very tight labor markets in the early 1970s, turnover rates began to rise, and people predicted that the system would come to an end as firms bid workers away from one another. That speculation ended when economic growth decelerated after the mid-1970s and labor market conditions softened. When the labor force began aging in the 1980s, seniority-based pay came under pressure as once-cheap work forces became more expensive. While the slope of wage profiles was modified, however, the system remained intact into the 1990s. The one sector where this system has diminished is finance, where anecdotal evidence suggests that midcareer moves motivated by offers of higher pay for trained specialists (especially for moves to foreign financial institutions) have become noticeable in recent years.

Now the system of lifetime employment is part of the debate over systemic reform. Is lifetime employment viable in a slow growing, aging economy? Will firms face increased pressures from shareholders or lenders to cut costs and raise profits by reducing labor inputs more quickly through layoffs? These were major questions by 2000, but as chapters 3 and 6 will demonstrate, predictions of the system's demise are premature. The belief that longevity of service produces greater loyalty and higher productivity is far from gone in Japan.

Industrial Policy

All governments are involved in economic affairs, some more explicitly than others. The government of Japan has been especially active in pursuing policies aimed at enhancing the growth and development of the economy. Considerable controversy has surrounded the efficacy of those policies in accelerating industrialization over the course of the twentieth century in Japan. Whatever the answer to that difficult question might be, the important consequence for this study is that the outcome was a pattern of government intervention in the economy that is relatively distinctive, especially in comparison with the United States.

Part of what the government has chosen to do is unremarkable. Education has long been a priority in Japan, producing high levels of literacy and a large

supply of undergraduate degrees in engineering. In addition, during the first
two decades after the Second World War, public works spending was skewed
toward producing the public infrastructure necessary for industrial development—such as improved harbor facilities, railroad facilities, and highways
(initially assumed to be primarily for trucks rather than passenger cars) rather
than amenities for the public (such as suburban sewer systems). At the
macroeconomic level, a government operating in the context of an economy
that had an enormous appetite for private-sector investment in the 1950s
and 1960s wisely chose to follow a balanced budget policy (thereby preventing the government from competing with the private sector for the finite
supply of domestic savings).

However, at the center of what is usually considered industrial policy is a
set of microeconomic policies. In the case of Japan, a central government that
was distrustful of markets chose to follow a path of informal and indirect
influence over the allocation of resources in the economy. Involved in this
approach was a complex (and sometimes contradictory) set of policies in
the following areas in the first several postwar decades:

—Protectionism. The government provided protection from both imports
and direct investment by foreign firms to enable domestically owned firms to
prosper.

—Regulation of the financial sector. The financial sector was heavily regulated, and the bank-centered pattern of financing enabled the government
to exercise informal or indirect influence over the allocation of loans.

—Government financing. Through the Fiscal Investment and Loan Program (FILP), the government provides subsidized loans for policy-related projects, including partial financing of firms in favored private-sector industries.

—Research and development. The government provides direct financial
support for R&D and has pushed private industries into cooperative research
projects in order to be eligible for government financing.

—Relaxation of antitrust rules. In industries where the government felt
competition could be detrimental to its development goals, it passed laws
explicitly permitting cooperative behavior. More broadly, government tolerated or encouraged the collusive business environment discussed earlier.

—Favorable tax treatment. Tax breaks were often aimed at very specific
development goals (such as accelerated depreciation allowances for very specific types of new production equipment).

—Aid for export development. Believing that exports would encourage
industries to meet international levels of productivity and quality, the government provided various forms of support (such as tax breaks) related to
exporting.

—"Administrative guidance." Government established and maintained a route of informal communication with (and pressure on) industry, going beyond its influence on the financial sector. Enhancing this informal route of contact has been an organized system of placing retiring government officials in private-sector firms.

Just as important as what the government has done has been what it has not done. Unlike European or some other governments, the Japanese government never nationalized many industries. The bulk of the rail network was nationalized in the early twentieth century, telecommunications belonged to a government-owned organization, and cigarettes were produced and sold by a single government monopoly, but government began to ease out of these direct ownership positions after 1985. In the postwar period the manufacturing sector and other services remained in the hands of the private sector. Rather than taking over direct control of some industries, as happened in Britain, for example, the Japanese government chose to exercise its influence over industry through its set of more indirect policies.

Some of the policy tools of the earlier postwar period listed above faded over time. As a result of thirty-five years of negotiations with the United States and other nations, official protectionism has waned. Official trade barriers have been lowered and the investment controls eliminated, though a web of other less formal entry barriers has kept manufactured imports and direct investment at much lower levels than in other industrial nations.[31] Official relaxation of antitrust laws through special industry legislation has waned, and the number of officially sanctioned cartels has dwindled. Tax breaks have also dwindled since the early 1970s. Explicit aid for export market development is largely gone, or at least no longer distinctively large in comparison with that of other industrial nations. All industrial nations provide some support for R&D.

What remained by the 1990s that was distinctive were government financing, research and development support, and informal administrative guidance. Protectionism—through regulation and tacit support for domestic collusion directed against foreign firms—also appears to remain as a tool, even if it is generally less powerful than in the past. Continued use of these remaining tools reflects the confidence of the government in the value of its interventions. Government may have lost some of its most powerful tools, but its desire to meddle in markets continued largely unabated.

Of the remaining tools, consider government financing first. Much of the money that the government invests directly in policy projects has little to do with a narrow definition of industrial policy. Nevertheless, the overall structure of how the government raises and invests these funds is important

Figure 2-4. *The Fiscal Investment and Loan Program (FILP),*
Outstanding Amounts, March 31, 1999

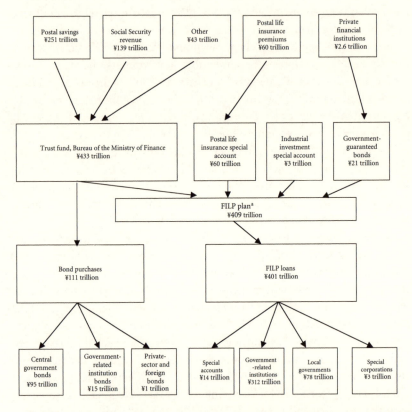

Source: Ministry of Finance, "FILP Report '99, How Does the Fiscal Investment and Loan Program Work?"
www.mof.go.jp/zaito/zaito99/p0607e.htm (April 9, 2001); "Appendix: Financial Data; Outstanding Balance for the
FILP at the End of FY 1998," www.mof.go.jp/zaito/zaito99/p37_45e.htm#04 (April 9, 2001); and "Trust Fund Bureau
Special Account and Trust Fund Bureau Fund," www.mof.go.jp/zaito/zaito99/p46_49e.htm#03 (April 9, 2001).

a. There is a small discrepancy in the amount reported for the FILP plan, based on the amounts reported by each
source of funding (¥409 trillion) and the total of FILP loans taken from a separate table (¥401 trillion).

because the mechanism is distinctive. As chapters 3 and 6 will argue, the nontransparent nature of this mechanism has led to distortions and waste. As
originally conceived and operated in the early postwar period, though, this
system would provide both crucial funding for the public infrastructure necessary for economic development (such as highways and harbor facilities)
and funds for favored industries or firms as part of what would be defined
more narrowly as industrial.

The mechanism for the government's direct investment in the economy is the Fiscal Investment and Loan Program (FILP). Figure 2-4 shows the flow of money through the FILP. The government collects funds from the public, mainly through savings deposits in the Postal Savings system, premium payments through the Postal Life Insurance system, and social security contributions collected through payroll taxes. These plus the other sources shown provide the funds that are then lent by the Ministry of Finance to a wide variety of public policy institutions and projects and used for the purchase of government bonds.

In this manner, the government acts like a large financial institution—borrowing from the public and lending to public and private-sector projects. However, this is a very special financial institution. The allocation of loans is very much determined by public policy interests rather than simple determination of risk and return, and the lending occurs at subsidized interest rates. The portion of the total flow of funds available to the private sector that is intermediated by the FILP was relatively modest—with the ratio to GDP around 5 percent in the final high-growth years in the early 1970s, and 15 percent as a ratio to total domestic fixed investment (discussed further in chapter 6 and shown in figure 6-3). Even this modest level gave the government some direct voice in the allocation of investment. Furthermore, in the early postwar decades, that voice was amplified by the stamp of official approval demonstrated by these loans. That is, companies or industries favored by government loans had an easier time obtaining additional credit from private-sector financial institutions that viewed government lending as one of the signals to guide their own behavior.

The public policy institutions that borrow funds from the FILP are shown in table 2-3. As is obvious from this list, the range of activities the government supported is quite wide. Over time the emphasis has changed. Whereas industrially useful investments were dominant in the 1950s (such as lending to electric power utilities, gas utilities, and the steel industry), the largest borrower from the FILP today is the Housing Loan Corporation, which provides low-cost mortgages.

Most of these recipients represent another distinctive aspect of government intervention in the economy: the public policy enterprise. Governments can build and operate public investments directly, or they can run them through semi-independent agencies or enterprises. Such enterprises are not uncommon in the United States, especially when independent revenue is involved. Airports conceived by local governments, for example, are often run by some separate organization, which is responsible for issuing

Table 2-3. *Major Recipients of FILP Loans, 1998–99*

Millions of yen

Organization[a]	New funds, fiscal year 1998	Outstanding balances, March 1999
Special accounts (10)		
Consolidation of specific national property	93	631
National hospitals	76	859
National schools	136	1,014
Land improvement projects	84	1,175
National Forest Service	145	910
Airport development	32	1,029
Postal savings	12,000	55,150
Government financial institutions (12)		
Housing Loan Corporation	6,238	71,853
People's Finance Corporation	3,260	9,054
Japan Finance Corporation for Small Business	1,735	7,164
Environmental Sanitation Finance Corporation	324	1,097
Agriculture, Forestry, and Fisheries Finance Corp.	260	3,947
Japan Finance Corporation for Municipal Enterprises	1,931	15,282
Hokkaido-Tohoku finance Public Corporation	295	1,516
Okinawa Development Finance Corporation	238	1,648
Japan Development Bank	2,877	15,554
Export-Import Bank of Japan	2,225	9,340
Other government-affiliated bodies (36)		
Housing and Urban Development Corporation	1,055	14,273
The Pension Welfare Service Public Corporation	3,923	35,473
Teito Rapid Transit Authority	22	513
Japan Regional Development Corporation	88	547
Social Welfare and Medical Service Corporation	371	2,252
Japan Highway Public Corporation	2,260	21,244
Metropolitan Expressway Public Corporation	371	3,927
Hanshin Expressway Public Corporation	258	3,199
Honshu-Shikoku Bridge Authority	178	2,172
Japan Railway Construction Public Corporation	98	1,647
Corporation for Advanced Transport and Technology	28	4,367
Water Resources Development Public Corporation	88	1,406
Japan National Oil Corporation	38	809
The Overseas Economic Cooperation Fund	512	4,623
Postal Life Insurance Welfare Corporation	2,500	13,373
Local governments	10,041	78,260
Special firms (11)		
The Electric Power Development Company	150	1,649
Total	54,370	400,798

Source: Ministry of Finance, FILP financing totals: Plans/Results for FY 1998, www.mof.go.jp/zaito/zaito99/p37_45e.htm#03 (March 13, 2001).

a. Excludes organizations receiving less than ¥100 billion of new funds and having less than ¥500 billion in outstanding loans from the FILP. The total number of organizations in each category is indicated in parentheses.

bonds to finance construction and then charges fees to raise funds to operate the airport and repay the bonds.

The rationale for separating some government-related activities into such
semi-independent agencies is mainly one of efficiency and responsibility.
Harbor facilities, airports, hospitals, and highways (among others) are all
examples of public infrastructure commonly built by governments that serve
specific parts of the public. Because they all have some characteristics of public goods, most nations rely on governments rather than private markets to
build and operate such facilities. However, they have enough characteristics
of private goods to lead to imposition of specific user fees to finance them.
Creating separate organizations accountable for the construction and operation of such facilities is a means of enforcing efficient choices; the managers
of these organizations must operate the facility to meet their goals while raising sufficient revenue to pay operating and construction costs.[32]

In addition to this potential rationale, such organizations fit clearly within
the general pattern of strong bureaucratic control and industrial policy in two
important ways. First, most of these organizations are constrained to borrowing from the FILP rather than seeking independent, market-based funds.
In the United States, a local authority seeking to build a new airport must at
least face a market test through the issuance of bonds. Should the investing
public disagree with the economic rationale for the airport, the authorities
might have difficulty raising funds. In Japan, however, financial markets have
no input into the financing of government-related enterprises. If the central
government decides an airport should be built, then it will provide financing
through the FILP. Even when government-related organizations do issue
bonds, many of the bonds are purchased by the FILP rather than by investors
in the private sector. For example, as of the end of fiscal year 1998, government-related corporations (both financial and nonfinancial) had issued ¥68
trillion in bonds (or about $600 billion), of which government-owned finan-
cial institutions held ¥42 trillion, or 62 percent.[33]

This system of close financial control over public enterprises fit well with
the development needs of the nation in the high-growth years of the 1950s
and 1960s. Faced with scarce financial resources and a clear economic development agenda, the central government wanted dominant control over public infrastructure. There was an obvious and urgent need to build
expressways, harbor facilities, railroads, and other public infrastructure essential for the continued growth of the economy. In some cases, furthermore, the
private sector was not addressing real social needs. Convinced that it knew
best how public investment resources should be allocated, the government

preferred lending to these projects through the FILP rather than making them face a market test by issuing bonds.

The second major distinctive piece of government involvement in markets remaining today is administrative guidance. This vague term describes the web of informal connections between government and private-sector firms. Sometimes specific legal authority buttresses guidance by the government. Often, however, there is no specific authority and no written record. Influence in these cases depends on the general prestige and power of the government.

A key element of administrative guidance is its informality. Often there is no written record of requests to the private sector since much of the contact is verbal—often conducted at night in bars and restaurants. An attempt was made in the 1990s to require that formal administrative guidance be put into writing, but enforcement of this law is questionable. A corporate manager standing on the principle of the law by demanding that a request be put into writing might well learn that a peeved government official could find ways to make life uncomfortable for the firm.

Whether administrative guidance always represents an activist government trying to bend the private sector to its wishes is doubtful. Some have suggested that the influence is often in the opposite direction—aggressive firms petitioning the government to pursue policies beneficial to them. The direction of influence does not alter the implications for this study. What matters is that the government has had an important role as an arbitrator or mediator in private markets. Firms in many industries either expect the government to set parameters for their competition and development or they expect to be able to use the government to legitimate essentially collusive decisions of the industry.

All societies have some degree of this sort of lobbying in both directions. The situation in Japan may sound quite similar to the relationships between defense contractors and the Department of Defense in the United States. What distinguishes Japan from the United States is the pervasiveness of the informal connection between government and the corporate sector, the informality of the process, and the weakness of countervailing consumer lobbying. Japanese are often amazed, for example, to hear from U.S. government officials about the severe limits on gifts and meals that constrain American bureaucrats.

A critical element of this system of influence is *amakudari* (descent from heaven), the retirement of career government officials into private-sector jobs. The United States has a so-called revolving door, in which people take appointed positions in an administration and then return to the private sector. In Japan the flow is largely one directional—from career government positions to the private sector. More important, the process is organized, and this is what most distinguishes the Japanese from the American revolving door. Individuals do not simply look for postretirement jobs on their own; the minister's secretariat is responsible for placing people in jobs. This makes the movement of a bureaucrat into a corporation a matter of negotiation between the government and the corporation. The practice is also pervasive. The Japanese government is composed almost entirely of career officials; only the minister and parliamentary vice minister are appointed; all of them retire relatively early (virtually all except the administrative vice minister are out by age fifty-five or earlier); all of them need postretirement jobs. Academic studies have focused on high-level officials, who presumably are in the best position to influence corporate behavior, but the system involves lower-level employees as well.[34]

The *amakudari* system provides a critical part of the glue that connects government to the private sector. At the very least, these former officials enhance the communications pipeline between government and the private sector. Whether their presence improves the firm's ability to influence government policy in its own direction or whether they enhance the government's ability to influence the firm matters less than their presence.

In summary, the Japanese government has been extensively engaged with the economy through what may be broadly called industrial policy. The government lost a number of the tools it could use in the 1950s and 1960s to provide a guiding hand over the allocation of resources in the economy, but it retained significant tools—continued protectionism, funding for research and development, general government financing for infrastructure and other public policy purposes, and administrative guidance—in the 1980s and 1990s.

Although the U.S. government has also been involved with the economy at a microeconomic level, the overall picture is quite different from Japan. Like Japan, the United States practices some protectionism, provides research and development funding, provides general government financing for public policy purposes, and even engages in jawboning the private sector. However, the Japanese government remains more closely engaged and pursues its engagement through different or more intrusive mechanisms than is generally the case in the United States.

Belief in the necessity or value of industrial policy stemmed from a concern that markets are inefficient or wasteful. Why allow markets to allocate investment funds to industries or firms that duplicate unnecessarily what others are doing? Why allow markets to finance resort hotels when the nation really needs increased steel capacity? Why allow markets to finance separately the research on competing new technologies of a dozen firms when they could all cooperate on a single approach at less cost? Such doubts about the efficiency of markets drove the government's desire to maintain a guiding hand over the economy.

This fundamental aspect of the Japanese economic system has been questioned in the 1990s. What seemed appropriate in a catch-up development phase was less appropriate in an advanced industrial nation. Markets might make mistakes, but could bureaucrats really outperform or out-guess markets about the shape of the future? Chapter 3 explores some of these new concerns.

Attractiveness

Each of the distinctive features of the economy just explored has been buttressed by strong beliefs concerning desirability and superiority. Having believed for several decades that core features of their economic system were superior to American or European approaches, the Japanese are struggling to change their attitudes toward reform. To be sure, the economic malaise of the 1990s undermined support for the existing system. Old beliefs die hard, however, and the problems of the 1990s did not touch the lives of most Japanese very directly.

While there is certainly envy over the rigor of American venture capital markets and general equity financing of small-cap firms, there remains suspicion over the short-term flows of equity and bond markets. If patient bank financing was a presumed advantage for Japanese firms for several decades, why should it not be an advantage now?

The same is true of corporate governance. The public has witnessed some examples of spectacular management failure, including the Long-Term Credit Bank, Nissan Motor Company, and Sogo Department Store. However, do people believe more broadly that stock market investors are better equipped to govern corporations than the managers themselves?

Vertical *keiretsu* were an ingredient in the emergence of excellence in quality control and manufacturing cost reduction. If vertical *keiretsu* were important to the rise of Toyota Motors as one of the leading automobile manufacturers in the world, why discard the system now? Are there not still cost and quality advantages to quasi-permanent subcontracting relationships?

After decades of decrying "excess" competition and accepting limits on price competition, why should competition suddenly be accepted as desirable? Certainly discontent over high prices mounted as consumers became more aware of lower prices abroad, and corporations recognized the liability of their high cost structures. Competition implies winners and losers, uncertainty in the marketplace, and possible instability in prices, however. If these were unsettling aspects of competition in the past, why should they be viewed more positively now?

For decades firms believed that lifetime employment engendered increasingly productive employees at both the blue-collar and managerial level. If the system enhanced productivity and productivity growth, why abandon it now?

Having the not-so-invisible hand of government in the marketplace was widely believed to be one part of the explanation of superior economic growth. Indeed, in the early 1990s, the Japanese government was pressing the World Bank to study the Japanese economic model and accept the proposition that other Asian countries were succeeding by adopting it. Although the public attitude toward bureaucrats deteriorated in the 1990s, no one was clamoring to disband government-affiliated financial institutions.

Japanese have been proud of other aspects of their economic system as well, especially in comparison with the United States. A combination of tax policies and corporate salary systems yielded an income disparity between rich and poor that was considerably smaller than in the United States or other industrial nations. The Japanese have long had a negative popular image of the United States—disapproving of CEOs, athletes, and entertainers being outrageously compensated while some people are homeless. The Japanese media have associated income disparity, unemployment, and the casual cruelty of market outcomes for losers with American social ills like violent crime and divorce.

When deregulation got under way, one group of opponents published two forceful articles in a leading policy magazine highlighting the supposedly negative effect of deregulation on the United States.[35] A long-term advocate of the Japanese system, Eisuke Sakakibara (a career Ministry of Finance official who served as vice minister for International Monetary Affairs in the late 1990s), maintained his beliefs through the 1990s. In 1997 he wrote: "I, for one, have long defended the Japanese-style market economy, and my position remains unchanged."[36] In 2000 he was saying much the same thing, rejecting what he called "market fundamentalism."[37] In 2000 the president of a Japanese wine company active in business leaders groups warned of the dangers of deregulation for consumer safety (in which unfettered competition leads firms to cut safety in their quest for profits).[38] Also in 2000 the director of Kyoto University's Economic Research Institute advocated that Japan adopt a "third way" that would reject "the handcuffs imposed on it by the 'market-economy' mantra."[39] These voices are typical of the considerable doubts about deregulation and the American economic model. Deregulation has also had strong advocates, but it is important to recognize that important voices like these speak either against it or for a cautious approach.

Thus, while the failings of the Japanese economic system may seem rather obvious from the outside, they are not so obvious or certain to the Japanese. The Japanese perception of an American model toward which they might converge is by no means as favorable as Americans might think. Some of the discussion of the Japanese economic model in this chapter may have been idealized or theoretical, but it is this idealized model and its theoretical benefits that many Japanese have in mind when they contemplate reform. If they believe the ideal, then they may exhort the individuals who make the system work to behave properly rather than to dismantle it in favor of a more market-based system that many have viewed with some distaste for the past several decades.

Interconnections

Much of the public discussion in Japan of structural reform in the 1990s has focused on individual parts of the existing economic system. However, the features discussed in this chapter form an interconnected whole. Trying to alter one piece of the puzzle without rearranging all the rest of the elements is very difficult. Either the immobility of the other pieces ultimately counteracts the effort at change, or the rest of the system must shift to accommodate the change.

Figure 2-5 shows how the various elements of the Japanese economic model relate to one another, as well as across the boundaries of households, corporations, and government. Consider the flow of government influence, beginning with its desire to informally guide investment allocation. A financial sector skewed toward banking enhanced government influence over investment. This financial configuration also led directly to the pattern of corporate governance, with weak boards and shareholders. This relative weakness of shareholders opened greater opportunities for administrative guidance by government since government did not face potential challenges from pesky bondholders and shareholders who might be disgruntled when the companies in which they invested pursued policies in accordance with government guidance rather than profit. Management's compliance with administrative guidance, coupled with overall protectionist trade and investment barriers erected by government, enabled reduced competition. The more stable corporate existence possible with collusive behavior enabled long-term vertical *keiretsu* relationships and paternalistic labor policies such as lifetime employment. Risk-averse households, in turn, preferred the sta-

Figure 2-5. *Interconnected Nature of the Economic System*

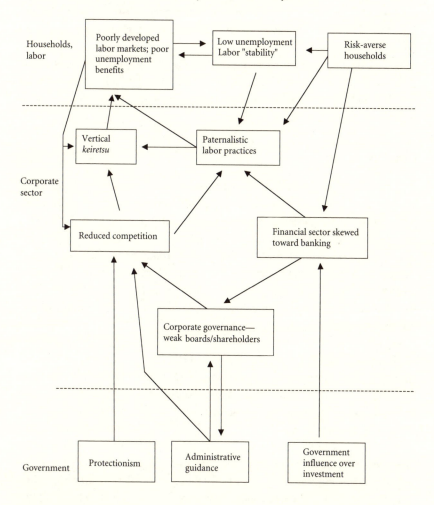

bility of lifetime employment and willingly stuffed their savings into low-return bank deposits in the bank-centered financial system established by the government.

Because these features are so interconnected, change is difficult unless pursued across all elements of the system. For firms to announce an end to lifetime employment in the face of poorly developed labor markets and a risk-averse labor force is not a winning proposition. Financial reforms aimed at altering the flow of funds away from banking toward bonds and equity are doomed to failure unless they change the nature of corporate governance (so that shareholders can behave like owners), accept a major loss of government influence, alter lifetime employment, or persuade households to be less risk-averse. In the long run, the "big bang" financial reforms now occurring, for example, could still leave a financial sector that is heavily dependent on banking.

This caution concerning the implications of interconnectedness does not mean that change is impossible. It does mean that individual efforts at reform are likely to have less impact than often supposed—or that the reform process will take much longer than imagined.

Conclusion

Embarking on a radical political and economic transformation, the Meiji government embraced capitalism in the late nineteenth century. The economy continues to operate in a basic capitalist setting; the government never moved as far as the Europeans in a socialist direction, and it has made at least some moderate attempts to privatize railroads, tobacco, and telecommunications. However, the government's general restraint in actually taking control of industries should not be seen as a sign that freely operating private markets dominate the economy. This chapter has demonstrated how different the overall architecture of the economic system has been from that of the United States.

Much of what differentiates Japan from the United States has to do with the role of the government. The government (meaning here mainly the career bureaucracy, not elected officials) distrusted markets and believed in its own ability to guide the economy on a path of growth and industrial development. While lifetime employment and its associated behavioral practices grew out of the private sector itself, a conservative government certainly appreciated the potentially beneficial effect that corporate allegiance and dependency would have on diminishing organized labor protest. The regulation of the financial sector deliberately pushed the flow of finance through a banking system over which the government could have some influence. Corporate governance shorn of the profit-minded interests of shareholders resulted in corporations that would be more pliable to government pressures. Restraints on competition were a deliberate result of government actions that either explicitly or implicitly permitted collusive behavior, believed by many in government to be better for the long-term growth of the economy than unrestrained competition. Industrial policy added a variety of other government actions and policies to explicitly promote industrialization.

This aggressive hand of government has been cloaked to a considerable extent in indirection, informality, and opaqueness. Determining whether a particular economic outcome is the result of government policy or of private-sector vitality is often difficult because the role of government is obscured. Although there are certainly specific examples of industries that defied explicit government policy initiatives, the overall picture remains one of continuous government involvement in the microeconomic affairs of the nation—to an extent well beyond what exists in the United States.

All societies change, and Japan is no exception. The postwar era began with an economy that was still quite explicitly controlled by government, a legacy of wartime mobilization. Change, in the direction of deregulation and reduction of the government role, has been under way since the 1960s. One must ask, however, what has changed and what has remained. The features of the economy discussed in this chapter remained very much in evidence during the 1990s. Despite predictions dating to at least the late 1960s, lifetime employment still exists. Banking still dominated the financial sector in the 1990s. Corporate governance remained in the hands of managers with weak oversight from their main banks. Restrained competition still exists in industries ranging from construction to telecommunications. Government continued to pursue initiatives to interfere in the workings of the market.

What about changes at the turn of the century? The pace of reform and restructuring accelerated in the late 1990s. Lifetime employment is once again being proclaimed dead. Banks have been in distress since the early 1990s, and financial flows could shift toward bonds and equity; the initiation of two new small-cap stock markets to provide financing for start-up firms received much publicity in 2000. Companies have announced an emphasis on return on equity. Hard times reduced the willingness of companies to stick to collusive arrangements and the willingness of buyers—both households and corporations—to tolerate high prices. Some newly successful industries (such as computer games) appear to have no relationship to government at all.

Part of this picture of accelerated systemic reform is accurate. However, the rest of this book will argue that the force of those changes remains rather weak and that the eventual outcome is unlikely to be an economy that embraces or operates on open market principles to the extent of the American economy.

3

The Argument for Change

Reform to reduce the economic role of government, motivated by public dissatisfaction with economic performance, has been a dominant story in many countries over the past quarter century. Heavy-handed government involvement in the economy eventually failed to enhance economic growth and led to increasingly obvious distortions and inefficiencies in a number of countries. In the United States, for example, deregulation grew out of economic analysis of the distortions, inefficiencies, and misallocation of resources caused by the regulatory system. In other countries, like Britain, state-owned enterprises were increasingly inefficient, soaking up ever-larger taxpayer-funded subsidies. Some countries experienced escalating inflation stoked by the monetization of government deficits incurred to finance red ink at inefficient state enterprises and welfare systems that were too generous. In Japan, however, the economic system continued to perform well through the 1980s.

During the 1980s many outsiders looked at Japan with admiration, envy, or fear because the economic system appeared to perform better than that of other industrial nations, and leading Japanese manufacturing firms steadily gained market share in global markets. Robust growth, low unemployment, and low inflation continued throughout the decade. The Japanese themselves believed that their version of capitalism and government intervention avoided the problems of both the United States (such as wide income disparities) and Europe (such as excessive welfare guarantees). If the system functioned so well for almost a half century, why change it?

Despite the appearance of success, problems were building. The speculative bubble in stock and real estate prices in the second half of the 1980s burst at the beginning of the 1990s. The rest of the 1990s brought slow growth and recession, a gargantuan mountain of bad debts in the financial system, rising unemployment, and increased worry about the future. The poor performance of the 1990s provides the proximate cause for discussion and action on systemic reform, even though the immediate reason for the economic malaise of the decade was, arguably, a macroeconomic phenomenon and not a structural one.[1]

Other factors also argue for change. First, major areas of the economy are operating inefficiently relative to other industrial nations, and the continued financing of those sectors represents misallocation of resources in the economy. While continued growth would be possible without fixing these problems, their negative impact tended to grow over time, and by the end of the 1990s, some aspects of inefficiency were quite startling, holding the potential to damage future growth and dampen income levels for society as a whole. Second, the existing system contained some inherent weaknesses or flaws. Indeed, some of these flaws provide at least part of the explanation for the emergence of the speculative bubble of the 1980s and the poor policy and business response to its collapse in the 1990s. Third, the globalization of economic activity implied that the advisability or capability of maintaining an economic system so different from those of other nations was becoming doubtful. The increasing presence of foreign investors in Japanese financial markets, for example, pushed the discussion of raising returns on equity and other changes in corporate behavior.

All these factors fed into discussion and pressure for reform during the 1990s, but none of them was sufficiently powerful to yield radical change. Dissatisfaction stemming from poor macroeconomic performance was modest because performance was far from a disaster—gross domestic product (GDP) did grow, albeit slowly for the decade as a whole. Furthermore, while sustained economic recovery required systemic reform, short-run cyclical recovery (as occurred in 1995–96 or in the first half of 2000) masked this need. To be sure, the financial sector experienced a debilitating bad debt problem and teetered on the brink of disaster. Overall, however, the average household was better off at the end of the decade than at the beginning.

This is true of the other factors discussed in this chapter—they represent problems or distortions sufficient to provoke concern, discussion, and some tinkering, but they were hardly disastrous enough to yield extensive reform. Many of the inefficiencies in the economy, for example, were more evident to outside analysts than to the Japanese themselves, and none was sufficiently debilitating to foster political revolt and extensive economic reform. Inherent weaknesses were exposed by the bad debt debacle, but whether the desired response was true reform or just admonition to bureaucrats and businesses to behave better was unclear. "Global standards" became a faddish term at the end of the decade, but often with little operational content; it was offset by an underlying desire to maintain past practices. The combination of all these forces was certainly producing something new; no one can question the reality of the atmosphere of change by the end of the 1990s. However, the force of these factors still did not appear to be pushing Japan toward major systemic reform.

Public dissatisfaction with the economic system in a democracy becomes actual reform through the workings of the political system. How and why the political system failed to produce voter revolt, a change in political parties, and more reform policies is a complex and fascinating story. That analysis is beyond the scope of this study, which focuses on the underlying economic developments that fed into political debate. Others have dealt with the arcane, dysfunctional aspects of Japanese politics—the skewed districts that give rural voters a disproportionate voice, the extraordinarily heavy emphasis by politicians on bringing home public works projects to their constituents, and the strength of the career bureaucracy vis-à-vis elected politicians in establishing policy and writing legislation.[2] These aspects of Japanese politics are important in their own right as part of the explanation for the slow, hesitant pace of reform. However, the underlying economic factors did not provide as obvious or powerful a motivation for reform as those viewing them from abroad might expect.

The Macroeconomic Spur to Change

The immediate spur to structural reform in Japan has been the deterioration in economic growth, especially the relative stagnation of the 1990s. Structural flaws in the economy are part of the explanation of the macroeconomic problems of the 1990s. Japan will not return to a sustained growth path until deregulation unleashes investment in industries that have been constrained by regulation. However, much of the stagnation and recession of the 1990s had purely macroeconomic causes, undermining this rationale for structural change. Government officials and politicians could blame the problems on the unfortunate collapse of asset prices and focus on macroeconomic fixes for the problem (through expansionary monetary and fiscal

Figure 3-1. *Real Growth of GDP, 1955–99*

Percent

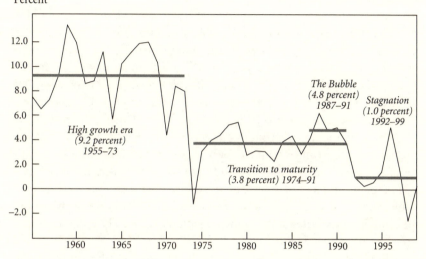

Source: GDP data are from Japan Economic and Social Research Institute, www.esri.cao.go.jp/en/sma/qe004/
gdemenue.html (April 9, 2001), (downloadable spreadsheet), "Changes from the previous year at Constant Prices."

policy). Upturns in economic growth—as in 1995–96 or in 2000—then became excuses to downplay the reform agenda.

However, the case can be made that structural features of the economy contributed to the creation of the speculative bubble in asset prices in the 1980s and delayed the recovery process during the 1990s. Economic recovery without substantial reform would be unfortunate. Times of recession and economic distress play a useful role in rooting out inefficiency and weakness in all economies. Should that process not occur, then the economy is likely to underperform in the future and run the risk of another crisis.

Figure 3-1 shows economic growth from the 1960s through 1999. From an average level of almost 10 percent in the 1960s, growth dropped to an average of 3.8 percent from 1974 through 1991. The high growth of the 1960s and early 1970s represented a continuation of a successful, high-growth catch-up era that had begun in the early 1950s. Then the average growth of the economy decelerated sharply to a 3.8 percent annual average from 1974 through 1991. The main cause of this decline in growth from the mid-1970s was economic maturity; having largely caught up with the leading industrial economies of the world, the economy could no longer grow at extremely high rates.[3] Even this lower growth rate remained considerably above that of the United States, which grew at a 2.4 percent annual rate over the same period.[4] Furthermore, the 1980s ended with a burst of higher growth that averaged almost 5 percent from 1987 through 1991. During this bubble period, confidence about the nation's ability to outperform other industrial nations blossomed. The features of the economy identified in chapter 2 were widely believed to represent a superior form of capitalism, yielding higher economic growth, more rapid productivity gains, lower unemployment, and greater income equality than the economies of other industrial nations.

The euphoria of the late 1980s was short lived. During the rest of the 1990s average annual real economic growth averaged only 1.0 percent. Eventually the economy slipped into a recession for the first time since 1974, with negative growth for calendar year 1998 and two consecutive negative quarters in the second half of 1999. This growth performance was a strong psychological blow and completely unexpected in the early 1990s, when the government anticipated only a short growth recession. The confidence and hubris of the 1980s evaporated.

Behind the stagnation of the 1990s lay the speculative bubble in real estate and stock market prices in the second half of the 1980s. When the Japanese economy was hit with the rapid appreciation of the yen from 1985 to 1987, with the yen doubling in value against the dollar, economic recession loomed as exports were hurt and imports grew. Governments facing recession can use either monetary or fiscal policy to provide economic stimulus. Because the government was in the midst of a determined long-term policy of reducing the government deficit, after a bout of fiscal expansion in the 1970s, officials were in no mood to use fiscal stimulus. Instead they used monetary stimulus, lowering interest rates and encouraging banks to lend. One result was the acceleration of real growth of the bubble period.

Arguably this spurt in growth exceeded Japan's long-term potential growth, and it certainly resulted in very tight labor markets. Normally this would have led to higher inflation, but yen appreciation had put manufacturers under strong price pressure, either because they needed to absorb a large part of yen appreciation to maintain market share abroad or because they faced new pressures from imports at home. Rather than general price inflation, Japan got asset price inflation, shown in figure 3-2. With limited growth in demand for funds by manufacturers, banks lent more for real estate and stock market investments. Even traditional borrowers—including manufacturing firms borrowing to speculate on the stock market, and department stores developing golf courses—began borrowing for these purposes in the late 1980s. The Nikkei average index of stock prices tripled in value from

Figure 3-2. *Stock and Land Price Indexes, 1985–98*

1985 = 100

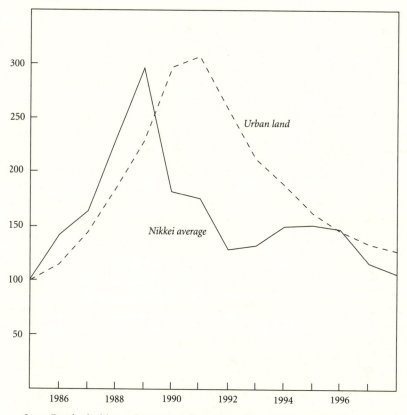

Source: For urban land data, see Statistics Bureau, *Japan Statistical Yearbook 2001*, p. 558; for Nikkei average, *Japan Statistical Yearbook 2001*, p. 475, and *Japan Statistical Yearbook 1995*, p. 481.

1985 to the end of 1989, while the official index of urban real estate prices in the six largest cities also tripled in value between 1985 and 1991.

These gains were not underwritten by any new technological impulse that raised long-term profits, investment, and productivity growth—unlike the situation a decade later in the United States. Indeed, the economy as a whole had completed the catch-up phase of development and faced a future of convergence on the modest growth of other mature economies. The unique technological impulse in Japan—engineering and organizational innovations in manufacturing (such as the vertical *keiretsu*) that lowered the cost of production while simultaneously increasing quality—dated to the 1960s and had largely played out as an explanation for superior performance relative to other mature economies. By the early 1980s these technological innovations meant some leading manufacturers were expanding their global market shares, offering products of lower price and higher quality than their western competitors. By the late 1980s these innovations were rapidly diffusing to other countries, erasing much of the advantage of Japanese firms. Furthermore, the sharp appreciation of the yen after 1985 was not a temporary phenomenon. All Japanese manufacturers had been aided in the first half of the decade by an unusually weak currency, giving them an added price advantage in global markets. With that advantage gone, firms faced a future of lower profits and growth. The tripling of stock market and real estate prices was, therefore, not justified by underlying economic factors.

By 1989 the Ministry of Finance (MOF) decided that speculative bubbles in real estate and stock prices truly existed and that they were unsustainable. At the time MOF officials seemed to be very confident that they could engineer a modest price decline in the two markets, which would hurt only "evil" speculators. Instead, figure 3-2 shows that virtually all of the gains in both the stock and real estate markets were lost, with real estate prices still falling through 1999.

One natural consequence of the collapse of these asset prices was economic stagnation, as would be the case in any economy. The fall in asset prices affected the ability of nonfinancial companies to borrow (by shrinking the value of assets they could use as collateral) and of financial institutions to lend (because of a rise in losses on nonperforming loans that had been secured by inflated collateral). The initial response to this major decline in asset values was actually relatively mild. After a year of close to zero growth in 1993, the economy appeared to be gradually recovering through 1996, propelled in large part by an increasingly stimulative fiscal policy.

What appeared to be a recovery was snuffed out in 1997. Believing the economy to be recovering, the politicians acceded to Ministry of Finance desires to raise taxes in the spring of 1997, including elimination of a temporary income tax cut, an increase in the national consumption tax (that is, sales tax) by 2 percentage points (from 3 percent to 5 percent), and an increase in national health care premiums. This policy change drove the economy into recession from late 1997 through 1998. With criticism emanating from domestic quarters and pressure coming from the U.S. government and other G-7 nations as well, the government reversed its fiscal policy stance once again in mid-1998. By 1999 it was injecting a much larger dose of fiscal stimulus through tax cuts and spending increases.[5]

Figure 3-3. *Government Fiscal Balance, 1990–2000*

Percent of GDP

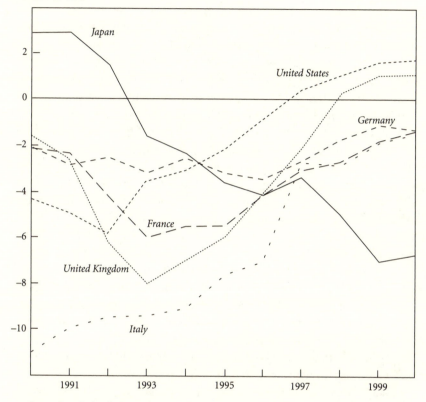

Source: Organization for Economic Cooperation and Development, *OECD Economic Outlook 67*, June 2000, p. 272.

Figure 3-3 illustrates the movements in the government's fiscal stance over the 1990s. These nominal figures reflect the result of both the effect of changing economic growth on taxes and spending and deliberate fiscal policy choices. After expanding through 1996 to a temporary peak of 4.2 percent of GDP, the deficit contracted in 1997 (3.3 percent of GDP) only to expand again by 1999 (7.0 percent of GDP). The contrast to other major countries is also noticeable. In fact, by 1999 Japan's overall government deficit was much larger as a percent of GDP than that of any other member of the Organization for Economic Cooperation and Development (OECD). Countries such as Italy that had been known for large government deficits had reduced them as part of the requirement for establishing a unified European currency. Thus by the end of the 1990s the government had finally heeded criticism from home and abroad, undertaking a truly massive effort to stimulate the economy.

With stagnation and recession, other economic indicators had deteriorated during the 1990s as well. Unemployment, which had been only 2.1 percent in 1990, hit a peak of 4.9 percent in mid-1999, a postwar high. Perhaps more telling, employment peaked in 1997; by 1999 it had fallen 1.5 percent, and it was still shrinking slightly through mid-2000. This had not happened since the 1940s.[6] These were discouraging developments for a population used to low unemployment and expanding job opportunities.

The second major consequence of the collapse of the asset bubble was a mountain of bad debt. Those who had borrowed to finance real estate development or stock speculation in the late 1980s were unable to repay their loans. Business failures due to economic recession left banks with collateral often worth much less than the amount of the nonperforming loans. In the summer of 1998 the newly established Financial Supervisory Agency (split off from the Ministry of Finance) calculated the "problem" debt figure to be ¥87.5 trillion ($630 billion at then-current exchange rates), to which should be added ¥35.2 trillion ($253 billion) in loans already written off by banks—making a total of ¥123 trillion ($880 billion).[7] To put these numbers in perspective, the ratio of bad debt to total bank loans was more than 17 percent, and the ratio to GDP was 25 percent—high levels for any nation to absorb. Even this admission was a step forward; government policy since the early 1990s had been to downplay the size of the problem while hoping that economic recovery would cause it to diminish.

Finally the government moved to deal more decisively with the banking situation by passing two laws in the fall of 1998. One law was to nationalize insolvent banks, a mechanism somewhat like the operation of the Resolution Trust Corporation in the United States, created in 1989 to deal with failed savings and loan institutions. The second provided government money to recapitalize weak—but presumably solvent—banks. While these developments could still be criticized as inadequate, they at least pulled the banking sector back from the brink of widespread failure.

The weak economic performance of the 1990s and the dilemma of coping with bad loans could be attributed to macroeconomic factors. The speculative bubble of the 1980s was due largely to excessive monetary ease and administrative guidance to banks that encouraged them to lend for real estate and stock market investments. The collapse of the bubble was due to deliberate monetary tightening. The stagnation in the first half of the 1990s occurred because of the government's delay in responding in the 1992–94 period, when it resisted calls for fiscal stimulus. Recovery in 1995–96 occurred on the strength of (belated) fiscal stimulus in the form of tax cuts and increased spending on public works. Recession in 1997–98 was the direct result of the tax increase in the spring of 1997. Finally, at least a weak, temporary recovery in 2000 began as the government reversed its fiscal policy stance once again.

If most of the economic gyrations of the 1990s could be attributed to standard macroeconomic developments, then presumably structural reform of the economic system was not necessary. Rather than deregulation and other reforms, all Japan needed was a more sensible set of macroeconomic policies to put the economy back on a self-sustaining growth path.[8] That notion became an excuse to downplay the need for systemic reform. The nation should simply wait for a dose of fiscal stimulus and monetary ease to reignite private-sector growth in classic pump-priming fashion. The government made a serious mistake in 1996 in assuming that the self-sustaining recovery in the private sector was already under way, and it removed fiscal stimulus too early. If the government could avoid such mistakes and keep the stimulus going long enough, then the desired recovery would occur and the "lost decade" of the 1990s would come to an end. At least this was what the government hoped.

This macroeconomic explanation of the problems of the 1990s certainly represents part of the truth, and part of the correct policy prescription, but it ignores deeper issues.

First, the description above of the causes of stagnation and recession is a snapshot of the government's bungling policy. The economy was whipsawed first by the excessive monetary ease of the 1990s, and then by the on-again, off-again fiscal policy stimulus during the 1990s. When the government did pump up fiscal stimulus, the tendency was to use large doses of public works spending, which some voters recognized as wasteful and corrupt. Meanwhile, the government presented a shockingly slow and weak response to the bad debt crisis that was building in the banking sector. This included the humiliating spectacle of being hectored by the United States and other G-7 countries in the spring of 1998 as banks slid closer toward mass insolvency. Instead of presenting an image of excellence and competence, bureaucrats looked more like a bunch of bumbling bumpkins, and politicians seemed to be their foolish handmaidens. Thus this was not just a simple macroeconomic story, but one that undermined public faith in the government.

Second, the collapse of the asset bubble spawned a number of shocking scandals, some of which involved government bureaucrats. Japan has periodically had scandals involving the private sector and politicians, but exposure of bureaucratic malfeasance has been relatively rare. The 1990s brought revelations of illegal and unethical behavior at both the Ministry of Finance and the Bank of Japan. The scandals that emerged in the 1990s revealed truly shocking episodes of indiscretion and illegality, or at least they were shocking in frequency, as much of the revealed behavior seems quite unsurprising.

Favored investors at securities firms received guarantees of high positive rates of return on their equity portfolios, and an embarrassed government continues to refuse to release the list of names on Nomura Securities "VIP" list since it includes politicians and career bureaucrats.[9] Huge loans went to small businesses for speculation in real estate and the stock market—including the infamous bankruptcy of a small restaurant owner in Osaka, who defaulted on debts worth $3 billion. The supposedly staid Industrial Bank of Japan was her largest lender.[10] Large banks eagerly introduced crooked clients to subsidiary banks or credit co-ops in order to keep questionable loans off their own books while hoping to benefit from the illicit business, relationships revealed when some of these credit co-ops went bankrupt.[11] Financial institutions (and other corporations) continued to pay off *sokaiya* racketeers who threatened to reveal negative information at annual shareholder meetings. In exchange for lavish entertainment and other favors, Ministry of Finance officials told banks when they would be making "surprise" inspections.[12] Those examinations were often perfunctory at best, enabling firms to hide their imprudent, unethical, or illegal activities, as happened in the Daiwa Bank scandal in New York.[13] Allegations were made concerning Ministry of Finance explicit approval of (or even administrative guidance recommending) illegal schemes to hide financial problems at Yamaichi Securities.[14] Even Bank of Japan officials were implicated in providing advance information on the bank's market operations to friends in the private sector.[15] These scandals were far beyond isolated incidents; their occurrence paints a picture of widespread routine corruption and incestuous relations among financial firms, their clients, government officials, and politicians.

These scandals implied that the bubble and its aftermath involved more than just a simple speculative mistake that could hit any economy. The causes included extensive unethical and corrupt behavior within the existing system—behavior that was difficult to detect until outright corporate failure revealed an inner rot. The existing economic system did not cause unethical or corrupt behavior, but the nontransparent nature of many of the relationships (such as those between bank and borrower or government and business) certainly put temptation before businessmen and government officials.

Scandals also undermined the faith of the public in the integrity of career officials, arguably contributing to a mood favoring deregulation. That is, if government officials are not capable of making unbiased judgments, then one solution is simply to eliminate the need for their decisions through deregulation. Clear rules and open competition could be a substitute for the rather heavy guiding hand of the government. This point should not be pushed too far, however. Japan has such a long tradition of strong government it is doubtful whether the public wanted anything more serious than for the bureaucracy to repent and return to (supposedly) impartial decisionmaking.

This point gains some credence since the duration of the bureaucratic scandals was quite short. While other scandals related to the bubble and its aftermath that involved politicians and private-sector actors began in the late 1980s (with the Recruit Scandal) and continue today, the bureaucratic scandals emerged in 1997 and came to an abrupt end in the spring of 1998, when the zealous prosecutor pursuing these cases was reassigned to rural Shikoku. With no new occurrences, at least the country could sustain a surface image of a chastened bureaucracy that had returned to its traditional selfless, dedicated role of serving the public interest.

Beyond bungled policy and individual malfeasance, the problems of the 1990s were partly due to, or exacerbated by, weaknesses in the existing economic system. Some of the structural flaws in the system discussed later in this chapter created an environment in which the bubble of the 1980s was more likely to occur. Speculative bubbles can occur in any economy, mainly because of the inherently unknowable nature of the future. This may lead occasionally to badly mistaken valuation of assets that become evident only in retrospect. However, one should ask why forecasts were so wrong, or why investors went so far in driving up prices. Behind the surface confidence of the late 1980s was an economic system that was not performing as well as believed. Lack of transparency, continued industrial policy despite economic maturity, weak corporate governance, and other problems implied that Japan was not embarking on an era of outperforming other industrial nations. Growth was built on a weak base, but the weaknesses were not apparent because of the lack of transparency coupled with a broad public determination to ignore weaknesses and problems.

In any case, there can be no doubt that the many problems of the 1990s— stagnation and recession, huge bad debts, occasional bank failures, recognition of structural problems, and exposure of an unusually high number of scandals—all contributed to a sour public mood and led to discussion of deregulation as a solution. From 1993, during the administration of Morihiro

Hosokawa, some voices in society argued that the nation would not return to a healthy economic growth path unless thorough deregulation took place. According to this thesis, regulation and other government interference had been locking up resources in inefficient sectors (such as agriculture) and delaying the growth of the industries of the future (such as telecommunications). While this view was occasionally exaggerated, it was largely correct. The existing economic system harbors growing inefficiencies and inherent flaws. Recovery on the basis of fiscal stimulus is certainly possible, but the longer-term health of the economy would be better were substantial reform to occur.

The fact that the malaise spawned calls for reform is encouraging. The continuing puzzle to many foreign observers has been the lack of vigor in that process, but the reason for that may also lie in the overall economic situation. As discouraging as the 1990s were for a society that was used to rapid economic growth, the decade was hardly the disaster often portrayed in the press. For the vast majority of Japanese, life remains very comfortable, and problems are something they read about in the newspaper or view on television. In 1990, per capita GDP was ¥3.5 million and by 1999 had risen almost 12 percent to ¥3.8 million (adjusted for inflation), yielding an annual growth rate of 1.2 percent. While this was a much slower rate of increase than in previous decades (3.4 percent in the 1980s), it was still positive rather than negative.[16] That is, on average the Japanese people were better off (in income) in 1999 than in 1990. Even at purchasing power parity exchange rates, per capita GDP in 1998 came to $24,109, the eighth highest among OECD members (and not far behind the $30,514 of the United States).[17]

Even with slow economic growth, a number of indicators of material well-being continued to rise. The automobile market suffered major declines in sales during the 1990s. Even at reduced levels of sales, the stock of registered automobiles continued to grow at an average annual rate of 4.6 percent from 1992 through 1997, exceeding the growth of population between the ages of twenty and seventy (only 0.6 percent annually over the same time period) and the increase in the number of households (1.5 percent annually). By 1998 Japan ranked high in the world in diffusion of household appliances such as air conditioners, color televisions, VCRs, and cellular phones.[18]

Furthermore, unemployment, though in 1999 at its postwar high of 4.9 percent, was still low in an absolute sense. For the vast majority of adults, potential unemployment was a vague worry, but not a personal reality. After all, 4.9 percent employment implies that 95.1 percent of all adults desiring work are employed. Certainly some adults had dropped out of the labor force, discouraged by the dim prospects of finding a job, but they remained largely invisible in society.

These indicators of personal welfare provide a large part of the explanation for the lack of vigor in pushing reform. Unless and until a broader segment of the population feels economically inconvenienced, why change? In the early postwar period, when people were poor, rapid growth was the key to a better life. Today that better life has arrived and masks the problems or flaws in the system that jeopardize the future. Life is just too comfortable to push vigorously for reform, especially when many still believe in the value of the existing system.

Economic stagnation in the 1990s certainly spawned discussion, debate, and some action on deregulation and other economic reforms leading in the direction of less government intervention in the economy. Obviously many in society were disgruntled over the weak economic performance, rising unemployment, scandals, and policy mistakes. Some were clearly worried about the future, even if they were not unemployed. However, the mildness of economic pain blunted the drive. Ultimately what many want is not a fundamental reshaping of the economic system, but for bureaucrats, corporations, and financial institutions to behave "better"—with greater morality and fewer mistakes.

Inefficiencies

Over time a number disparities have emerged between Japan and other industrial nations. Most of these have not been obvious to the public and have not fed into domestic debate over the need for deregulation. Viewed from abroad, however, some of these inefficiencies are rather startling for an advanced industrial nation.

Excess Investment

One of the disparities between Japan and the rest of the world is the high level of investment and cumulative capital stock. In the 1980s some American manufacturers worried that high levels of plant and equipment investment meant their Japanese competitors would have newer and more productive factories, giving them an advantage in global competition. By the end of the 1990s the overall result appeared to be extraordinarily low returns on capital and extensive inefficiency in the use of capital stock. In broad terms, investment was too high and was a drag on the economy rather than a boon.

Figure 3-4. *Gross Fixed Capital Formation as a Percentage of GDP, OECD Countries, 1997*

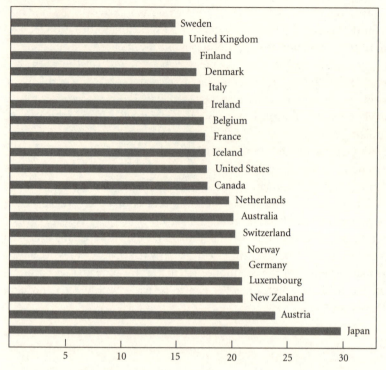

Source: Organization for Economic Cooperation and Development, www.oecd.org/std/nahome.htm (March 28, 2001), "Gross Domestic Product Table."

In 1997 gross fixed investment as a share of GDP was the highest in the OECD, as shown in figure 3-4. At 29.7 percent, the ratio of investment in Japan was well above the next highest OECD member (Austria, at 23.8 percent) and 68 percent higher than the level in the United States.

Figure 3-4 includes all fixed investment—private residential, private nonresidential (business investment in plant and equipment), and government (public works) investments. In earlier years, when the economy was growing quickly and the nation was upgrading both housing and public infrastructure, a high level of fixed investment relative to that of mature industrial nations was logical. But by the late 1990s, the economy was mature, the housing stock was no longer as inadequate as it had been a decade or two earlier, and public infrastructure (such as roads, bridges, sidewalks, and libraries) was relatively well developed. As a result, total fixed investment should have

Figure 3-5. *Private-Sector Fixed Investment in Japan and the United States, as a Percentage of GDP, 1960–98*

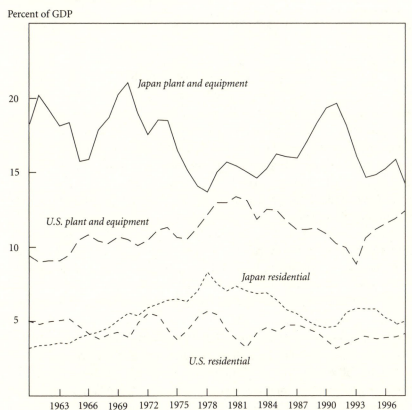

Sources: U.S. data are from U.S. Department of Commerce, *Survey of Current Business*, vol. 79 (December 1999), p. 132; Japanese data are from downloaded GDP table, Japan Economic and Social Research Institute, www.esri.cao.go.jp/en/sna/qe004-2/gdemenue.htm (May 3, 2001).

diminished as a share of GDP to the level of other economies. In addition, 1997 was a recession year, which should have further depressed private-sector investment.

What about the components of fixed investment? Both residential and business investment has been high relative to the United States. Figure 3-5 shows the ratio of plant and equipment investment and residential investment relative to GDP in both the United States and Japan.

While plant and equipment investment has fluctuated between 9 and 13 percent of GDP in the United States, it has ranged from 15 to 20 percent in Japan. Such a high level was consistent with the 10 percent economic growth of the 1960s, but it was excessive for the slower growth of the 1980s and 1990s. On average, plant and equipment investment did decline somewhat—it averaged 18.2 percent of GDP in the 1960s and 15.9 percent in the 1980s. However, at the peak of the bubble in the late 1980s, plant and equipment investment actually returned to the level of the high-growth era. At the time, some saw high investment as providing Japanese firms with a competitive advantage in global competition, but the record of the 1990s suggests otherwise. Finally in the late 1990s, as real recession hit the economy during the 1997–99 period, the share of plant and equipment investment sagged—to 14.0 percent in 1999. Even this level remained slightly higher than in the U.S. economy, where the prolonged economic growth and associated information technology investment boom brought the ratio up to 12.9 percent. That the United States could generate accelerated economic growth with that level of investment while Japan needed more in stagnation is indicative of the inefficient use of investment.

Residential investment as a share of GDP was noticeably low until the mid-1960s. During the era of high growth, upgrading residential housing was a secondary priority. Industrial policy pushed financing toward industrially useful private-sector investment and public investment in infrastructure useful for the business sector (such as harbor facilities). Once the economy achieved economic maturity in the 1970s, it is not surprising that residential investment as a share of GDP moved higher than the U.S. level. Having successfully built a modern industrial base, government presided over a shift of resources toward housing, enabling households to make up for the relative deprivation of the earlier postwar years.[19] Also keep in mind that this investment does not include land purchases; these figures are not affected by the inflation in land prices. The burst of residential fixed investment tapered off after the mid-1980s, suggesting that the deficiency in housing had come to an end. However, the ratio remained somewhat higher than that of the United States until the late 1990s. Only in 1998 and 1999 did the recession-induced drop in housing investment bring the ratio down to the U.S. level.

The ratios for both residential and plant and equipment fixed investment imply inefficiency or waste in the use of capital stock. Why should a slow-growing Japan require such high levels of annual corporate investment to sustain output? If these investments enhanced the productivity and technological prowess of Japanese companies, why were they not doing better in competition with their global rivals? Part of the answer lay in the nature of the economic system. Lack of pressure from profit-sensitive shareholders has enabled corporations to invest even when they expected little or no positive return on those investments. Banks providing both the loans and the supposed oversight of corporate behavior were satisfied as long as corporate borrowers met their interest payments and the loans were secured by real estate that the banks believed would rise in value regardless of whether the economic activity resulting from the loan produced an operating profit.

One concrete way to visualize how or why investment is inefficient is to look at the use of trucks and automobiles. In Japan's geographically compact economy, with about two-thirds the GDP of the United States, the fleet of registered commercial trucks is actually slightly larger than that of the United States. In 1995 the average for-hire truck (that is, those operated by trucking companies) carried only 42 percent as many tons of freight and produced only 10 percent as many ton-kilometers of freight haulage as those in the United States. For own-use commercial trucks, these percentages are higher: 83 percent as many tons, but only 15 percent as many ton-kilometers. This disparity is obviously affected by narrow, winding roads that limit truck size to some extent (though Japanese trucks are no longer so obviously smaller than their American counterparts), but it is also a result of inefficient truck use, debilitating traffic congestion, poor road design, and regulation. Regardless of causation, though, the fact remains that the Japanese economy gets considerably less output from its fleet of trucks, necessitating higher investment in the fleet of trucks to run the economy.

Furthermore, for both trucks and automobiles, the pattern has been to discard vehicles much earlier than is the case in the United States. The average total lifetime of trucks in Japan was only 8.2 years as of 1998 (up somewhat from 7.2 years in 1980), compared with 15.4 years in the United States. With a shorter lifetime and fewer miles per year, the average truck in Japan is being discarded after being driven only 38 percent as far as the average American truck. Similarly, the average lifetime of an automobile in Japan is 11.5 years, compared with 17.1 years in the United States, implying that Japanese cars are discarded with only 35 percent as much mileage (since they are driven far less per year). Both trucks and automobiles, therefore, are discarded long before the end of their economically useful lives. In quality, vehicles in Japan are at least the equal of those in the United States, and arguably they face less severe climatic conditions (including less extreme temperature variations and no use of salt on roads in the winter).

Trucks and automobiles, therefore, provide a glimpse of how capital is used less productively than in the United States. The causes of the less efficient use of trucks and the shorter lifetimes of trucks and automobiles may lie in many factors. Consumer taste may matter; perhaps people just like to have newer cars than Americans do because they are more style conscious and are willing to pay the price. As noted above, geography might affect truck size. Government behavior matters as well, however. Costly car inspections that encourage people to discard cars rather than pay high repair costs to pass inspections shorten the average lifetime of cars. Cars that are from three to nine years old must undergo inspection every other year; beyond nine years, inspections are annual. Poor road design and inadequate investment in road capacity lead to extensive traffic jams, lowering truck productivity. Whether variables like geography and consumer taste explain the differences or not, the result is a high capital-output ratio. Nevertheless, to the extent that the explanation involves regulation and poor public policy, this high capital-output ratio is unnecessary and wasteful.

Domestic consumption of iron and steel—a key input for physical capital stock—is another vivid example of just how inefficient or overbuilt capital is in Japan. In 1992 apparent domestic consumption of steel in Japan was 81 million metric tons, virtually identical to the 84 million tons consumed in the United States—an economy twice the size of Japan. Even after a 14 percent slide in consumption due to economic stagnation, by 1998 Japan was consuming 27 percent more steel per unit of GDP output than the United States when comparing the two at market exchange rates. Using purchasing power parity exchange rates, Japan was consuming an incredible 58 percent more steel per unit of GDP.[20] To be sure, part of the difference is due to the relative importance of heavy steel-consuming manufacturing industries (especially automobiles and shipbuilding). However, the disparity is especially evident in construction. According to input-output tables for the two countries, iron and steel inputs represent 8.0 percent of construction sector inputs and 0.95 percent of total GDP in the United States; in Japan iron and steel is a whopping 34 percent of construction inputs and 2.8 percent of GDP. Even admitting the structural demands of an earthquake-prone economy, it seems rather incredible that Japan would be devoting triple the share of GDP to iron and steel in construction projects. However, this huge disparity is not so incredible to anyone who has seen the massively constructed highways, bridges, railroads, and buildings in Japan.[21] If all of this steel is truly necessitated by earthquake risks, then the Japanese economy is simply condemned to high capital investments in its structures. A more likely conclusion is that this outcome is due to a half-century of collusion and incestuous relations among steel companies, construction companies, politicians, and bureaucrats, all of whom equated increasing use of steel with the strength of the nation.

Inefficient Labor

Japanese manufacturing firms have been known in global markets over the past two decades for high quality, low-cost products, partly as a result of efficient use of labor. High labor productivity in some parts of the manufacturing sector, however, is offset by very low labor productivity in other areas. Disparities in productivity are wide, and laggard sectors appear quite low relative to other industrial nations such as the United States.

Figure 3-6 shows the level of labor productivity (measured as output per hour of labor input) across the manufacturing sector. Taking the level of productivity in the United States as 100 for each industry, the level of productivity in Japan varies widely. Two industries—basic metals (mostly iron and steel) and the petroleum and chemical industries—had levels of labor productivity that exceeded those in the United States. Others, however, lagged well behind, and some of them, especially textiles and the food, beverage, and tobacco industries, actually lost ground relative to the United States over the course of the 1980s.

In a well-functioning economic system, some variation across sectors is to be expected (due to the inherent nature of the technology of different industries), but for such a wide gap to exist in Japan *relative to the United States* is quite startling. In 1990, for example, the level of productivity in the food and beverage industry was only 35 percent as high as that of its American counterpart, while basic metals were 145 percent the level of American productivity. Since the Japanese have access to the same technology as American firms and have equally high-cost labor, the failure of some industries to raise labor productivity more than they have is a serious failing of the economy.

Figure 3-6 presents evidence only on the manufacturing sector, but similar results should follow from looking at nonmanufacturing industries as well. As noted elsewhere, the construction industry is notoriously inefficient, as are agriculture, the distribution sector, and domestic transportation.

To visualize just how inefficient labor use can be, consider gasoline retailing. As many foreign visitors to Japan know, buying gasoline is akin to making a pit stop in the Indy 500: a crew descends on the car to pump the gas, wash the windows, check the oil and tire pressure, handle payment, and even direct traffic back onto the road. These stations are also numerous. Despite its having a compact geography, half the population of the United States,

Figure 3-6. *Comparison of Japanese and U.S. Output per Hour of Labor Input, 1980, 1985, 1990*

United States = 100

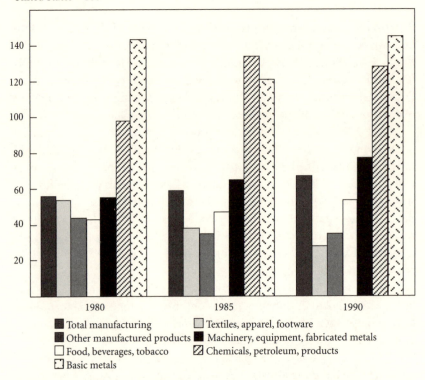

Total manufacturing   □ Textiles, apparel, footware
Other manufactured products ■ Machinery, equipment, fabricated metals
□ Food, beverages, tobacco   ▨ Chemicals, petroleum, products
▢ Basic metals

Source: Peter Hooper, "Comparing Manufacturing Output Levels among the Major Industrial Countries," *Industry Productivity: International Comparison and Measurement Issues* (Paris: Organization for Economic Cooperation and Development, 1996), p. 286.

and vehicles that are not driven as far each year, Japan has 60 percent as many gas stations as the United States. On average, each of those stations pumps only 18 percent as much gasoline (actually less if the higher mileage per gallon for Japanese cars is acknowledged). With their larger size (and generally greater variety of services (repair and convenience store retailing) American gas stations actually employ more people per station on average than their Japanese counterparts, but even so, Japanese employees pump only 30 percent as much gasoline per employee as do American gas stations.[22]

Do Japanese consumers simply prefer the convenience of many gas stations and pampering service? No one knows, because alternatives were not available until 1998; self-service stations were illegal until 1998, and the combination of stiff regulations and collusion have not encouraged many stations to experiment with this new form of service yet. When labor was cheap, heavy staffing of gas stations was economically rational, but the industry did not adjust as the relative cost of labor rose dramatically over the past half century. Government interference in the market lies at the root of this lack of adjustment. Until 1986 the government prohibited the import of gasoline, confining the market to the inefficiently produced, high-cost domestic product. Domestic gasoline was then sold in an informally cartelized market, tolerated by the Ministry of International Trade and Industry (MITI), that strongly discouraged retail price competition. A new law in 1986 theoretically liberalized gasoline imports, but only existing domestic refining firms got licenses (and they, of course, had no incentive to import).[23] Not until these regulations were eased in the late 1990s did gasoline imports begin in any quantity. Meanwhile numerous government regulations affected the nature of gasoline stations (such as a requirement to have a car wash facility on the grounds). All of these factors led to a gasoline retailing industry that had no incentive to change its marketing practices as labor became more expensive. This story is also one of inefficient capital use; gas stations in Japan represent not only low labor productivity, but also low capital productivity. Requirements on size and equipment raise the capital cost of each individual gas station, and the excessive number of stations results in low output for each facility.

By the end of the 1990s, recognition of the embarrassingly large inefficiency in this market was leading to some change. Removal of the restrictive rules on imported gasoline plus legalization of self-service stations led to announcements of a shake-up in the nature of gasoline retailing.[24] The shift, however, got off to a slow start, and a number of years are likely to pass before behavior in this industry will appear to be economically efficient.[25]

Inherent Flaws

In addition to inefficiencies visible in statistics concerning the economy, the postwar economic system harbored several potential flaws or problems. These flaws emerged mainly when the economy had reached maturity; features of the economic system that were useful (or at least not very harmful) in a high-growth development setting were a liability once the economy matured. These include the increasing irrelevance of industrial policy, inflexibility in vertical *keiretsu* relationships, nontransparency, and technical weakness in finance.

Irrelevance of Industrial Policy

Chapter 2 argued that industrial policy broadly defined may have been helpful during the high-growth era and at worst was not much of a drag on the economy overall. Government provided public infrastructure to prevent serious bottlenecks as the economy grew, and the informal, partial guidance over the allocation of resources certainly did not slow the economy by forcing too many inefficient choices. When the government did advocate inefficient choices, its limited controls enabled industries to circumvent some of its pressures. However, the very concept of industrial policy depends on the special conditions that prevailed in the earlier postwar period—a lower-income nation determined to catch up with the industrial leaders. Those conditions had ceased to apply by the mid-1970s; Japan had achieved a century-long goal of becoming a leading industrial nation.

At the global economic frontier, Japan's brand of industrial policy became a liability. How is government supposed to partially guide the allocation of investment and guide the direction of research and development when the future direction of the economy is unknown? Only private markets can react flexibly and quickly to embrace promising industries or technologies while withdrawing resources from those that do not pan out. Governments tend to be too narrow and conservative in making choices about future winners, and they are often unwilling to drop support for economic losers. Markets cannot predict the future, but they provide a more robust way to cope with uncertainty—with the vast multitude of approaches that markets fund, some blossoming and many withering—than the stifling hand of government bureaucrats.

In Japan government officials continued to believe that corporations and markets were not capable of making economically rational decisions. As in other countries, however, vast improvements had occurred in the capabilities of private corporations and markets as the economy developed in the first several decades after the Second World War, further lessening the need for government officials or quasi-governmental organizations to fulfill these functions.

While the rationale for Japanese industrial policy withered, the government continued its traditional hands-on policies through the 1980s and 1990s. The formal tools available in the earlier era had diminished somewhat over time, but the impulse to meddle remained. Chapter 6 explores the extent to which the government continued its involvement at an industry level in the midst of supposed efforts at deregulation during the late 1990s.

The point here is two-fold: that this involvement is so entrenched in the bureaucracy that it is difficult to remove and that industrial policy is increasingly problematic for the economy, harboring a greater probability of misguided policies.

Even if industrial policy had become less relevant, dismantling it would take serious effort. The two-way communication and flow of influence between government and the private sector is deeply entwined with the system of *amakudari*—officials "retiring" to private-sector jobs. Unless or until retirement ages are raised considerably, ministries face a continuing need to find jobs for their retirees, and the resulting personal connection to industry will remain. Whether these handy channels of contact are useful for the economy or not, it is difficult to imagine that government officials would not use them to maintain an involvement with the private sector that goes well beyond the situation in the United States. Continuation of this system seriously undermines the very notion of deregulation.

Public Works

Closely related to the continuation of industrial policy is the undue bias in Japanese politics toward public works spending. With a strong bureaucracy, politicians have a diminished role relative to their American counterparts on many national policy issues (such as education, industrial policy, science and technology, and others). However, the bureaucracy has permitted them a strong voice on public works projects; politicians can deliver visible projects to their voters.[26]

No task is more important for elected members of the national Diet than to participate in this process. Kakuei Tanaka's ability from early in his political career to deliver on approvals and funding for projects in Niigata Prefecture made him a very successful politician.[27] Others may not have Tanaka's ability, but the need to play this role in intervening with the central government bureaucracy remains paramount and is an obvious incentive for corruption. Tanaka began his political career sincerely believing that an uncaring central government was unfairly skewing public investments away from rural areas like Niigata Prefecture. Attempting to pressure the political system to reallocate public works spending is a legitimate political aspiration in any democracy; allocating public financial resources is at the heart of democratic politics.

While Tanaka's efforts made sense in the 1950s, the emphasis on public works as a means for politicians to deliver benefits to the people has gotten out of hand. There are actually two related problems from this system in

Figure 3-7. *Public Works Spending as a Percentage of GDP, OECD Countries, 1997*

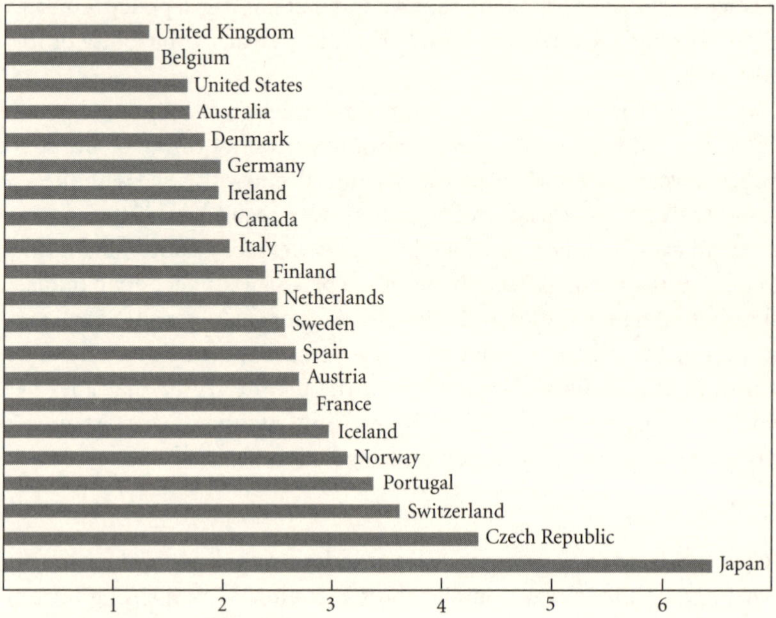

Source: Organization for Economic Cooperation and Development, "Issues and Developments in Public Management," Survey 1996–97 (Paris, 1997), pp. 304, 311, 315.

Japan: excess public investment and excess central government control. Consider the contrast between the level of public investment relative to the rest of OECD member countries. At 6.4 percent, the ratio of public investment to GDP in Japan for 1997 was well above that of other OECD countries (figure 3-7). Even Switzerland—a mountainous country where tunneling for roads and railroads conceivably raises the overall cost of public works—had a ratio of public investment to GDP just over one half that of Japan's. The United States, which certainly provides an overall adequate level of public investment (even though the fractured political process leaves some gaps), had just one-quarter the level of spending relative to GDP as Japan.

In the earlier postwar period the lack of basic infrastructure for a rapidly growing economy provided an urgent justification for a high level of public investment. The economy needed dredged harbors and other harbor facilities, highways, railroads, subways, water supply and sewage lines, paved roads, streetlights, and other public infrastructure. By the 1990s, though, Japan was a mature industrial nation with a well-developed public infrastructure and a very slow growing economy. What could possibly justify such a high level of investment? The answer is a combination of high costs (due to an inefficient and corrupt construction industry) and wasted spending on unjustified projects. The money is available (through both the general account budget and the Fiscal Investment and Loan Program), the politicians are stuck in a political game that involves bringing home projects, so the money will be spent whether it is needed or not. Thus the high investment in public works is more than just an inefficiency; it represents a flaw in the system for organizing the provision of public infrastructure. This system had delivered important improvements in infrastructure in the high-growth era, but then the spigot could not be turned off.

The second distortion is too much centralization. Some 36 percent of prefectural revenue in 1995 came in the form of revenue sharing from the central government, some of it as straight revenue sharing and some of it for special projects. This ratio appears to have been relatively stable over time. Revenue sharing from the central government is particularly important for relatively poor rural prefectures. Okinawa, Miyazaki (in rural Kyushu), and twelve other rural prefectures receive more than 50 percent of their total revenues in the form of revenue sharing. Niigata (49.7 percent) and Hokkaido (49.0 percent), two other rural prefectures long known for wasteful public works projects, are just below the 50 percent level. In addition, the central government can step in to purchase bonds issued by local governments when they need to finance deficits. As of March 31, 1999, central government–affiliated financial institutions held 31 percent of all outstanding local government bonds.[28]

Central government officials may not have any clear notion of local needs and, therefore, saddle local jurisdictions with projects or project designs that are inappropriate or unwanted. One of the frequent complaints one hears when visiting regional cities in Japan is about unwanted projects or the failure of the central government to accept input on project design. Local officials and businessmen believe the central government forces unwanted, unneeded, or poorly designed projects on them out of insensitivity or a desire to push particular technologies or to help particular firms or industries.

Complaints by local officials should also be taken with a grain of salt, however. They know the money is available from the central government, and they know that their jurisdictions have weak economic bases, so any projects they can fund with outside money are to their benefit. Occasionally protests over environmental damage or other ills from proposed projects succeed, but the overall incentive to local governments in rural parts of Japan is to play this game to the maximum extent possible.

One result of the game is that local officials, politicians, and business people spend an inordinate amount of time cajoling central government officials to obtain funds for local projects. Among the scandals emerging in the 1990s were examples of excessive wining and dining of central government officials by local visitors.[29] Why should anyone be surprised at this? Given the nature of the system, local jurisdictions have little choice but to use any means possible to obtain approval and funds for local projects. However, the extreme dependency of local areas on these central government funds and approvals skewed the system too far, providing incentives to engage in various corrupt practices to sway the system.

Inflexibility of Keiretsu

Long-term contracting involves real efficiencies. The Japanese manufacturing sector captured those efficiencies as the vertical *keiretsu* system came into being over the course of the 1960s. Once established, however, the system became quite inflexible. Economists extolling the virtues of long-term contracting do not intend "long" to imply "permanent." The advantages of long-term contracting still imply a need for periodic reopening of the bidding process to all potential suppliers. That essential aspect of long-term contracting has been neglected in Japan.

Making close contracting relationships work properly involves constant personal monitoring in a Japanese setting. The golfing, drinking, and other entertainment involved create personal relationships that are difficult to break. That is, long-term contracting involves the use of social behavior that tends to make relationships rigid. After years of drinking and golf, breaking a business relationship becomes more difficult because what may have begun as a coldly businesslike effort to monitor a business partner closely (and get beyond the facade of good news that often surrounds formal meetings) can become a relationship of friendship and personal obligation.

Parts suppliers also serve to absorb employees from larger firms as they reach the mandatory retirement age, creating an additional social tie. Having sent one's former employees off to work at a *keiretsu* parts supplier, ending the business relationship becomes more difficult. These social obligations and their impact on *keiretsu* and other features of the existing system are explored further in chapter 5. The flaw that matters here is that a sensible and innovative business system—long-term contracting—had to operate in a Japanese social context that led to permanent ties that went well beyond the original concept and introduced an element of inflexibility that may cancel out the economic efficiencies.

Two of the most difficult trade issues between Japan and the United States involved such relationships in telecommunications equipment and auto parts. The government-owned (until its partial privatization after the mid-1980s) telecommunications monopoly, Nippon Telegraph and Telephone (NTT), purchased its equipment from a particularly tight-knit "NTT family" of suppliers and resisted any newcomers—and especially foreign newcomers. The auto industry also proved exceedingly difficult for foreign parts suppliers to penetrate (even with equal product quality and lower prices) because of exceedingly rigid relationships between Japanese auto firms and their existing domestic suppliers.

The dilemma of such inflexibility had become evident by the 1990s. When the yen was strong, foreign firms could often substantially undercut existing prices in Japan for industrial parts. However, in the automobile industry, for example, American suppliers often found that Japanese firms did not even want to talk with them. When Renault purchased a strong minority ownership of Nissan, with a supposed mandate to rescue the failing company, the president of Renault immediately argued that the *keiretsu* system had saddled Nissan with high parts costs.[30]

What began as a means of cutting costs and reducing product defects had ossified to the point of actually raising costs. The extent to which this flaw implies a desire for radical change, though, is unclear. Firms could dismantle the whole *keiretsu* system and develop shorter, more explicit contracts with suppliers, moving to a system closer to the ideal of long-term contracting with open bidding systems. Alternatively, firms could carry out a one-time adjustment—casting out inefficient parts suppliers on the grounds of extreme corporate distress, but then reestablishing an indefinitely long-term relationship with a newly selected set of suppliers, with the same gradual overlay of personal ties.

While this discussion has centered on vertical *keiretsu* in the manufacturing sector, the same problem bedevils the banking sector. Bankers faced the same need to monitor borrowers as major manufacturers in monitoring their parts suppliers. The banks followed the same pattern of wining, dining, and weekend golf. They also dispatched retiring employees to work at borrowers, where they would presumably have even better inside knowledge of the firm, which would facilitate the bank's role in providing corporate governance. Among the scandals of the 1990s, however, were disturbing episodes of connivance between bankers and troubled firms. In 2000, for example, bankrupt Sogo Department Stores almost managed to get its indulgent bank lenders to forgive a large part of its existing debts without formal bankruptcy or stringent restructuring requirements, a scheme prevented only by the refusal of the new foreign owners of the former Long-Term Credit Bank to play along.[31]

Nontransparency

The Japanese economic system has depended on a number of nontransparent mechanisms in critical parts of the system. Financial systems that rely heavily on bond and stock markets for allocating investment resources and influencing corporate governance depend on an open, transparent flow of information from corporations to all participants in the market. The bank-centered system in Japan, however, depends on a very private, nontransparent transfer of information between the borrower and the managers of the bank.

Nontransparency also characterizes both general corporate behavior and the relationship between government and business. Arguably this aspect of the economic system suited the government's goals for economic development during the past half century, as noted in chapter two. The bank-centered financial system could be more easily influenced by government than broad capital markets. Corporations, without the oversight of market investors, could pursue market-share goals or fulfill industrial policy objectives that were at odds with generating profits. The government considered these features beneficial to economic growth and industrial development goals. Nontransparency also meant government could handle trouble spots (such as a failing bank) quietly, without worrying the rest of the private sector or the broader public. In this manner, government could avoid dampening the optimism that helped underwrite the high investment levels producing economic growth and industrial transformation. Furthermore, the lack of transparency meant government could pursue its industrial policy goals while maintaining a public facade of market reliance, an approach that was especially useful in international trade disputes or for quelling domestic political critics.

Nontransparency, however, poses considerable dangers for the economic system. A great deal depends on the trustworthiness or ability of the small subset of players with access to information. Even they may not always have accurate information, a condition that may lead to bad decisions. The main problem concerns the transmission of unpleasant information. When the economy was growing at 10 percent annually, most information about corporations was positive, so this problem did not arise very often. However, in a mature, slowly growing economy, some companies or industries may be doing well while others suffer from losses. It is critical for the economic system to continuously reallocate resources away from the losers toward the winners. Markets, too, may make mistakes in interpreting information, but they are generally self-correcting when there is a continuous stream of information to enable reevaluation of past decisions. A nontransparent system, however, makes it very easy to conceal the bad news that is such a critical part of this process.

Part of what companies were concealing relates to the window dressing of corporate financial statements. Such behavior is a direct result of the same desire to hide problems, coupled with the weakness of accounting rules. Even worse has been the cooperation or collusion among those with privileged access to information to conceal bad news. The Ministry of Finance, for example, connived with Yamaichi Securities to hide the firm's losses as it was failing.[32] Banks and other financial institutions failed to declare loans to deadbeat borrowers as nonperforming, and they often participated in schemes to lend them more money to cover the interest on past borrowings.[33] Thus the very participants in the economic system who should have a keen eye for sorting out winners and losers participated in protecting the losers in the economic system.

Lack of transparency and weak shareholder oversight of corporations even led to a peculiar Japanese problem—the *sokaiya*, shadowy thugs preying on the corporations' desires not to reveal negative information to their shareholders. In the early postwar period, corporations hired *sokaiya* to intimidate shareholders from asking questions at annual shareholder meetings. The *sokaiya* became adept at seeking out corporate scandals or news at odds with official corporate financial statements. During the 1990s some corporations were finally revealed as preferring to pay bribes to *sokaiya* rather than to let their own shareholders know what was really happening inside the firm. The practice was made illegal in the early 1980s, and a government crackdown got under way in 1997–98. A slew of highly publicized cases involved a number of leading Japanese companies—Mitsubishi Electric, Mitsubishi Estate, Daiwa Securities, Nikko Securities, Matsuzakaya (a leading department store), Yamaichi Securities, and Dai-Ichi Kangyo Bank.[34] With all these revelations coming over the space of a few months, the public was treated to a glimpse of the seamy underside of the corporate world. Somewhat unfortunately, though, the news on all these *sokaiya* scandals focused on the illegality of asking for or paying bribes. No one asked what these companies were trying to hide that made them so willing to pay bribes in exchange for silence.

The story of the *sokaiya* may seem to be a quaint peculiarity of Japanese society, but it is a peculiarity that demonstrates a flaw in the system. Nontransparent systems can easily generate a disparity between the facade of public information and a less pleasant reality. The prevalence of that disparity created a ready market for the *sokaiya*.

Some pressure for reform has emerged from recognition of this flaw. Forthcoming accounting rule changes should inject greater reality into published corporate financial statements, for example. How far the system will move toward greater transparency, though, remains very much in doubt (see chapter 6). As with *keiretsu* ties, the most likely outcome is a one-time recognition of problems and failures accompanied by great fanfare over installing new, more transparent systems, followed by a slide back toward less transparency.

Inept Financial Institutions

The system of reliance on banks to mediate financial flows and provide corporate governance appears to have worked well from the 1950s to the 1970s. Money flowed from savers (households) to investors (corporations) without many problems due to failed investments. Since the economy grew quickly, not very much of the flow could have been misdirected to unproductive uses.

Despite its success, bank-centered finance had a flaw separate from the lack of transparency discussed above, this one stemming from tight regulation or control by the government. With controlled deposit and lending rates, no new entry to banking permitted, and no real recession for more than twenty years (until the recession of 1974), banks had comfortable profits in the first three decades after the war. As long as they kept a weather eye on government industrial policy signals, they were largely assured that their loans to corporate customers would be safe. The Ministry of Finance kept a tight reign on innovation in the interests of maintaining stable financial flows and the assigned place of different kinds of banks and other financial institutions. Deregulation of the financial sector began in the late 1970s, but it proceeded so slowly that financial institutions continued to live in a comfortable cocoon until the 1990s.

This protected environment had a devastating effect on banks and other financial institutions in the 1980s and after. Put simply, they missed much of the innovation and change that occurred in American and European financial markets over the preceding quarter century—including both advances in risk-management theory and the proliferation of new products and management decisionmaking concepts that flowed from these theories.[35] The relative lack of sophistication proved to be dangerous as market conditions changed.

The skills of the banks may even have deteriorated over time. Since non-performing loans were few during the high-growth era, presumably banks were suitably cautious or astute in their lending. However, continued success may have lulled banks into less initial credit analysis and less careful monitoring of borrowers. The presumption that real estate collateral would always rise in price (as it had almost continuously during the twentieth century) also meant that analyzing the credit of the borrower or the viability of the proposed investment was not considered very important. Personal relations with borrowers had existed for so long that maintaining close relations per se, with their overlay of entertainment, became more important than using relationships to carry out hard-nosed monitoring, as noted earlier.

Bankers interviewed by one analyst revealed that they actually have incentives not to monitor credit worthiness. Banks that serve as the main bank for a corporation, or even the two or three next-largest lenders after the main bank, reap substantial other business from borrowers (various kinds of fee-based services and an inside track to providing banking services for the firm's employees).[36] Thus the main bank system, which supposedly provided corporate oversight in lieu of shareholder control, actually was biased away from careful corporate monitoring. Given the nontransparency of the system and the existence of theoretical models touting its efficacy, however, the flaw was largely invisible.

These latent problems became actual problems when economic growth decelerated after the mid-1970s. As a result of the slowdown in growth, loan demand from traditional manufacturing and other major clients did not grow as quickly as before. Searching for new, growing markets for loans, banks moved in two important directions: real estate and overseas. In both cases the Ministry of Finance accommodated the pressures with regulatory changes. For real estate, the MOF encouraged the large commercial banks to create nonbank subsidiaries (a set of firms known as the *jūsen*) to engage in real estate lending in the late 19070s. Internationally, the MOF presided over piecemeal changes in foreign exchange controls, which were ratified by revision of the Foreign Exchange Control Law in 1980 and driven further by bilateral negotiations with the United States, leading to the Yen-Dollar Accord of 1984. By the mid-1980s, foreign direct investment into and out of Japan was completely liberalized; Japanese banks and insurance companies could lend or invest abroad and establish foreign branches; and controls on foreign portfolio investment into Japan were largely gone.

Table 3-1 shows the impact of changing bank behavior. Bank lending to the manufacturing sector grew at a modest 5 to 6 percent annual pace (meas-

Table 3-1. *Annual Growth in Bank Lending by Selected Sectors, 1976–90*

Percent

Years	Total	Manufacturing	Real estate	Overseas
1976–80	9	5	7	11
1981–85	11	6	18	25
1986–90	11	0	20	5

Source: Edward J. Lincoln, "Japan's Financial Problems," *Brookings Papers on Economic Activity 1998:2,* p. 354.

ured by the change in outstanding loan balances) from the mid-1970s to the mid-1980s and then was flat (despite the acceleration of the economy in the second half of the 1980s). Lending overseas accelerated from a high—11 percent—annual pace to 25 percent per year in the first half of the 1980s. Real estate lending had been growing at a modest—7 percent—annual pace in the second half of the 1970s, accelerating to 18 percent in the first half of the 1980s and to 20 percent in the second half of the 1980s. These growth rates imply a major change in the direction of bank activity.

Banks were relatively unfamiliar with both real estate and overseas lending, and the result was dangerous. Lending to the real estate market implied new clients or riskier behavior on the part of existing clients. Banks did not behave with any caution or prudence in approaching this market. Their lack of caution was actually spurred by the government, which had advised establishment of the *jūsen* and increased real estate lending in general, and sent *amakudari* officials to head all of the *jūsen*. This action increased moral hazard. Banks believed that the government stood firmly behind their advance into the real estate market; administrative guidance plus the arrival of a coterie of *amakudari* officials could hardly have provided a clearer signal of support. Furthermore, banks believed that the government continued to stand behind the viability of the banks. No bank had failed in the postwar period (though a few had been merged into others to avert possible failure), and there was no reason for banks to think this support policy would change. The result was a rush of incautious (and sometimes unethical or illegal) excess lending for real estate.

Overseas, financial institutions faced a somewhat different problem. In American and European markets, Japanese banks faced savvy competitors with superior training, management decisionmaking, or investment technologies that quickly recognized Japanese financial institutions as neophytes that could be conned into deals dangerous for the Japanese and highly profitable for Americans and Europeans.[37] Like manufacturing in the 1950s, financial institutions could have been expected to learn the game quickly and thereby become more competitive in international markets. Since Japanese institutions hired staff from American institutions, presumably these people would provide the bridge for technology transfer. However, little learning appears to have occurred. Japanese institutions believed that they actually had an advantage in foreign markets—large amounts of money from low-interest bank deposits at home that were available to invest around the world. The advantage of low-cost funds led Japanese banks to undercut international lending rates to gain market share. Grabbing market share at any cost had worked as a strategy for manufacturing firms in the high-growth era, but it did not work for banks. In their effort to gain share and become major international players, banks gave scant regard to risk or return. The outcome in the 1990s was that many banks downsized or exited from American and European markets.

This story is primarily one of banks, but similar stories characterize life insurance and securities. Life insurance companies were permitted to include overseas investments in their portfolios after the early 1980s. Encouraged explicitly by the MOF, they became heavy purchasers of U.S. Treasury bonds, which saddled the companies with large losses when the yen appreciated against the dollar after 1985. Securities houses also moved into American and European markets, partly on the strength of *keiretsu* ties that gave them a ready business as underwriters of euro-bond issues by Japanese nonfinancial corporations. However, they, too, failed to learn as much as expected from their international experience.

Why Japanese financial institutions failed to "catch up" with western institutions over the course of the 1980s and 1990s, in contrast to some manufacturing industries in previous decades, is unclear. Certainly the specific mistakes of the financial institutions are well documented, but the contrast with manufacturing is startling.[38] Part of the answer may lie in the underlying expertise of management. Much of what manufacturing needed to absorb was engineering, and manufacturers were well staffed with capable, technically trained engineers who could absorb and manipulate foreign technologies. However, the technical advances in finance over the past several decades have involved sophisticated mathematics and an understanding of the dynamics of open markets. Few Japanese managers at financial institutions appeared to have the appropriate training, and their career experiences in entertaining clients was a poor basis for absorbing the new financial sector technologies. Decades of comfortable life as a regulated industry left them unable to adjust or to catch up quickly.

The weaknesses revealed during the 1990s by the debacle in real estate and the failures abroad might be expected to lead to pressure for change in the system. To some extent that appears to have been the case. Only in a more openly competitive market, in which financial institutions no longer feel they are protected by the cocoon of government-guaranteed existence, are institutions likely to shift to new investment strategies or management organization. The strength of this pressure is unclear, however. The Ministry of Finance proceeded with the "big bang" financial deregulation, despite the problems of bad debts, presumably wishing to force more competitive behavior. Financial institutions have mixed reactions, however; some aggressive institutions welcome change, but many have much to lose.

Globalization

The final potential source of pressure for change comes from the general globalization of economic markets. Despite efforts to continue protection, Japanese markets for goods, services, and finance are more open today than a decade or two earlier. As barriers fall, maintaining a separation between Japan and the rest of the world becomes more difficult. Either foreign companies begin to play a larger role within a Japanese setting, bringing different modes of behavior into the Japanese market, or Japanese firms in their expanded presence abroad find they must adapt to the standards of the outside world in order to succeed.

This theme of the need for greater conformity between Japanese practices and those elsewhere was epitomized by a faddish phrase in the late 1990s—"global standards," meaning that Japanese firms should adopt the standards of the outside world rather than insisting on Japanese uniqueness. As is often the case with such phrases, this one was rather vague. The reality is that, in general, few global standards exist in the economic realm. Certainly, however, some common practices that pervade other industrial nations could provide a model for Japanese firms to adopt.

In some cases the pressures may be real. Some Japanese corporations have their shares listed on the New York Stock Exchange. So doing imposes on them a requirement to have their accounts audited by outside accountants and to conform to stringent Securities and Exchange Commission (SEC) regulations concerning financial disclosure. Those firms, therefore, have published financial information that is more reliable than is the norm for domestic firms. Similarly, foreign investment banks have expanded tremendously in Tokyo over the past fifteen years. The analysts of these firms bring sharper analytical methods to reporting on Japanese firms and making decisions about what to buy and sell. As a result, there is at least some potential for the

Figure 3-8. *Foreign Direct Investment Flows into Japan, Fiscal Years 1985–99*

Billions of yen

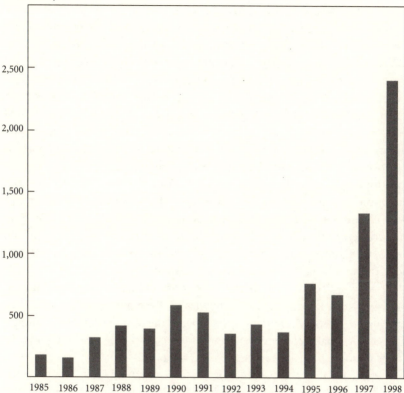

Source: Ministry of Finance, *Okurasho Kokusai Kin'yukyoku Nenpo* [Annual Report of the International Finance Division of the Ministry of Finance], no. 14, 1990, pp. 447, 467; no. 16, 1993, pp. 483, 504; and www.mof.go.jp/english/fdi/e1c008f5.htm (March 28, 2001).

Tokyo Stock Exchange to shed its reputation for unethical practices (such as artificially ramping up the price of particular companies to favor certain clients).

Foreign financial institutions are not the only ones to expand their presence in Japan. Overall inward direct investment rose sharply late in the decade, as is visible in figure 3-8. The surge in direct investment included some headline acquisitions, such as Renault's purchase of a 37 percent stake in Nissan, or Ripplewood Holdings acquisition of the nationalized Long-Term Credit Bank. Before 1998, the annual inward flow of direct investment as reported by the Ministry of Finance had never exceeded ¥800 billion. In fiscal year 1998 the level doubled from the previous year to ¥1.3 trillion and in fiscal 1999 almost doubled again to ¥2.4 trillion ($21 billion).

A larger presence of foreign firms within Japan opens the possibility that they will have a stronger demonstration effect on the rest of the economy. To the extent that they are successful, and bring with them different business practices, domestic firms will feel more competitive pressure to change their own behavior. However, the rise in the presence of foreign firms comes from a very small base, and the scale of their presence even with this surge is small relative to the situation in the United States or other industrial nations. Furthermore, one wonders how far this new endorsement for adopting foreign practices will extend. Japan has undergone a number of waves of enthusiasm for adopting foreign technologies and practices, stretching back at least to the adoption of Buddhism and Chinese written characters in the sixth century A.D. In most cases the operative term is adaptation and not adoption. Foreign concepts and technologies generally undergo transformation when they enter Japan. Indeed, the current economic system represents an adaptation of western capitalism. Why should the current wave be any different?

The visibility of some of these acquisitions, coupled with the need for the foreigners to restructure these companies to make them viable entities, has provided a sense of change at present. Even if the overall presence of foreign firms is still small, Japanese firms appear to be more receptive to the idea of adopting some of their practices.

Presumably the presence of foreign firms in Japan makes a difference this time. Even with the rise in inward foreign direct investment, however, the impact of these firms remains unclear. In market share, their role remains small. Citibank and Merrill Lynch are interesting players in the retail finance market, but they are small relative to the household financial services market. The extent to which Japanese financial sector institutions will respond to the competitive example of the foreigners, therefore, remains doubtful.

Conclusion

Taken together, all the pressures explored in this chapter have contributed to a vigorous discussion of fundamental change in the existing economic system. Discontent and concern about the existing overarching architecture of the economic system was clearly visible during the decade of the 1990s. Given the relatively poor performance of the economy and the accompanying scandals, it would be surprising if there were *not* agitation for reforming the system. Some analysts in Japan exposed the inefficiencies and distortions in the system. Some railed against the foolishness of continued government involvement in the machinery of the economy through industrial policy and other means.

Viewed from outside, this ferment of discussion and complaints looks quite similar to arguments made in the United States, Britain, and other countries over the past quarter century that fed into political processes resulting in substantial systemic reform. Nevertheless, this chapter has emphasized the mildness of the pressure. Discussion or debate occurred, and some changes took place, but the pain imposed by the failures of the system was simply not sufficient to induce a stronger political reaction or reform process. Some flaws were more evident to foreigners than to the Japanese (like the gasoline station inefficiencies discussed earlier). Some flaws were perceived as the individual lapses of bureaucrats or corporate managers that could be remedied by repentance among decisionmakers. Other flaws appeared to lead more easily to one-time corrections, after which the system as a whole could return to performing as it had in the past.

Concern among many in Japanese society was certainly genuine, and the discussion of reform was real, but discussion and action are different. Discontent did not lead to any "Thatcherite" or "Reaganite" political tsunami. Quite aside from the general mildness of the failings that might lead the political system toward systemic reform, various factors continue to impede reform in Japan. These factors are the subject of the following chapters.

4

Vested Interests

Vested interests can be a problem for change in any society. Some individuals, groups, and organizations profit from the current configuration of rules, regulations, taxes, and other aspects of the framework for the economic system. If changing that framework would hurt their economic interests, they have no reason to support change and may actively oppose it. In democratic societies, they have the power of the vote to support their positions, and, if they are well organized politically, they may exercise a political voice stronger than might be suggested by their numbers alone.

Over time, groups may also use their political power to create the laws and regulations that protect their special economic interests. Economist Mancur Olson proposed in the early 1980s that such behavior may act gradually to stifle growth, as the increased protection of existing economic interests diverts attention from policies to produce growth and stymies the reallocation of economic resources necessary as growth and development occur. The principal special interest Olson had in mind was organized labor, whose power in postwar Britain and elsewhere led to nationalized industries and a generous welfare state that reallocated income toward workers and gave them job security, but turned out to be detrimental to growth. Organized labor has not been very strong in Japan (at least since the power of the postwar unions was broken by the mid-1950s), nor did policy proceed as far along the road toward a welfare state as occurred in Europe. Nevertheless, diverse groups have ample reason to fear major reform of the current economic system, even though higher economic growth rates unleashed by reform would ultimately make them better off. There may be some truth in Olson's proposition that the extended period of peace and prosperity of the past half-century has enabled these groups in Japan to become more entrenched and more of a negative influence on economic growth.[1]

The earlier high-growth era involved a major transformation of the economy that was also disruptive or disadvantageous for some in society. At that time vested interests did not block change. Why? The government willingly compensated or bribed the losers in this transformation in order to buy their political acquiescence to the overall process of change. When growth was high, these bargains were not very costly relative to the economic benefits of rapid industrialization. When economic growth subsided, these special benefits caused increasing distortions in the economy. Once special rights, protection, or subsidies are put in place—no matter what the economic logic may have been at the time—the beneficiary groups have a vested interest that they can often maintain or enlarge for years at the expense of the rest of the economy.[2]

In some societies, even those who have profited from the existing configuration of the economic system change their minds about opposing change because the system eventually fails to perform as expected. This dissatisfaction enables democratic political processes to produce impetus for substantial change, as was the case in Great Britain in the 1980s. Nationalized industries, job security, and extensive welfare benefits initially worked to the advantage of many in British society, but weak growth, stagnant wages, frequent strikes, and deteriorating services drove many to recognize that the system was not generating further increases in their economic well-being. Similar experiences have occurred in other nations, with a rising drain on public finance from state-owned enterprise deficits, weak economic growth, and other obvious, painful failures. Therefore, groups that might have initially favored extensive government intervention changed their minds in Britain and elsewhere. A vested interest in a failing system is not worth protecting.[3]

The situation in Japan is quite different. Those with vested interests in the current economic system do not appear to be as disgruntled with the system as has been the case in other industrial countries. In Great Britain and other societies, people became dissatisfied with malfunctioning systems that had ceased to provide the anticipated benefits, and they voted for change. Many groups in Japan have little reason to believe that the system is fundamentally broken, however, and they fear that major change would jeopardize their benefits. Many see those parts of the system that do not involve them personally as possibly malfunctioning, but not the parts that do affect them. As pointed out in chapter 3, on average people were better off at the end of the decade than at the beginning. Most of the stories in the press concerning scandals or other problems are about events that have little impact on people's personal lives. This helps to explain why many people support deregulation and reform as a general principle, but lose their enthusiasm when it comes to the details.

To be sure, the average person is anxious about the future even though his or her own current economic situation has not deteriorated. People may worry about unemployment even though they are not unemployed. They may worry about what will happen to their future social security and pension benefits if the economy does not shake off the relative stagnation of the past decade. For some people these anxieties are sufficient to support systemic reform. Any outside observer of Japan can report conversations with individuals—academics, business people, and bureaucrats—who are worried about their own future and that of the nation and who genuinely believe that deregulation, with greater reliance on transparent markets and less reliance on government, is the only choice. Their convictions have been—and will be—sufficient to produce at least a moderate transformation of the overarching architecture of the economic system.

However, fear of losing current economic benefits is palpable. Even if people know that change should ultimately make them better off by producing higher economic growth, they are uncertain about whether such benefits will really materialize, against which they weigh the certain or likely loss of their current benefits. American society has its own vested interests, but they have not had the same stifling effect on economic restructuring in the past several decades. Workers in the "rust belt" in the 1970s and 1980s obtained little in the way of import protectionism or welfare, certainly not enough to appreciably slow the rapid restructuring of the economy. Deregulation in the 1970s demolished the protected interests of railroads, trucking firms, airlines, and other regulated industries. The government removed AT&T's monopoly rights in long-distance communications almost thirty years ago and aggressively broke up the firm in the 1980s. Japan, however, is not the United States. Society in general has been more protective of potential losers, and vocal special interest groups seem adept at getting the rest of society to fulfill such social obligations.

Groups in Japan with a vested interest in the existing configuration of the economic system are also far larger in number and political weight than often assumed. Viewed broadly, a majority of Japanese adults may well belong to one or more groups in society that stand to lose from major reform of the sys-

Table 4-1. *Groups with Vested Interests in the Existing
Economic System, 1993, 1995, 1996*

Group	Percent of total employment (1996)
Workers in agriculture, forestry, and fishing	5.5
Workers covered by lifetime employment[a]	20.0
Government workers	3.3
Construction sector workers	10.3
Workers at smaller wholesale and retail establishments[b]	9.8
Workers at small manufacturing firms[c]	5.0
Total	53.9
	Share of total population (1995)
Households in rural areas[d]	35.3
	Share of total households (1993)
Homeowners	59.8

Source: Statistics Bureau, *Japan Statistical Yearbook 1998* (Tokyo, 1997), pp. 27, 38, 84, 288, 394, 599.

a. Author's estimate.

b. Employees of small wholesale and retail establishments defined here as those with fewer than ten employees (with the share of total distribution of employment based on the 1994 census).

c. Employees of small manufacturing firms defined here as those with fewer than twenty employees (with the share of total manufacturing employment based on 1995 census data).

d. Defined here as the percentage of the population living outside densely populated districts (those with more than 4,000 inhabitants per square kilometer).

tem. This breadth of vested interests becomes an important factor in holding back real reform. Opponents of change may not prevent all reform efforts, but they will certainly delay and weaken those efforts. This chapter considers the broad sweep of different groups in society that still have a vested interest in preserving the current configuration of the economic system and explores what they have to lose.

Table 4-1 presents a summary of principal groups that have vested interests in the current system. Some of these groups are well known; others are less obvious. People trying to explain the failure of the system to change more rapidly or thoroughly have often picked on farmers as an obvious politically powerful group that benefits from protectionism and heavy subsidy, but an exclusive focus on farmers would be misguided. Employment in the collection of groups listed in table 4-1 totals 54 percent of all workers in Japan; the connections among these sectors and others suggests that the actual number of employees benefiting may be higher still. From a different perspective, the table notes that 60 percent of households own their own dwelling unit, and 35 percent of households live in rural areas of the nation. Collectively these groups represent a potent force to delay and moderate change.

Totaling employment in different groups may be unfair. Workers with lifetime employment may strongly favor ending subsidies to farmers, for example. However, consider the implications of the old adage, "Those in glass houses shouldn't throw stones." Those with a strong vested interest to press for vigorous change elsewhere in the system could create an antagonistic political environment in which their own benefits were challenged. Politicians representing such interests, therefore, may hesitate to join coalitions in favor of reform, or they may end up endorsing reform in name only.

This chapter highlights the principal groups in society that benefit from the current configuration of the system, what they get from the system, and how large they are. How their behavior in the political system affects reform is a different and more complex question, largely beyond the scope of this study. Some—such as farmers and small shopkeepers—are well organized in the support base for the Liberal Democratic Party (LDP). Others—such as the amorphous group of workers covered by lifetime employment—are not organized at all. How these groups vote in elections is uncertain, since voters are motivated by many factors in casting votes. Nevertheless, there is a puzzle to be explained. No political party championing thorough economic reform has captured sufficient voter support to remove the Liberal Democratic Party from power. The LDP's support has eroded—it was out of power for one year in 1993–94 and has governed with smaller coalition partners since then. In 1998 the newly formed Democratic Party of Japan (DPJ) appeared to enunciate a reform platform, but it remains far from ousting the LDP. In explaining this puzzle, vested interests play a role; people know what they might lose and are far less certain what they might gain under reform. The overall explanation of political developments is more complex (including the difficulty of building new parties, skewed voting districts, or limits on campaign advertising), but these vested interests are part of the story.

The Rural Sector

Table 4-1 notes that 5.5 percent of all workers in Japan are in agriculture, forestry, and fishing. While this percentage is not high, these workers have long been presumed to have a disproportionate political voice because of skewed boundaries for voting districts for national Diet seats: rural districts have fewer voters than urban ones, giving each rural vote a disproportionate weight, despite a redistricting effort in 1996. Perhaps a better way to view this sector, though, is as a rural sector rather than just focusing on those engaged in agriculture, forestry, and fisheries. Table 4-1 also shows the proportion of households living in rural areas, defined somewhat arbitrarily as those in cities, towns, or villages with fewer than 4,000 people per square kilometer, with areas above this level identified in the data as "densely populated."

What do people in the agricultural sector want to protect? Agriculture import barriers (quotas, tariffs, phytosanitary standards, and testing procedures) that keep food prices high in Japan are one obvious benefit, though those barriers have been gradually lowered over the past thirty years, causing a gradual increase in the proportion of foreign food in domestic consumption. Despite Japan's being an affluent society, its people still spend 23 percent of their household income on food, compared with only 14 percent in the United States.[4] This difference is most emphatically not due to any preference of the Japanese to eat out—Americans actually spend a much higher proportion of their lower level of food expenditures on eating out at restaurants (37 percent) than do the Japanese (16 percent). Thus the difference is a function of the much higher level of food prices in Japan than in the United States.

The same situation is true in forestry, where trade barriers have inhibited import of lower-priced foreign processed wood products. Years of trade negotiations have gradually lowered these barriers, but the domestic forestry industry and the wood processing manufacturing industry remain protected to some extent.

Equally important, rural areas benefit from subsidies. The most obvious direct subsidies accrue to farmers, who are subsidized mainly through state-administered high prices for farm output. Among member nations of the Organization for Economic Cooperation and Development (OECD), Japan's agricultural subsidies are particularly high—the equivalent of $49 billion in 1998. With subsidies expressed as a ratio to the presubsidy market value of farm output ("farm-gate value," in OECD parlance), Japan's subsidy ratio comes to 63 percent, a level exceeded by only Norway and Switzerland, and well above the 45 percent ratio for the European Union (EU) and the 22 percent ratio for the United States. Including import protection, the annual real cost to Japanese consumers of domestic agriculture protection and subsidy is a much higher $73 billion—higher than the $71 billion cost to EU consumers and the $4 billion cost to American consumers.[5]

Rural areas also benefit from subsidies defined more broadly, such as public works spending. Data on public works spending by prefecture do not show any large overall bias in favor of rural areas. For example, the correlation between prefectural population density and the value of public works spending in 1995 was a positive .63, implying that more densely populated areas do get more public works spending (rather than the reverse). While this correlation is positive, however, it is certainly far from perfect. Furthermore, a significant negative correlation (minus .54) exists between prefectural population density and the proportion of the labor force engaged in the construction industry. The skewed distribution of construction employment must be due to both some skewing in the location of projects and the employment of workers from rural areas in construction projects in more urban areas.[6]

These data imply that a cut in rural public works projects or the national level of public works spending would affect workers in rural areas disproportionately. In 1995 construction represented 9.2 percent of nationwide employment, but it was over 12 percent in nine rural prefectures. Niigata—home of former prime minister Kakuei Tanaka and his finely tuned public works machine—not surprisingly topped the list at 13.2 percent.[7] These percentages are considerably higher than those for employment in agriculture, forestry, and fishing.

Chapter 3 showed that government spending is skewed toward rural prefectures through taxation as well. Revenue sharing disproportionately benefits rural prefectures—distorting government spending toward rural areas. Furthermore, groups other than farmers obtain subsidies in rural areas. Principal among these have been coal-mining districts that have received welfare support for decades as part of the social bargain in slowly closing inefficient domestic mines. Thus, in a variety of ways, workers and households in rural areas benefit from a political economy that disproportionately distributes subsidies, revenue, and other government benefits to rural areas.

Rural areas may also be more resistant to change because of a disproportionate presence of small manufacturers (discussed in detail later in this chapter). Much of the manufacturing presence in rural areas consists of relatively labor-intensive industries with small firms: textiles, stainless steel flatware, wood processing, and others. Greater market openness to foreign corporations, deregulation, and an end to vertical *keiretsu* practices would disproportionately affect workers and firms in rural areas.

These broader concerns of those living in rural areas of Japan explain better why the skewed voting districts matter. Farmers have long been blamed for too many problems and distortions in Japan; rural groups that currently benefit from the configuration of the economy are much broader than just farmers. In fact, "farmers" is becoming an increasingly uncertain designation; in 1996 only 15 percent of "farm" household income came from farming, the rest coming from nonagricultural employment (61 percent) and social-security or other nonearned income (23 percent).[8] The existing eco-

nomic system has benefited rural households considerably through government public works spending, agricultural subsidies, and protection of small,
inefficient manufacturing firms. They have ample reason to resist change,
represent a sizable minority of the total population, and benefit from
enhanced voting power.

Lifetime Employees

As noted in chapter 2, the exact number of workers covered by lifetime
employment is unclear since the system does not involve written contracts.
Table 4-1 picks a conservative estimate of 20 percent (with estimates by analysts varying between roughly 20 percent and 30 percent). These workers are
largely separate from the other groups identified in table 4-1, since they are
predominantly in large firms (though employees at large construction firms
listed elsewhere in the table might be included). They also include both
(unionized) blue-collar workers and all of management. Small firms not
practicing lifetime employment but tied to large firms through subcontracting arrangements probably should be included as well. Their employees gain
job security from the firm's *keiretsu* tie to a large buyer, and at least part of the
work force comprises lifetime employees of the large firm finishing out their
careers after passing the mandatory retirement age.

These workers committed themselves to the demands of the lifetime
employment system described in chapter two. They jumped successfully
through educational hoops that carried the reward of good jobs; they passed
a stiff entry selection process; they accepted a seniority wage or salary system
that burdened them with unduly low pay in the early years of their careers;
and they gave a large part of their personal lives to their companies in
exchange for the promise of long-term employment. These are rather hefty
personal commitments or costs paid by those participating in the system, suggesting the high value they attach to the job security and higher pay later in
life that are the reward for their commitment.

If lifetime employment were to come to an end, most of these people
would still be employed at the same firms. Some might lose their jobs, however. In the second half of the 1990s, major firms did downsize, though
almost entirely within the limits of their lifetime employment commitments—using attrition and some buyouts of those approaching retirement,
plus reduction in temporary employees (as discussed in chapter 6). Few
workers at firms practicing lifetime employment have actually been fired as
part of downsizing, though certainly stories abound in the press of workers

pressed hard by management or peer pressure to "retire" or quit. Despite the rarity of real firings, fear or anxiety about the possibility of being fired if the system were to end is palpable.

The concern of these employees is not simply the direct consequence of ending lifetime employment per se. More broadly, workers at such firms are concerned about changes in other aspects of the economic system that currently underwrite lifetime employment (recall the interconnections shown in figure 2-4). Reliance on patient bank finance, stable business ties though vertical *keiretsu*, tolerance of horizontal collusion, trade barriers, management dominance of corporate boards, and the weak role of shareholders all contribute to an environment in which firms can maintain greater stability in employment, and probably a higher overall level of employment, than would be possible in a more open market with more profit-conscious firms. An unforgiving stock market and shareholders able to exercise corporate governance to maximize profits could cause firms to be more conscious of maintaining leaner staffing in general and to downsize more quickly in bad times. A more vibrant market for corporate control could bring in new owners who would replace management and eliminate jobs without consideration for lifetime employment practices.

Whether employees at firms practicing lifetime employment actually have the power to maintain their vested interests is unclear. Labor unions have been very weak and have shown a declining interest or ability to engage in strikes to protect their interests. Only 43,000 employee-days were lost to strikes in 1996, a minuscule number compared with either the past (8 million in 1975) or other countries (4.9 million American employee-days lost in 1996).[9] However, consider that the senior management of all major firms comprises lifetime employees who have worked their way up through the system. Surely they would prefer to maintain the system in which they prospered, and until or unless major changes in the financial system yield a set of shareholders, bondholders, or lenders who put them under extreme pressure to change management behavior, there is no reason to expect them to advocate real change.

What about the other 70–80 percent of workers in Japan who do not benefit from lifetime employment? Would they grow to resent the job security and higher pay of the minority? They might feel resentful, but they also know that the main reason they are not in the system has to do with their own personal failings—their educational credentials are not as good, their zeal to work is not as evident, or their personalities are not as attractive. That is, entry to the golden world of lifetime employment is theoretically open to all (males) in society, so failure to make the grade is the fault of the individual and not the system. In the hierarchical world of Japanese society (discussed in chapter 5), those who fail to make the grade are more accepting (albeit sometimes grudgingly) of their lower wages, lessened job security, and inferior social status. If they truly want entry to this world, they can always put pressure on their children to do better academically.

In this manner, the attitude toward lifetime employment is quite different from the similar lifetime employment at nationalized industries in Europe. In the European case, the rest of the public could feel resentful at the cushy deal for workers in nationalized industries, such as coal mining or steel, who were often perceived as lazy or underemployed. Coal miners in Britain, for example, were a highly contentious group obstructing change at the obvious expense of the rest of the nation. Such a charge would be much more difficult to sustain against those who benefit from lifetime employment in Japan. Those with lifetime employment represent the cream of the crop, with blue collar employees working in the most productive factories and with managers who put in long hours at high-pressure jobs with the most prestigious, internationally competitive companies. Nevertheless, those with lifetime employment in Japan play much the same role in obstructing change as did the workers in inefficient, nationalized industries in Europe, since altering the economic framework would jeopardize lifetime employment practices as they currently exist. As large firms have downsized since 1997, some change may be occurring, with new, young workers hired without the implicit guarantees of lifetime workers, but chapter 6 will cast doubt on how major a change this is.

Government Workers

As shown in table 4-1, only 3.3 percent of all workers in Japan are in the government. This percentage is not large (compared, for example, with 14.4 percent of American workers who are in government), though almost as large as that for workers in agriculture.[10] As discussed below, this number may be somewhat underestimated, since the government is surrounded with many quasi-governmental organizations uncounted in the narrow definition of government. While small, the career government sector represents a significant vested interest in the existing system.

Major economic reform that reduces the role of government in the market would surely lead to some reduction in the number of these direct and indirect government workers as well. Most jobs would continue, but, as with lifetime employment, the real issue is the fear of becoming redundant. Perhaps equally important, a decline in the economic role of government would reduce the social status or prestige attached to government employment; in a government with less clout in the marketplace, those on the elite professional track would not enjoy the respect and deference from far older executives in the private sector that they have had in the past.

Government workers have a particularly strong political voice in maintaining their narrow employment and prestige interests. Their strong role in policy formation has left them in charge of deregulation and administrative reform, a central topic of chapter 6. While they will engage in vicious turf battles in this process, it is highly unlikely that they will preside over any major reduction in the role of the government in the marketplace. Over the past twenty years they have not entirely prevented deregulation, but the pace has been slow, and formal deregulation has often been accompanied by informal mechanisms to keep government engaged.

The extent of the government worker group may be somewhat undercounted by the official employment statistics. Government ministries are surrounded by ostensibly nongovernmental organizations that are really just appendages of the ministries. Many postal workers, for example, are civilians at technically private post offices operating with government postal contracts. Other quasi-governmental organizations include serious operational units, such as the Kan'i Hoken Fukushi Jigyōdan (Postal Life Insurance Welfare Corporation), which runs various recreation and other facilities for its policyholders and invests part of the Postal Life Insurance reserve funds. These organizations range down in size to small offices that are in charge of publishing statistical books (such as the Japan Statistics Bureau, which publishes the *Japan Statistical Yearbook*). As noted earlier, quasi-government organizations are a distinctive feature of the economic system. Jobs and organizational existence in this amorphous sector would also be jeopardized if a wave of efficiency were truly to sweep through the government sector.

Peripheral organizations are also a favorite dumping ground for *amakudari* officials "retiring" from government. The practice of *amakudari,* an important feature of industrial policy but one of increasingly dubious value, is part of the vested interest of government workers. In the private sector, lifetime employment carries an informal commitment on the part of the employer to find postretirement jobs for those employees reaching mandatory retirement age or for those who need to be downsized. *Amakudari* is the government equivalent of that commitment, one that conveniently furthers the government's industrial policy goals as well. Therefore, government officials have two important interests in maintaining the system.

First, they fear the perceived loss in ability to engage in industrial policy if the *amakudari* system disappears. They want the personal connections between government and private sector to grease communications channels with the private sector. Stripped of a cadre of their own people in private-sector firms, the job of communicating with, coordinating with, or hectoring those firms would be more difficult.

Second, they fear the loss of a managed labor market. In fact, government workers may have even stronger fears about facing the job market on their own than do their private-sector counterparts with lifetime employment. Private-sector workers—both blue and white collar—presumably have marketable skills in an open labor market. Government workers may fear that their skills are not so marketable since they have never worked in a competitive, private-sector, profit-driven setting. In the absence of a continuing industrial policy regime that causes at least some firms to desire the personal connections to the bureaucracy, and without their ministries' arranging those jobs, government employees might have a difficult time finding postretirement jobs.

One possible solution to the *amakudari* problem would be postponement of retirement ages. Today, virtually all government officials retire by age fifty-five except the administrative vice minister and a handful of others who survive to the very pinnacle of the promotion pyramid. If the retirement age were pushed back to age sixty-five or seventy, those needing or desiring postretirement jobs would presumably diminish to a small number. A recent change allows officials to stay until age sixty-five, but at only half pay after age sixty. Later retirement might work for those employees on the lower or middle career tracks, but not as well for bureaucrats on the elite track. They begin leaving their ministries as the promotion possibilities shrink toward the upper management ranks. This weeding out would still occur (albeit at a somewhat older age). Therefore, extension of retirement ages would moderate but not eliminate the *amakudari* problem. Bureaucrats would still see the system as a necessary and desired part of their career package.

As alluded to above, the imperative for *amakudari* also feeds the interest of bureaucrats in preserving at least some form of industrial policy. As long as the government continues to interfere in private market affairs, private firms will need a personal route of contact and communication with government to protect or further their own interests. This desire remains true even in a world of "soft" industrial policy in which government listens to industry as much as it tries to impose its own will; in either case, communication is important. If government were to drop industrial policy, therefore, the need to have these routes of communication would be greatly diminished. In the absence of industrial policy, government ministries would have difficulty putting pressure on firms to accept *amakudari* employees. Thus bureaucrats have a motive to maintain not just the *amakudari* system itself, but also the broader system of industrial policy in which it is embedded.

The vested interest of government bureaucrats is further reinforced by social hierarchy. If private-sector workers with lifetime employment represent an elite, government bureaucrats are the elite of the elite. Those on the top career track attended the very best of elite universities and passed an extremely difficult entrance exam to obtain their government positions, an exam many of their classmates failed, leaving them with private-sector jobs as a second choice. The public may resent their arrogance, officiousness, and condescension, but no one can deny their credentials. Thus their high prestige and status offset their very small numbers in the labor force, even though that prestige was marred by scandals in the 1990s.

Younger bureaucrats supposedly favor real deregulation and reform of the economic system, and some undoubtedly genuinely hold such intellectual positions. But one wonders if this group really sees its special interests in the current system as not worth preserving. Do they really want to eliminate their own jobs and face a private-sector labor market on their own? Do they really want to invalidate the importance or prestige of the difficult path they followed to enter elite government careers? Some radicals may truly hold such beliefs, and they may well leave the ranks of government on their own, as some always have in the past. The majority, however, are unlikely to favor radical change and will become more conservative over time.

Overall, bureaucrats represent a rather potent vested interest. If they do not favor radical change, their central position in policymaking enables them to successfully obstruct the process. Since Japan is a democracy, an angry public or their elected representatives could presumably force changes on a reluctant bureaucracy. The scandals involving bureaucrats in 1997–98, as well as the broader sense of government's bungling on macroeconomic policy and the bad debt problem, certainly irritated the public. But the reality is that the bureaucracy remains a powerful unelected force within government, able to resist pressures from politicians and the public to a much greater extent than is the case in the United States.

The Construction Sector

The construction sector includes both private sector construction and public works projects. Construction firms and their employees benefit from the current economic system in both their private and public works business. Illegal but commonly accepted collusion among construction firms has led to high construction costs, enhanced by nearly total closure of the market to foreign construction firms. On the public side, the construction sector benefits from the excessively large amount of annual public works spending and the collusion and bribery accompanying it.

Table 4-1 shows that 10.3 percent of all workers are employed in the construction sector, a level that is high in comparison with the United States, where only 6.4 percent of employment was in this sector in 1997.[11] The ratio has risen a bit over time, since 7.7 percent were in the sector in 1970, suggesting that the relative inefficiency or distortion has increased over time.[12] This upward shift is all the more remarkable considering that 1970 was during the high-growth era, when construction demand was high (including both new factories or other offices and the public infrastructure necessary to underwrite expanded economic activity). The number of employees is high for two somewhat separate reasons.

First, inefficiency pervades the sector because collusive bid-rigging behavior known as *dango* enables construction firms to maintain very high prices. This lack of price competition leads directly to slow technical change and wasteful practices, including excessive employment. Backing up this collusion have been severe restrictions on competition from foreign construction firms. Japanese construction sites are impressive to behold: always extremely clean and orderly, with a small army of employees to direct road traffic and pedestrians around the site. Esthetics does not necessarily yield efficiency, however; the marginal productivity of lighted-baton-wielding guards directing traffic at nighttime road construction sites may well be less than zero, since their waving light sticks often provide very confusing or ambiguous signals to drivers.

Second, the political system in Japan has resulted in a great reliance on public works spending. Politicians, and especially those from rural areas, have learned that the game of creating political support consists largely of bringing home large public works projects. Along with the highest ratio of public works spending to GDP in any OECD nation comes an excessive level of employment in construction. Public works is a major part of the business of construction firms; in 1995 public works represented 38 percent of all construction firms' domestic business (a ratio that is only 23.8 percent in the United States).[13]

If the construction sector were subjected to greater competition, or if the political system stopped focusing on public works spending, then the size of the construction sector would shrink. Employment would be down, and some firms would go bankrupt. Clearly workers and managers of construction firms have a strong interest in maintaining the current system of wasteful and excessive construction.

The negative effects of deregulation would actually be more widespread than in the construction industry per se, including those manufacturing industries that supply the principal inputs to the construction sector. Steel, cement, construction equipment, and wood processing industries all have something to lose from greater competition in construction and a more rational public works system. Thus the vested interest includes some very powerful players other than construction firms themselves, including such industrial giants as Nippon Steel, Mitsubishi Heavy Industries, and Komatsu.

Because the special interests of the construction sector and those industries supplying it work to the detriment of the rest of society and the economy, protest and reform would be a logical outcome. Scandals in the 1990s exposed some of the corruption and collusion involved in public works contracting. However, protest has been muted. When the government turned to fiscal stimulus in the 1998–2000 period to pull the economy out of recession, it once again relied heavily on pumping up public works spending.

Why has the construction sector been so successful in protecting its vested interest? Part of the answer lies in politics. Despite the upheavals in politics in the 1990s (with the temporary dethronement of the LDP and the advent of coalition governments), the basic model of pork barrel–centered politics remains unchanged. Part of the answer may also lie in public ignorance. Not many people are aware of how excessive public works spending is in comparison with other countries, or how excessive even housing construction costs are, and they are susceptible to arguments about special technical factors since Japan is a mountainous country with earthquakes and typhoons. After all, construction sites are esthetically pleasing in Japan; most people have no concept of the price they pay for that visual pleasure. Politics and ignorance, therefore, imply that the construction sector may well continue to protect its special interests in the current system.

The Distribution Sector

As any visitor to Japan realizes quite quickly, small retail shops remain ubiquitous. Historically, the heavy reliance on small stores has been the result of high population density, low automobile ownership, low wages, wide wage disparity between large and small firms, and a preference for very fresh materials in Japanese cuisine. High population density meant that small retail shops or wholesale establishments could have a sufficiently large customer base nearby. Low mobility constrained most people from traveling very far to shop and limited their purchases to what they could carry by hand. Low wages in general and the relatively lower wages of small establishments lessened the cost advantage of large, labor-efficient stores. Finally, the premium on fresh food materials implied local stores to which customers could have easy access on a daily basis, a phenomenon that was reinforced by the small refrigerators most people had.[14]

These conditions have changed drastically in the past forty years. The shift to an affluent, high-wage, automobile-owning society should have produced a shift toward much greater reliance on labor-saving large stores and wholesale establishments. To some extent that shift has occurred, but it has been hampered by government policies protecting small establishments. The vast number of small shop owners comprises a powerful vested interest that has obstructed regulatory change and continues to do so today. The outcome of their effort has been unnecessarily high retail prices for goods and services, representing an efficiency drag on the economy.

Overall, some 22 percent of the labor force is employed in the distribution sector, wholesale and retail. Those who would be hurt by reform are mostly those in smaller establishments. Table 4-1 defines this group somewhat arbitrarily as workers employed in wholesale and retail establishments with fewer than ten employees. This group represents an amazing 9.8 percent of all employment in Japan.

By way of comparison, some 20.7 percent of American workers are in the wholesale and retail sectors, but far fewer of them work in small establishments. Only 2.6 percent of all American workers (just one-quarter the proportion in Japan) are employed in wholesale or retail establishments with fewer than ten workers.[15] While geographical, demographic, or cultural factors would keep the Japanese ratio from falling as low as that of the United States, the disparity suggests that employment in small establishments would indeed decrease in a more open, deregulated market.

Table 4-2. *Size Structure of the Retail Sector, 1985 and 1997, and Comparison with the United States, 1995*

Percent unless otherwise specified

| Number of employees | Japan | | United States |
	1985	1997	1995
1–4	46	32	5
5–9	19	18	7
10–19	12	17	9
20–49	12	16	...
20–99	...	...	20
50+	12	16	...
100+	...	...	58

Source: U.S. Census Bureau, *Statistical Abstract of the United States: 1998* (Government Printing Office, 1998), p. 548; Ministry of International Trade and Industry (MITI), *Chūshō Kigyō Hakusho*, Heisei 2000-Nenpan (2000 Medium-Small Business White Paper), statistical supplement, p. 19.

Table 4-2 shows the structure of the retail sector in comparison with the United States. In 1998, 32 percent of employment in the Japanese retail sector was actually in tiny shops of one to four employees, compared with only 5 percent in U.S. retail sector employment. Higher shares for Japan also characterize stores employing five to nine workers and those employing ten to nineteen. As a result, only 33 percent of Japanese employment was in stores with twenty or more employees, compared with 79 percent in the United States. In fact, the disparity is even more startling at the largest size category. Although size categories are dissimilar in Japanese and American data, only 16 percent of Japanese retail employment was in stores of fifty or more employees, but stores with one hundred or more employees composed 58 percent of retail employment in the United States.

A common response to such disparities in size is to point out the crowded conditions and high land prices in Japan, which might militate against establishing large stores (because they cost too much to establish).[16] However, economically the opposite ought to be true. If land is expensive, then there should be an added incentive to use it efficiently. One way to increase efficiency is to build one large, highly efficient store with high turnover rather than maintaining a set of small, less inefficient, lower volume operations.

The record of retailing demonstrates one of the major dilemmas in interpreting Japan. On the one hand, change has clearly taken place over time, as visible in table 4-2, or as is obvious to anyone who has visited Japan at various times in the past two decades. More large stores are opening, and small "mom and pop" stores have declined in number (as can be seen in the drop of the share of workers in stores with one to four employees). Small independent retail stores and coffee shops are being replaced by franchised stores such as Seven-Eleven and AM PM convenience stores and Pronto and Starbucks coffee shops. On the other hand, change has been slow, and Japan retains a remarkably large number of small retail outlets for a high-wage country. In the eleven years from 1985 to 1996, employment at stores with fifty or more employees rose only modestly, from 12 to 16 percent of all retail employment.

As wages rose rapidly in Japan over the past fifty years, labor-intensive business operations in any industry became a liability. In addition, affluence brought explosive growth of automobile ownership and use. The combination of these two developments should have had a profound effect on the distribution sector, just as it did in the United States. Large-scale chain stores possess clear efficiency advantages, and greater mobility enabled their location away from congested, expensive, downtown areas.

A trend away from small stores toward larger stores has certainly proceeded in Japan, but two decades of response has left Japan with a size structure for retailing that is still remarkably skewed toward small shops. Among the factors involved are the vested interests of both manufacturers and small store owners. One of the distinctive trends of the early postwar period was the attempt by manufacturers to establish clear control over the distribution of their consumer products. This process is known in Japanese as the *keiretsuka* of distribution, or the process of pushing distribution into long-term vertical *keiretsu* relationships. Manufacturers established either captive retail chains (such as the nationwide network of small "National"-brand stores selling the household electric products of Matsushita Corporation) or exclusive distribution relationships with "independent" stores in which the manufacturer exercised control over retail prices and had de facto power over the ability of the store to carry rival products. This change in the relationship between stores and manufacturers was a major trend of the 1950s and 1960s.

These new, tighter relationships between manufacturers and retail distributors did not necessarily involve an equity link, but they evolved into close relationships of mutual benefit and obligation. In addition, manufacturers could reinforce the ties by using associated distributors (both wholesale and retail) as dumping grounds for their retired or downsized employees.

As a result of these developments, manufacturers were tied to maintenance of the existing system for two reasons. First, they now had networks of wholesalers and retailers related to them in ways that would be difficult to break quickly. *Keiretsu* are not just about long-term contracting, but also about social obligation. Having forced distributors into unequal relationships, the manufacturers acquired an obligation to look after their welfare. Second, the whole thrust of these networks was maintenance of high retail prices without discounting. New, independent large-scale stores were a threat to this cozy, profitable system, something for manufacturers to resist.

In addition to this vested interest of the manufacturers in maintaining a distribution system based on close relationships extending from the manufacturer down to small retail shops, the store owners themselves have been a major force of resistance. Small retail stores are an important part of organized political support for the Liberal Democratic Party. If all politics is local, then these stores are a core part of the LDP's local effort. Working through the LDP, small store owners had resisted the inroads of large stores throughout the postwar period, beginning with the restrictive Department Store Law of 1956 and through the Large Scale Retail Store Law of 1974.[17]

The vested interests of the manufacturers and small store owners have not prevented change, but they have surely slowed its pace. The counter argument of some economists that the current structure of retailing in Japan can still be explained by unique Japanese conditions (such as high population density with crowded streets, or a preference for very fresh fish and vegetables) is simply not tenable. The restraints imposed by the regulatory framework are very obvious, and it is highly unlikely that they have not affected the actual structure of the industry. A perfectly free market environment for retailing might well be the result in a nation that continues to rely on stores that are smaller, on average, than those in the United States. But surely that structure would be quite different from what currently prevails in Japan. Therefore, small shopkeepers have reason to fear change and actively work against it.

In 1999 the Large Scale Store Law was eliminated, a move that ought to have signified true deregulation of the retail sector. However, the Ministry of International Trade and Industry (MITI) simultaneously encouraged prefectures and local governments to pass laws regulating the opening of large stores on the basis of environmental, noise, and congestion concerns. While the new laws would theoretically have nothing to do with economic regulation, the opportunity for abuse through manipulation of standards was enormous. Indeed, by devolving control over the issue from the national to the local level, a potential existed for the drift toward a more rational retailing structure to actually decelerate.

The distribution sector thus appears to have been quite successful in defending its special interests in the current configuration of the economic system. Gradual change will continue, eroding the profits and employment of small wholesale and retail establishments. In another two or three decades, perhaps their voice will be largely extinguished, mainly as elderly shop keepers retire from business and their children do not choose to maintain the family business. However, their power to delay and diminish the process of change will be a continuing drag on economic efficiency for a number of years to come.

Small Manufacturing Firms

Small manufacturers, especially those at the very bottom of the size scale, would also be hurt by true deregulation of the economy, especially if deregulation were to include easier access for imported products. These small firms have existed within the context of the vertical *keiretsu* system and the variation in wages by size of firm that has characterized labor markets. Small firms, with their lower wages, have supplied labor-intensive parts to larger firms in the vertical hierarchy of *keiretsu* groups. If reform of the economic system resulted in dismantling the *keiretsu* system, enabling large manufacturers to move more aggressively in substituting imported parts for those currently purchased from small domestic manufacturers, this segment of the manufacturing sector would contract.

Small firms have existed in other industries, such as textiles, that are less tied to vertical *keiretsu* chains, that also have been sheltered from foreign competition, and that would have difficulty competing in an open market. For example, only 1.1 percent of U.S. employment in 1996 was in the textile and apparel industries, compared with 2.1 percent in Japan. Note that in the absence of protection, employment in the American textile and apparel industry would probably be even lower than it is, providing some notion of the greater impact of protectionism in Japan. Even with protection, the textile and apparel industry in Japan has shrunk over time, declining from 3.3 percent of total employment in 1980.[18] However, protection has slowed the adjustment process and the current comparison with the United States implies that a further downward shift is justified.

As noted in table 4-1, employment at manufacturing firms with fewer than twenty employees represents 5 percent of total employment in Japan. Viewed in the context of the manufacturing sector, employment at these firms in 1999 was 23 percent of total manufacturing employment. By way of comparison, only 0.5 percent of U.S. employment was in manufacturing firms with fewer than twenty workers.[19] Most manufacturing processes

Table 4-3. *Size Structure of Manufacturing Establishments, 1985 and 1998, and Comparison with the United States, 1996*

Number of employees	Japan		United States
	1985	1998	1996
1–9[a]	13.9	12.5	3.4
10–19	10.7	10.4	3.9
20–99	30.2	30.9	14.9
100–299	17.0	18.6	...
100–499	...	...	16.2
300+	28.3	27.5	...
500+	...	...	61.5

Sources: U.S. Census Bureau, *Statistical Abstract of the United States: 1999* (GPO, 1998), p. 556; MITI, *Chusho Kigyo Hakusho*, Heisei 8-Nenpan [1995 Medium-Small Business White Paper], statistical supplement, p. 7; and *Chūshō Kigyō Hakusho*, Heisei 2000-Nenpan [2000 Medium-Small Business White Paper], statistical supplement p. 13.

a. The Japanese data include only 4–9 workers with no data reported on firms with 1–4 workers; the U.S. data are 1–9 workers.

involve sufficient economies of scale that firms with fewer than twenty employees simply make no sense economically. This suggests that a more deregulated and internationally open environment would drive down employment in such firms in Japan. Thus small manufacturers and their employees have a vested interest in maintaining the current system.

Table 4-3 puts the difference in the size distribution of manufacturing firms into stark perspective. In 1998, 12.5 percent of Japanese employment in manufacturing was in firms with only four to nine employees (with no data collected on those with fewer than four employees, although the number is presumably greater than zero), compared with 3.4 percent in the United States in the smallest size category of one to nine employees. At the other end of the scale, only 27.5 percent of employees were in "large" firms with three hundred or more employees. In the U.S. data the dividing line is at five hundred or more employees, and these firms account for 61.5 percent of American manufacturing employment. The common perception of Japan as a nation of efficient workers toiling in the giant factories of firms like Toyota, Matsushita, or Sony is quite simply untrue. A more accurate picture is one of a lucky elite in large, well-paying firms, supported by a mass of workers in small manufacturing shops—often with low wages and undesirable working conditions.

Even without major structural reforms, small manufacturing firms have been in a difficult position during the past fifteen years. The combination of a stronger yen and modest improvements in market access for foreign products has put pressure on small firms. Some have gone out of business, some have had to relocate their factories overseas, and stories about their distress have been prominent in the media since the mid-1980s. Nevertheless, the data indicate only minor change. In 1985 employment at small manufacturing firms with fewer than twenty workers was 24.6 percent of total manufacturing employment, so the share of these firms fell only 3 percentage points over the succeeding decade and a half.

Part of the answer to this puzzle of a steady share versus stories of failing small manufacturers is a decline in the manufacturing sector as a whole, as some firms relocated production abroad. From 1985 to 1999, total manufacturing employment dropped by 4.9 percent, and, as a share of total employment, manufacturing slipped from 25.0 percent to 21.2 percent.[20] As part of this decline, small manufacturing firms have gone out of business. Employment at manufacturing firms with fewer than twenty employees dropped over this period by 426,000.[21] The most interesting aspect of this downward shift is that all sizes of manufacturing experienced a decline, so that by 1999 the size distribution of manufacturing employment was virtually unchanged from 1985. The smallest firms—and presumably least efficient—did not take a disproportionate share of the adjustment. Should real reform occur, therefore, additional loss of jobs in this segment of manufacturing would be quite likely.

Furthermore, each of these small manufacturing firms has an owner, since most small firms are family owned. These people represent part of the power elite in their communities, providing financial and other support for politicians. Small manufacturers may be especially important in rural areas, with the stronger political voice provided by skewed districts. Thus their interests are likely to receive substantial sympathy from politicians and bureaucrats.

Homeowners

Table 4-1 indicates that 60 percent of Japanese households live in dwellings that they own, a ratio roughly comparable to that in the United States. These households have a vested interest in the complex maze of taxes, fees, rights (such as sunshine rights), and zoning that has led to a pattern of tiny plots of land priced at very high levels. Those prices remain high despite the collapse of the real estate bubble during the 1990s; even with prices today back to about where they were in 1985, land is still overvalued.

Although not included in chapter 2 as a core part of the distinctive Japanese economic model, real estate is certainly a part of the system. Land has served as the predominant collateral for bank loans of all sorts (that is, not just for housing mortgages). Prices have often exceeded marginal productivity, implying that the actual use of the land generates less revenue than needed to finance its purchase. This pattern rested on a presumption over at least the past eighty years that real estate values would consistently rise over the long term. These features of the real estate market are both a distinctive feature of the economic system and a cause of economic distortion and inefficiency.

Any household owning a dwelling would not favor any changes that would lead to further declines in land prices. Most landowners have not been seriously affected by the collapse of land prices in the 1990s. Only those who purchased property near the peak of the speculative bubble have suffered major paper loses on their property, and, because the annual number of transactions is low, this is not a large portion of homeowners. According to Japanese data, 25 percent of households that owned their dwellings in 1993 had acquired them during the decade 1981 to 1990, yielding an annual acquisition rate of 2.5 percent.[22] This suggests that households that acquired their dwellings near the peak of land prices (roughly the five years from 1988 to 1992) account for only some 12 percent of total property-owning households. These households now occupy dwellings that in many cases are worth far less than when they purchased them. While perhaps angry with a system that resulted in such losses, this group surely would not want to see a deregulated, free-wheeling real estate market in which supply and demand could be balanced at even lower prices.

The other 88 percent of households owning dwellings made their purchases either before or after the peak. Most of them either have not lost value or, for those purchasing their dwelling before the 1980s, still face potential large gains when they sell. Still hoping for some financial gain (a hope of either the current owners or their children who stand to inherit the property), this group would be loath to see the rules changed in a way that might cause lower prices.

Meanwhile, the drop in land prices that has occurred already means that the 40 percent of households who do not currently own a dwelling have less reason to lobby for change. When land prices skyrocketed, prices began to move beyond the reach of those who wished to own a home, and there was agitation for changes in taxes and regulations. Those concerns appear to have abated. Presumably these households should still prefer change, since a more liquid real estate market with lower prices would enhance their ability to acquire a dwelling. However, several factors seem to have muted their voice. Some members of this group are younger households that will eventually inherit a family dwelling, which they can either occupy themselves or sell to finance the purchase of another dwelling. Others are benefiting from the extremely low level of interest rates, enhancing their ability to acquire housing at current real estate prices. Therefore, this group has not been very vocal in pushing change.

To give some notion of the low level of real estate transactions, consider the contrast to the United States. In 1997, 6.3 percent of existing owned dwellings changed hands, and newly constructed dwellings expanded the stock of owner-occupied housing by another 1.7 percent. This 8.5 percent acquisition rate is more than triple the 2.5 percent figure noted for Japan above.[23] Thus the American real estate market is much more liquid than that in Japan. The illiquidity of the Japanese market, combined with the thicket of regulatory and tax rules, results in very inefficient land use. Farms exist within the boundaries of the city of Tokyo, and ramshackle, two-story wooden houses sit cheek-by-jowl with gleaming skyscrapers in downtown areas. Illiquidity also feeds higher prices, since desperate buyers must cajole owners with premiums well beyond the real worth of the property, and their willingness or ability to pay the premiums then rests on the assumption of continued capital gains that will accrue from owning the land.

A large vested interest in the current state of land policy is a problem. An efficient economic system needs assets priced at realistic prices in accordance with marginal productivity. Land prices are clearly above this level in much of Japan. Many companies and financial institutions have not yet sold the property serving as collateral for nonperforming loans. Clearing the real estate market, to find the bottom price at which property will change hands and be put once again into productive and profitable use, is important. The thin nature of the market, reinforced by taxes, regulations, rights, and other problems, obstructs this process. Homeowners' large vested interest in continuing the current system works against this important change.

Conclusion

The groups analyzed in this chapter represent a large force arrayed against transformation of the economic system. If peripheral employment groups (such as the quasi-governmental sector or manufacturers supplying the construction sector) are included, an even larger majority of employees in Japan may have an interest in maintaining their particular pieces of the current economic system. Property-owning households, which are certainly a majority of all households, also have a vested interest in the system. None of these groups has reason to believe that the system has become sufficiently dysfunctional to require major reform or restructuring of their own sinecure.

Opposition by these special interest groups has certainly not absolutely prevented change. Small retail shops are slowly shrinking in number and importance. So, too, are tiny manufacturing firms. Employment in agriculture and textiles continues to shrink slowly. Bureaucrats have been humbled by scandals in the 1990s, and at least modest tightening of conflict-of-interest rules in awarding *amakudari* jobs has occurred. Large firms appear to be more vague about implicit "lifetime" employment guarantees to new, young employees. Homeowners have watched the real estate bubble collapse, and housing prices are still declining slowly. Rather than absolutely opposing reform, these groups have generally managed to delay and diminish it.

When the economy was growing fairly quickly, as in the 1980s, the dead-weight drag from the inefficiencies imposed by these special interests may have been less visible or less debilitating to the economy as a whole. Today the negative impact may be larger and, because of a new environment of very slow economic growth, is a more serious problem.

The contrast with other countries is also instructive. Some countries have managed to carry out major changes, reducing the role of the government in the economy despite strong vested interests. A significant portion of British society felt that striking miners at nationalized coal mines were holding the nation hostage to their narrow interests in the 1970s, and the outcome was the Thatcher political "revolution." Coal, steel, and other industries were truly privatized, and workers lost jobs. However, economic conditions have not been as bad in Japan, nor has it been as easy to point fingers at some of these vested interests. When the vested interests represent the cream of the crop of both blue and white collar workers, painting them as villains is more difficult. Finger pointing is also less prevalent when most in society remain well off.

One conclusion from this state of affairs is that overall economic conditions may need to deteriorate further before the impetus for change can overcome special interests. Those who are part of special interests need to feel that their interests are not worth preserving anymore, or that without reform the economy—and their special benefits—is in serious jeopardy. Others in society may need a more serious crisis to believe that their own economic future is being held hostage by those who receive special benefits from the existing system. Over the course of the 1990s, pressure to reform the economy faded every time economic growth began to recover. Should the government muddle through in the new decade without pushing the economy back into recession, then the prognosis for accelerating reform is not good.

One other possibility is simply that the vested interests are not sufficiently debilitating to the economy to justify reforming the system. The Japanese economy has drifted through the 1990s without a serious crash in the financial sector or major economic contraction. Very slow growth may not be exciting, but it is certainly better than the prolonged recession that could have occurred. If growth recovers a bit in the next decade, then why bother to dislodge these special interests? Japanese society does feel an obligation to protect its weaker members, including farmers, those in rural (less affluent) parts of the country, those in small-scale retailing, and those in small-scale manufacturing. All societies have important values other than economic efficiency, and Japan is no exception. Indeed, noneconomic values of fairness, social harmony, and social orderliness are particularly strong in Japan relative to the United States. Contradictions are likely—with consumers voting with their wallets for discount stores, while supporting policies that favor small shopkeepers.

Furthermore, the distortions identified in this chapter may not seem so debilitating to most Japanese. Small distributors will diminish in number gradually, and the current system does provide a privatized welfare safety net for them. Bureaucrats may continue to meddle in the economy more than justified, but as long as they are prevented from generating too many foolish development schemes, the economy will survive their efforts. Rural areas may continue to benefit from an excessive and inefficient construction policy, but as long as the bulk of the public does not mind having rivers paved over and roads built to nowhere, this system props up incomes in rural prefectures. The Japanese, like people in many industrial nations, have a romantic fondness for, or derive esthetic pleasure from, their inefficient, rice-producing rural hinterland.

Only time will tell whether the distortions resulting from the existence of these vested interests that hamper the economy are tolerable or not. If they are tolerable, there will still be a price in terms of forgone growth and efficiency; society could be better off than it is. This situation could last for decades, until the disparity in economic performance relative to other advanced nations leaves the public distraught at their diminished comparative affluence (much like the British in the twentieth century). If the distortions are more serious than the public believes, then the cost of coddling vested interests becomes a more critical problem. At some point recession, financial collapse, or other serious ills could galvanize public frustration and produce the political climate for more radical reform. At present, society remains short of that level of frustration.

5

Consistency with Society

The Japanese and American economies have many of the same economic institutions—corporations, industries, banks, securities firms, households, and government agencies. Those institutions have often behaved quite differently in the two countries, however. Differences in economic factors, unique historical developments and path dependency, or variations in the distribution of political power explain much of the difference in behavior and form the core of most analysis of Japan's political economy. Nevertheless, in explaining why societies make certain choices about how to organize and operate their economic systems, sociology matters as well.

Put simply, institutional systems for organizing economic activity vary among market economies in ways that are related to broad social norms and behavior. Indeed, since economic institutions and rules are created by political systems, it would be surprising if the outcomes were not influenced by social or cultural factors that shape political behavior. Rarely are economic choices made solely on the basis of economic efficiency. When a society experiences economic problems that are attributable to some aspect of the existing institutional or regulatory system, a desire to improve economic efficiency may well be an important driving force for change, and notions of efficiency may inform or partially shape the outcome. Nevertheless, noneconomic social factors also play a critical role in shaping change and should not be ignored in analyzing Japanese economic reform efforts.

Economics focuses on behavior that is largely removed from culture, and the inherent bias of economists is to assume that their models can explain behavior across societies. The theoretical concept of a downward sloping demand curve, which posits that people demand more of a product when its price is lower (under most circumstances), is not particularly culture-bound. Economists assume that much of the variation across different societies is empirically measurable. That is, while demand curves generally slope downward, tastes vary across cultures so that the slope of the demand curve for a particular product may be different in different nations. The difference in slope can be measured. This chapter argues that much more is involved than just differences in the coefficients of elasticity for demand and supply curves. Social factors affect the shape of the overall framework within which economic activity occurs—the nature of economic institutions, choices about kinds of economic activity, and decisions about how to organize economic exchange. As Yasusuke Murakami and Thomas Rohlen expressed this idea, "The mode of social exchange has diffused more significantly into the economic sphere in postwar Japanese society than in most other industrial societies."[1]

Economists and other social scientists are generally wary of invoking the term culture to explain differences across nations because it is often little more than a tautology. Saying that people are different because they are different is not very expressive. Social scientists have been especially wary of invoking culture in the case of Japan because of a domestic, nationalistic school of analysis called *nihonjinron* (the theory of Japaneseness), which posits that the Japanese have a unique and superior society, culture, history, and even physiology.

Nevertheless, nations or ethnic groups are clearly motivated by differing sets of social routines, values, and preferences that affect how people behave and interact. The fact that such differences are identified and labeled as characteristic of a society does not mean that all members behave at all times in accordance with those norms and rules. However, such generalizations or stereotypes can be justified because they represent strong tendencies in behavior that cannot be denied. The social characteristics identified in this chapter are certainly not deterministic of all social or economic behavior, but they influence, shape, constrain, or inform the choices made by the Japanese on many economic issues. To deny or marginalize the importance of these variations is as silly as accepting the excesses of the *nihonjinron* school.

Government is important in influencing these tendencies or manipulating them in pursuit of economic policy goals. For example, the government has emphasized certain social behavior patterns (such as the importance of group behavior) through the school system. Regulations and other rules have pushed behavior toward what government believed represented appropriate behavior. In a less manipulative sense, government has shaped rules and regulations in a way that would appeal to social beliefs and thereby be accepted more readily. Readers who find the appeal to sociological explanations for economic institutions and behavior unsatisfactory should bear in mind these ways in which government can use or manipulate norms of social behavior in pursuit of economic policy goals.

This chapter explores the ways in which Japanese social factors have affected the nature of the existing economic system and hold back or modify systemic changes that would bring the economic system closer to the current American or market-dominant model. Change or reform will be easier to the extent that it maintains or builds on underlying social norms and expectations, but such changes imply a system that will continue to be quite different from that of the United States. Adopting American-style institutions or behavioral norms is difficult because of real or perceived (on the part of Japanese elites, including the bureaucracy) differences in the underlying social implications of the American system.

The discussion deliberately avoids the loaded term culture, which connotes an unchanging set of distinctive values rooted in some distant historical mist. In any society, however, individuals are influenced by a wide array of values, expectations, preferences, rituals, and routines for acceptable or desired social behavior. At any moment in time, behavior by individuals in different nations varies across this array of social norms. A long and distinguished academic literature comparing Japan with the United States or with the West has analyzed and validated the existence of rather wide differences in social norms and behavior patterns.[2] When sociologists looked at Japan in the past, often they were seeking social explanations for the outstanding Japanese economic performance.[3]

Are the elements of behavior emphasized in this chapter becoming obsolete descriptors of Japanese society? Certainly social factors change over time. The baby boom generation in the United States created a social revolution in the 1960s, and the current generation of teenagers and young adults in Japan is having a similar effect. In both cases, these generations grew up in a much more affluent environment than their parents. While the media emphasize anecdotes of new behavior patterns among the young in Japan, it remains to be seen if this generation will be substantially different from its predecessors.[4] Young people may spend more time on individualistic pursuits such as electronic games, but they still grow up in Japanese families and are socialized in a Japanese educational system and in Japanese corporations. The intergenerational transfer of social patterns through family, school, and place of work still occurs, especially given the conservative nature of school supervision by the Ministry of Education. The young may be less careful in their usage of the nuanced variations of respect in the language, but hierarchical differences in language remain. Furthermore, young people today are part of a developing "baby bust" generation, meaning that they may not have the numbers to bring about the kind of rapid social revolution that occurred in the United States. The changes they effect on overall social values and behavior will be more gradual.

Economic growth and development itself can alter the direction or the speed of shifts in social beliefs or behavior. In Japan, automobile ownership and larger dwelling spaces have certainly enabled people to be more individualistic than earlier generations. However, many aspects of social behavior change rather slowly. The recognition that a particular institution or set of rules is economically inefficient occurs much more rapidly than shifts in the underlying social behavioral norms that would facilitate changing or correcting the inefficiency.

This chapter explores how social attributes first shaped the economic framework and now constrain its alteration toward patterns that American observers believe are necessary for greater efficiency and stronger economic performance.

The principal features of society considered here are: group orientation, hierarchy, reliance on personal relations, avoidance of uncertainty, the importance of facades, and preference for indirectness and informality. These aspects of social preference, expectation, and behavior are deeply ingrained in many aspects of the existing economic system, and they all represent dimensions of social behavior where both norms and average behavior differ significantly from those in the United States or the West. Since these features of society remain important, even if they have become somewhat less significant over time, the obvious inference is that changing the economic system in a manner that converges on an American model will be difficult.

Some systemic economic change is certainly occurring; the social factors considered here have not blocked reform. However, reform will be constrained or shaped by these aspects of society in ways that will leave Japanese economic institutions and behavior looking rather different from the patterns in the United States. The following sections consider the nature of these aspects of society, and then their impact on aspects of the existing economic system: labor practices, vertical *keiretsu*, the structure of financial markets, corporate governance, restrained price competition, and the role and nature of government industrial policy.

Social Features

All of the features described here can be found in American or western society. All members of Japanese society are not equally committed to these values and norms. Along a continuum of behavior patterns, however, the following aspects of Japanese social behavior are more pronounced or operate in a noticeably different manner on average than they do in the United States.[5]

Group Orientation

One of the most striking aspects of Japanese society to westerners is the dominance of social groups over the individual. This strong group orientation of society is critical for understanding several aspects of the Japanese economy, particularly labor practices, corporate governance and finance, and the vertical *keiretsu* structures among corporations.

The boundary between self and group, with the scope of the individual quite constrained, is very different from U.S. style. As soon as children enter nursery school, they are taught—gently and slowly but firmly—the importance of belonging to groups and the importance of attention to the nuances and dynamics of group behavior.[6] The central government—through the Ministry of Education—maintains a strong role in public education. Therefore, the government has played a role in encouraging what the Ministry of Education has seen as appropriate behavior. These goals of the government, however, obviously resonated with both teachers and parents.

The result of social education through family and school is that the desire to belong to one or more identifiable groups is powerful, and the sense of self-worth that comes from belonging and being accepted by the others in the group is strong. Family is one obvious social group, but so, too, are sports and other clubs. Rare is the college student without a club affiliation, and often students put far more effort into their club participation than into studying. Any individual will belong to a series of overlapping groups over the course of a lifetime—family, school, school class, school club, corporation, entering-year class at the corporation, sports club, neighborhood, and others.

Becoming an accepted member of a social group (except family) involves entrance rituals that are often elaborate, plus an apprenticeship akin to fraternity hazing in the United States. Having participated in a serious attachment ceremony or ritual, and having endured a period of apprenticeship with assignment to unpleasant or onerous tasks, individuals are more committed to the group (membership had to be worth enduring the apprenticeship), and they gain the full acceptance of the other members. The group may be rife with internal factions, disagreements, and struggles, but commitment to the overall group can be very strong and becomes a core part of the individual's sense of self-worth.

Despite the similarity between rituals of entrance and adherence or attachment in Japanese groups and some American social groups (such as fraternities or U.S. military academies), the practice seems broader or more thoroughly embedded in contemporary Japan. Furthermore, as a crude generalization, Americans both adhere to and disassociate themselves from groups more quickly and more easily than Japanese. If the purpose of the group is to accomplish a goal, Americans focus on the job to be done without as much need to develop or understand the human bonds among the group members. For the Japanese, the ability to organize the group effectively to accomplish the goal does depend on establishing group bonds and paying attention to the nuances of relations among the group members. Rather than acting on the basis of quick majority-rule decisions, Japanese groups generally rely on consensus. Discussion proceeds until all members accept the emerging agreement, at least on the surface—a process that can be lengthy.

The notion of Japan as a group society and the United States or the West as a society of individuals should not be exaggerated. Groups in the United States are extremely important. But the point here is that the relative importance to the individual of group membership as part of a satisfying life is greater in Japan; groups constrain individual desires (or actions) more frequently; efforts to make groups function occupy more of an individual's time; the sense of personal commitment to groups is generally stronger; and the internal dynamics of groups are different.

Reliance on Personal Relations

As might be expected in any society where groups are dominant and work on a principle of consensual decisionmaking, personal relationships among group members are very important. Behavior within groups is not simply a matter of taking votes and letting the majority rule, nor is it a matter of establishing hierarchical control and allowing those at the top to make the decisions. Making groups function becomes a process of establishing everyone's preferences, calculating the likelihood that a consensus can be achieved in any particular direction, and then cajoling everyone to move in that same direction. Personal likes and dislikes, possible compromises, personality conflicts among various group members, and other aspects of personal relationships become critically important in this process.

Personal relationships are also important in many cases outside group behavior. While many social and economic transactions are as casual and impersonal as they are in the United States (such as shopping in a supermarket), others are not. An individual is often less comfortable in entering a relationship—economic or social—unless or until he or she has developed an understanding of the other party, bringing a greater sense of personal connection, familiarity, or trust to the relationship or transaction. Francis Fukuyama has described Japan and the United States as both being societies with high levels of trust.[7] But while trust is important in Japan, and underwrites economic transactions, creating a sense of trust in which economic and other transactions can occur requires more effort to establish or maintain and involves a broader array of personal attributes than those directly related to the transactions involved. The Fukuyama argument, in fact, can be reversed; Japanese society is characterized by a lack of trust, so considerably more effort than in some other societies is necessary to establish sufficient trust to enable social and economic transactions. There is a desire or need to develop a broader positive social relationship in which to embed many economic or social transactions. What Americans would often perceive as either unnecessary or unwanted social interaction is a normal part of many Japanese transactions.

As one quickly learns in American society, personal relationships can also be very important in determining what does or does not happen in social groups, corporations, financial deals, and government. Nevertheless, there is a striking difference between the two societies. Japanese often refer to American society as "dry" and Japanese society as "wet," meaning that Americans seem capable of making dry decisions (that is, based purely on factual analysis), while Japanese often make wet decisions (that is, based on emotional human relations). Wet takes on a very literal meaning, since the process of establishing and maintaining personal relations in the business world often requires copious amounts of drinking at night in bars and restaurants. In the economic sphere, the emphasis on personal relationships has been a core aspect of the emphasis on banking in the financial system, the nature of corporate governance, and the reliance on and nature of vertical *keiretsu* relationships.

Hierarchy

Individuals and groups exist in a very highly defined hierarchical social structure. Everyone knows their place within this hierarchy, and that place affects behavior and infuses patterns of speech. Although the Japanese pride themselves on the small disparity in income between the top and bottom strata of society, they actually have a much stronger sense of social inequality than Americans do. One uses different language—both words and grammar—to speak to a superior and to an inferior, providing people with a constant verbal reminder of their relative status through language. Even siblings often call one another by terms like older brother (*oniisan*) rather than their given names, and members of other groups often refer to others in their group as being either their elders (*sempai)* or their juniors (*kohai*).

Related to these distinctions, the pervasive practice of exchanging business cards is important to people so they can establish their relative positions, choose the correct language, and have the right attitude toward the other. Individuals are eager to know all the relevant attributes of others in order to determine where they stand in social hierarchy: which schools they attended, when they graduated, what company they work for, how long they have been working, and their rank or title. Over the course of a lifetime, an individual may move up from the bottom to the top of the social hierarchy, although the possibilities for where one starts and might finish have a great deal to do with education and other social sorting devices.

In the ideal, vertical relationships should also be suffused with warm personal attachment in both directions, a characteristic known as *amae* (a term that has no direct English language translation, though "warm indulgence" comes close). The essence of this concept is an emotional mutual attachment akin to that of mother and child, in which the child has unqualified love for the mother and the mother is tolerant, indulgent, and protective of the child. Between adults, these relationships involve humility and obsequiousness on the part of those at the bottom, and paternalistic care by those at the top.[8] In a society where individuals live within a vast array of vertical relationships, obviously relatively few of these relationships are characterized (or need to be characterized) by *amae*. Nevertheless, the concept is deeply ingrained in the social consciousness as a desirable state of affairs. The pejorative imagery one associates with English-language terms such as obsequiousness, sycophant, or brown-noser is absent from this Japanese term in most circumstances, coming closer to the positive imagery of a term like mentoring.

The concept of *amae* frequently finds expression in the term *oyabun-kobun* (parent-child) to describe nonfamilial relationships.[9] This term conveys the sense of indulgence, guidance, and superiority on the part of the "parent" and the submissiveness, inadequacy, and receptiveness of the "child" in a relationship, whether it involves individuals, business ties between corporations, or the relationship between a government ministry and industry.

Both individual and group hierarchy play an important role in economic behavior as well. Just as individuals exist within a web of hierarchical relationships, so do economic organizations like firms. Weak, small organizations know their place within the hierarchy, but expect large organizations to look after their interests in a paternalistic (or, more properly *maternalistic*) manner. Understanding one's place in the web of hierarchical relationships is an important determinant of group behavior.[10] In addition, other corporate practices, including labor practices, vertical *keiretsu* relationships, and government-business relationships are all affected by a strong sense of hierarchy to a much greater extent than is the case in the United States.

Avoidance of Uncertainty

One of the seemingly contradictory aspects of Japanese society is a strong desire to avoid uncertainty. Any nation that manages to grow and industrialize as rapidly as did Japan in the first three decades after the Second World War must face and accept a great deal of uncertainty because so many aspects of economic and social life change so rapidly. Paradoxically, Japanese society attempts to minimize or avoid uncertainty.

Surprise or unexpected developments can be very troubling to Japanese individuals, generating a degree of anxiety that one does not usually see in a similar context in American society. Small deviations from an accepted plan or unexpected delays in a schedule can be the cause of deep concern. This anxiety may stem from the strong emphasis on routinization that is central to teaching young children to work smoothly within a group setting at school.[11] On the positive side, Americans are often pleasantly surprised at the amount of information provided in Japan. In the public transportation system, for example, displays in subway stations indicate where the next train is located, when it will arrive, and its final destination; highway signs indicate the location, length, and impact of traffic jams; and bus stops post a complete bus schedule. These kinds of information all reduce uncertainty and anxiety.

The troubling nature of uncertain or unexpected developments is more understandable in the context of group society and consensus decisionmaking. If the individual is attuned to the importance of the group, and aware of its routines or the time and trouble that were involved in making a decision, then developments outside the scope of expectations or agreed-on decisions imply an additional burden on the group. Being late for an appointment is an imposition on those who sent the invitation; developments not included in a plan imply another round of hammering out a consensus; or the unexpected development may confront an individual with the necessity of ad hoc individual action without the personal security of consulting with the group.

In economic theory, markets are an efficient means to cope with risk and uncertainty. At a single moment in time, the outcome of economic choices that affect the future is unknown and uncertain, but the market mechanism generally provides the most efficient means for allocating resources in these circumstances and reallocating them when new information becomes available. However, in many societies, including Japan, the uncertainty surrounding possible outcomes is very unsettling. Therefore, the dislike and avoidance of uncertainty has led to a number of features in the Japanese economic system, including those affecting labor market behavior, the structure of financial markets, the broader nature of corporate governance, vertical *keiretsu*, and industrial policy.

The Importance of Facades

Individuals and groups live behind masks to insulate themselves from the broader society. For the sake of social harmony, consensus, peace, and civility, it is not always appropriate to reveal one's true feelings or impart unpleasant information. As a result, the innermost aspects of the individual or group are often carefully concealed. In Japanese society, the importance of such facades, or the disparity between facade and reality, is often more pronounced than in American society.

The Japanese language has a variety of terms to express the existence of the sharp distinction between the public image and the inner reality. *Honne* (the truth) and *tatemae* (the facade) are two common terms. What one reads in the newspaper or hears in daily conversation is usually *tatemae*, and getting at the *honne* is often a time-consuming task—a task that can involve establishing a close personal relationship, joining the relevant group, or engaging an appropriate go-between. Another paired term expressing the same distinction is *omote* (the surface or face) and *ura* (the backside or inside). A somewhat similar distinction is in the paired terms *soto* (the outside) and *uchi* (the inside).

All of these paired forms are familiar and frequently invoked concepts in Japanese society, affecting behavior on a daily basis. Speculation over the nature of the reality or *honne* lying behind the *tatemae* is a common subject of conversation. This is particularly true when the pleasant, insipid, positive facade is thought to conceal a less pleasant or negative reality. Discovering the reality can be difficult.

What is true of individuals is also true of groups. Groups desire to present a favorable facade to the outside, concealing their internal disagreements or unpleasant information. Government, for example, has not, until new legislation passed in 1999, faced any legal requirement to disclose information to the public, and even the new law is quite weak. Doctors and hospitals have generally not supplied full information to patients because they are not part of the medical group, and they might be injured by hearing bad news.

One consequence of the effort to maintain a facade is that the general flow of factual information in society tends not to be as broad or open as in the United States (in contrast to the point made earlier concerning the large amount of public information concerning transportation and other routine facts). Accurate information is something to be shared carefully, generally along group lines. Many kinds of information may be shared quite freely among individuals within a group, but not outside. Groups provide bonds of affinity, trust, and familiarity that enable people to share their private information more willingly, and the knowledge that group membership brings access to information provides an additional incentive to belong.

The lack of more open dissemination of information also increases the need for go-betweens in society. If one lacks connections with an individual or group from whom one needs information, intermediaries who do have the necessary connections can provide the link. Americans are often amused, for example, by Japanese researchers coming to the United States who ask for personal introductions to people they wish to contact for interviews, a formality that is far more necessary in Japan than in the United States.

All of this may sound quite familiar to Americans. In all societies masks are important, and the truth is often concealed for reasons of social harmony. In the opposite direction, Japanese have been voracious readers of newspapers, the purveyors of news and information in society. Certainly there is a realm of factual information that resides in the public domain in Japan. The Japanese government publishes a very wide array of statistics and issues endless government reports and white books. However, the facade is often far more difficult to penetrate in Japan; the newspapers often fail to

convey more than the surface; and the government often withholds important information from the public.

The prevalence of facades also affects economic behavior, including the
bias toward bank-centered finance, since the information necessary for bond
and stock markets has often been unreliable. More broadly, it has affected the
nature of corporate governance and has been a factor in the reliance on
close long-term vertical *keiretsu* ties.

Preference for Indirectness and Informality

Direct debate and confrontation are uncomfortable for many Japanese.
Even the Japanese language has evolved in conformity with the preference
for indirectness. The language is replete with grammatical structures that
impart vagueness to statements, to the point that even Japanese attuned to
the nuances of their own society sometimes have difficulty deciphering what
is really meant. Furthermore, society evolved an elaborate reliance on go-
betweens as a mechanism for avoiding direct confrontation or negotiation.

This attribute of social behavior is one where government has played a
particularly strong role. Government has controlled the use of courts as a
mechanism for confrontation and resolution of problems by strictly regulating the number of judges and lawyers. Only a single government-run
school trains lawyers and judges, so the government has total control over
the annual entrants to these professions.[12] Recently there has been discussion
about the need for more lawyers and judges, but recommendations remain
vague. A report by a commission attached to the Ministry of International
Trade and Industry (MITI) recognized the need for more lawyers and judges,
but put no numbers on the increase.[13]

Indirectness relates very closely to the concept of facade. Individuals may
hide cautiously behind a facade, but to achieve viable decisions the underlying reality must eventually become known to others in the group or be
shared as necessary outside the group. The preferred route for this revelation
of the truth is indirect; neutral brokers or go-betweens can seek the information, negotiate, or assuage hurt feelings to prevent undesired, embarrassing direct revelations or unpleasant direct confrontations.

Informality becomes another aspect of the same phenomenon. Formal
settings, such as contact during the day in the corporate office, inhibit open
discussion and transfer of information. Individuals who want or need to
reveal their inner thoughts generally wait for a more informal setting—over
drinks in a bar or a meal in a restaurant with a comfortable collection of
close colleagues from the appropriate group. Informal settings such as these,

and the confidences shared, provide an essential ingredient for building the personal relationships identified earlier.

The preference for indirectness and informality affects a variety of economic behaviors. Reliance on banks—a go-between joining savers and borrowers—is one obvious example. So, too, is the prevalence of sending retiring personnel from banks to borrowers, to subcontractors in vertical *keiretsu*, or government officials to the private sector (*amakudari*) as part of industrial policy.

Implications for the Economic System

The features of Japanese social behavior just described create potential problems for a market economy. Markets need accurate information to clear properly, and they must have a constant flow of updated information so they can adjust properly, especially when expectations about the uncertain future are incorrect. Efficiency presumes an ability to juggle productive assets without regard for hierarchy, group loyalties, or other aspects of noneconomic personal relationships. Much of what was just described would seem to undermine the efficient functioning of financial markets, labor markets, or the corporation. However, the economic success of Japan since the late nineteenth century belies such a conclusion.

The answer to this puzzle is the evolution of economic institutions and behavior patterns that accommodated or deliberately played on these social features, and, in some cases, even turned them into a virtue. This evolution took time. When the Japanese government consciously began the process of modernization and industrialization in the 1870s, the initial approach was to import the new institutional framework from abroad, creating laws similar to those in western nations to permit corporations, financial institutions, labor markets, and the other basic building blocks of a modern economy. Over time, however, institutions and behavior patterns changed to deal with perceived problems. The set of distinctive features of the economy described in chapter 2 all reflect the conscious bending of western concepts, in part to conform better to social norms.

Labor Markets

Simple economic theory assumes that workers exist in a competitive labor market. They have varying attributes that affect their productivity ("human capital," in economists' parlance) and are hired to work at firms up to the point where the marginal productivity of the last worker hired equals the wage rate. If the business cycle results in excess workers at the firm, so that marginal value added is less than wage rate, then the firm reduces wages or fires workers until the equilibrium is restored. Simple theory also assumes workers with similar quality attributes to be interchangeable, working productively within the firm once hired.

The flexibility of this model is important for producing an efficient economic outcome, but it imposes a cost on workers. They face uncertainty in their personal economic existence, since they could lose employment at various times over the course of their lives. This imposes on the worker loss of income, the social stigma of unemployment, and the burden of searching for alternative employment, all adding to emotional stress. Many societies have found this stress to be socially unacceptable and have modified the operation of labor markets. This has been particularly true in postwar Japan, resulting in "lifetime" employment and a variety of distinctive labor practices within firms.

From the late nineteenth century until the 1920s, labor markets in the emerging modern corporate sector in Japan worked roughly in accordance with economic theory. A labor market emerged in which people sought employment and firms hired according to their economic need. However, over time new mechanisms emerged that modified labor practices to conform better to social norms of reducing uncertainty, group orientation, and hierarchy.[14]

Of these modifications, the most obvious is "lifetime employment," in which the firm hires young workers permanently (until a mandatory retirement age). Firms reacted to high labor turnover rates by instituting lifetime employment for core managerial employees beginning in the 1920s. The system spread to blue-collar employees after the war; this occurred in response to labor union pressure for job stability and management desire to build employee loyalty to undermine more radical union demands. This system has value to those workers covered by it, dramatically reducing the personal uncertainty in their lives. To the extent that Japanese society as a whole has a distinctive aversion to uncertainty, this system furthered broad social values, or at least the social values of those in jobs covered by lifetime employment.

Economists have argued that the system is closely related to the notion of firm-specific skills that workers acquire over time. If a worker who remains with the company for twenty years has continuously acquired new skills applicable only to the particular organization and technology of that firm, then the corporation reaps a productivity gain by inducing workers to remain with the firm.[15] However, it is highly likely that social factors affect the firm as well. Corporations are not just black boxes that convert inputs into outputs; they are groups of people working together. Getting a group to function effectively in Japan involves the creation of group consciousness. The notion of lifetime employment fits well with this need. Building commitment, loyalty, and group consciousness involves longevity of membership, a period of apprenticeship, and promotion from within. Companies, for example, have long training programs for new employees that serve both as initiation rites and as mechanisms to build a sense of membership, commitment, loyalty, and self-sacrifice for the good of the corporate group.[16] Participating in a familiar group setting will elicit commitment, thereby enhancing work effort or productivity over time.

This argument for the value of lifetime employment is quite different from standard human capital theories about continuous skill formation. In this social model, the skill or human capital that employees amass as they remain with the firm is not technical skill but a deeper understanding of the nuances of personal relations among their coworkers and other aspects of group dynamics, greater loyalty and commitment to the firm, and a greater willingness to trust others within the firm.

Bringing in employees from outside at a later point in their career or into the upper reaches of the corporate managerial hierarchy is difficult in this social context, particularly if those persons have been employed elsewhere in the same industry. Their loyalty or commitment cannot be the same as those who have built their careers within the firm, and, therefore, they cannot be as fully trusted, nor will they gain an equal amount of respect from those they manage. Since Americans adhere to new groups more quickly and with less of an overlay of ritual or apprenticeship, this is less of a problem in U.S. labor markets.

Long-term employment also implies that the corporation bears certain social obligations. Having promised, no matter how implicitly, not to fire an employee until retirement, and having gained the employee's total commitment, the firm has a social obligation to abide by its side of the bargain. Furthermore, the obligation extends to the employee's exit at the end of the "lifetime." In an additional practice that reduces uncertainty, firms have the social obligation to find their lifetime employees retirement positions (either when they reach the mandatory retirement age or if they need to be forced out of the organization before they are eligible for retirement). Thus an individual who gains a regular position with a firm that practices lifetime employment can largely eliminate personal anxiety about long-term well-being. Life may be anxious for other reasons, as the entering cohorts of new employees jockey continuously and intensely over the course of their careers for the best promotion slots. However, the downside risk of losing one's job and being left entirely on one's own to find a new job is theoretically absent. To the extent that workers in this system believed this risk was truly absent, the fraying of this commitment over the course of the 1990s was troubling. Some firms faced an overwhelming need to downsize as the economy stagnated in the 1990s, and the resulting pressures on senior employees to retire early has been strong—sending a chilling implicit message to younger employees.

Note also that lifetime employment also has implications for the role of government in the economy. In essence, lifetime employment brought a privatization of the social safety net. Rather than relying on unemployment insurance to support these employees in times of economic downturns, corporations have borne the cost of maintaining workers who might otherwise be let go. Even corporations supporting the presumed productivity advantages of long-term employment have certainly faced times when keeping their implicit commitment to these workers has been a financial burden. In exchange for bearing this cost, the government provided a domestic business environment of reduced competition, which put firms in a better position to bear this cost.

Not all working adults in Japan are covered by this lifetime employment, nor do all who are covered necessarily remain with the company they initially entered. Women, for example, have generally been excluded: they are expected to "retire" when they either get married or have their first child. However, a sufficient minority of workers is covered, and certainly the concept is deeply ingrained in the psyche of many Japanese as a desired condition. They see or imagine a wide gulf between, on the one hand, the familiar, embracing group-oriented employment practices of their own society, embodied in the concept of lifetime employment, and, on the other hand, a heartless American system in which individuals must suffer instability in employment and the necessity of searching for a job entirely on their own.

For those employees who are not at a firm that openly offers lifetime employment, the existence of the vertical *keiretsu* system may also provide a sense of stability. Those not well enough educated, or not lucky enough to land a job with a major firm practicing lifetime employment, can achieve some semblance of stability in their employment by working for a subcontractor of such a firm. Their lack of education, skill, or luck relegates them to a world of lower wages, but they can imagine that employment at a subcontractor to a major, growing manufacturer would be similarly stable. Life at a subcontractor to Toyota Motor Corporation, for example, might be very hard, with constant pressure to improve productivity, cut prices, and deliver according to very demanding schedules. However, the auto industry grew so rapidly that someone at a Toyota subcontractor should have faced little prospect of being laid off in the past fifty years. Since the early 1990s, however, the certainty of employment at subcontractors has diminished as overwhelming financial pressures have forced some desperate manufacturers to reconsider their vertical *keiretsu*. This was dramatically true of Nissan after its partial purchase by Renault.

The finely developed sense of hierarchy is also consistent with lifetime employment. Corporations are hierarchical organizations designed to put individuals together in a productive relationship. Some of those individuals must manage all or parts of the totality. In Japanese society, the authority necessary to occupy such managerial positions comes in part from the personal qualifiers accompanying lifetime employment: age and longevity of service. The managers may not exercise authority in the same manner as Americans, but their ability to gain acceptance from their subordinates in managerial roles certainly depends on the mutual acceptance of the social validity of these qualifiers. Given these expectations, it is more difficult for a firm to bring in an outsider to occupy a managerial position.

What does all this imply for Japan at present? The presumption of outside observers is that lifetime employment and exclusive reliance on internal promotion should come to an end or is coming to an end. Certainly there is much talk about the demise of lifetime employment in the media and among Japanese. But will this really happen? No. The system may be modified, but it is very unlikely to converge on an American model.

Fear or anxiety about potentially changing toward a system in which employment is uncertain and where one might have to seek reemployment alone is noticeable. This anxiety is not simply a matter of individuals' recognizing that life has been easier with the paternalistic care that came with lifetime employment. Rather, there is a sense of social injustice of a system in which individuals would have to confront the possibility of seeking employment entirely on their own more than once during their careers. In a Japanese social context, groups should bear the responsibility for the welfare of their members. Having once found employment, therefore, as a matter of principle people expect or hope that the corporations to which they belong will take care of their future needs, by either keeping them employed or finding them other jobs.

On the corporate side as well there are powerful reasons to maintain the general principles involved with lifetime employment. As long as corporate managers believe that employees continue to learn technical and interpersonal skills, develop commitment to the firm, and (thereby) become increasingly productive the longer they remain with the firm, why would the managers want to fundamentally change the system? The notion that individual firms have specific technologies that employees learn to use and improve over time is probably exaggerated in the economics literature on Japanese firm-specific human capital. However, managers know that an individual's adherence to a group is not a light matter in their society, and they believe that their employees will be more loyal, committed, and productive in an environment in which the employees sense that the firm treats them as long-term group members.

Labor force practices are under considerable strain at the turn of the century. The optimism of the 1980s led to excess hiring, leaving many companies overstaffed by the late 1990s. Recognizing that lifetime employment is an obstacle to rapid downsizing, outside observers have predicted an end to a system that is outmoded and should not be sustained. However, this view ignores the social context in which the system exists. Instead of outright abandonment, two scenarios are possible.

First, firms could engage in a one-time downsizing, as they did in the mid-1970s, the last time the economy experienced a sharp recession. Most of the adjustment can be made through attrition—not hiring new workers to replace those retiring, and offering early retirement packages. The adjustment may not be as rapid as is possible in the United States, but over a period of two to three years, corporations could reduce employment by nontrivial amounts. At the margin, desperate companies can lay off workers. When the alternative is bankruptcy, management can break its implicit social obligation to workers. In this scenario, the one-time adjustment would clear away the mistake of the late 1980s, after which the economy would revive, and firms could continue practicing the same labor policies as before. Chapter 6 considers recent corporate developments that suggest downsizing is generally modest enough to be done through attrition.

The problem with this first scenario is that it represents a *structural* change, but not a *systemic* one. Firms living in a slow-growth economy will continue to face slow labor force adjustments due to their commitment to lifetime employees. A one-time downsizing paves the way for a cyclical economic recovery, but the next economic downturn would leave them once again struggling to reduce labor costs. Meanwhile, the attrition process leaves firms with an older work force because they are not hiring young employees to replace retirees. This has a double negative effect on firms. Labor costs per employee rise because lifetime employment includes a strong seniority pay scale, so not bringing in new, cheap employees raises the average. In addition, this process leaves firms starved for bright, young, tech-savvy employees while they retain older, more conservative ones. Firms relying on attrition, therefore, are placing themselves at a disadvantage in both labor cost and technology, especially in the information technology field.

Second, the system could be modestly modified. Lifetime employment could be offered to a smaller subset of employees. Even in the past the practice did not apply to all employees at large firms, and the core could be narrowed to those blue- and white-collar employees deemed most important. Furthermore, the nature of the commitment could change, with a more explicit recognition that the firm might not be able to maintain employment until the retirement age, but would still promise to relocate employees to another firm should circumstances make downsizing necessary. In this way, the firm maintains its responsibility to care for the well-being of its members by not forcing them out into a cold, heartless labor market.

In reality, both scenarios may be operative. By 1999 firms were more actively downsizing, but with few outright layoffs. Furthermore, the rise in use of part-time and temporary workers and of women (whose unemployment rate in 1999 was lower than that of men) suggests some modification in corporate behavior. Sadly, this has occurred at some expense for women. In 1990, 28 percent of women worked part-time (that is, less than thirty-five hours a week), but that share rose to 35 percent by 2000 (and 50 percent of new hires), with the absolute number of women working full time falling 5 percent.[17]

None of these changes connotes an outright abandonment of lifetime employment and other labor force practices. Those who think that Japanese firms will converge on the American model by becoming far more nimble in labor adjustment over the course of the business cycle will be disappointed. Firms acquiring others will still face constraints on removing large parts of existing management personnel and installing their own people. In particular, any naive foreign firm acquiring Japanese firms that thinks it will be able to easily downsize management or bring in many new managers from the outside will be in for an unpleasant shock.

Vertical Keiretsu

The reliance on long-term vertical relationships between large manufacturers and their parts suppliers and distributors has a purely economic rationale, stemming from the economic efficiencies of long-term contracting. Chapter 2 argued that in the Japanese case, these vertical *keiretsu* relationships went beyond the theoretical notion of long-term contracting, becoming rather fixed. The realization that businesses have been locked into relationships with others that are no longer economically beneficial has led some observers to declare the *keiretsu* system dead. Firms will acquire and shed subsidiaries with greater ease and engage or dismiss suppliers and distributors on the basis of performance. Some companies, Nissan Motor Corporation in particular, have announced an official end to their existing *keiretsu*. In the Nissan case, parts suppliers seem resigned to the changes, blaming Nissan managers rather than the Renault leadership for having mismanaged the company over the past decade.[18]

However, the web of ties that constitutes vertical *keiretsu* relationships is deeply embedded in social practice. These practices are so familiar and fit so comfortably with broader social expectations that it is difficult to imagine the system's coming entirely unraveled. Just like individuals, firms (or the managers within firms) are uncomfortable doing business with strangers outside the group without an overlay of broader social ties to build familiarity and trust. American businessmen are often amused or appalled at the extent of personal information (such as complete resumes for the senior staff) that potential Japanese clients demand as part of the process of gaining familiarity. Americans often fail to spend enough time getting to know their Japanese counterparts socially. Nevertheless, these are routine aspects of doing business in Japan. Given the reliance on personal relations to evaluate a situation, Japanese managers want and need to develop a personal context in which to evaluate the worth or profitability of a business relationship. Since creating such a context takes considerable time and represents a considerable initial cost to the firm, this social preference or need supports the preference for long-term business ties. This aspect of Japanese social behavior does not appear to be changing much, so long-term business relationships such as those in vertical *keiretsu* will remain.

Another way to look at *keiretsu* relationships is as another form of group. Both the large manufacturer and its parts suppliers are more comfortable with the belief that the network of their ties represents a group, with all the familiar social expectations and routines. To evaluate potential business deals solely on their technical or cost merits, interact only long enough to negotiate a contract, and then put the deal immediately into operation is unsettling because the requisite elements of trust and familiarity are not there. Spending the time developing personal relationships that are necessary to build trust and then embedding the relationship in a long-term group framework by labeling it a *keiretsu* relationship creates an environment in which trust can continue to exist if monitored closely through continued personal ties. Even though the dominant player in these relationships has always had the power of termination as a threat to extract performance from suppliers and distributors, actually terminating a *keiretsu* relationship is not easy because of this overlay of social obligation and expectation.

The hierarchical inequality in these relationships often leads participants and observers to speak of them in *oyabun-kobun* (parent-child) terms, giving them the feeling of familial relationships and emphasizing the relatively unequal roles and expectations of the involved parties. Broadly speaking, in the United States assemblers and parts manufacturers do not generally exist in a tight hierarchical relationship, though there have been exceptions. Indeed, many large, diversified parts manufacturers are as large and sophisticated as the major assembly firms. In Japan, however, many parts supply and distribution relationships acquire a distinct vertical, hierarchical coloring. Although these long-term contracts are often with formally independent firms in which the large manufacturer has no equity stake, they perform essentially as subsidiaries of the parent company. This enables the large firm to make extensive demands on them and to interact closely with their staff. While the demands—price cuts, tight delivery schedules, or sudden design changes—might seem unreasonable, the junior partners in these relationships accept them in exchange for the long-term economic security the relationship provides. They may also accept the inequality simply because they know they are at the bottom of the hierarchy. Smaller in size, run by managers who did not attend equally prestigious schools, paying lower wages and salaries, these firms know they are both economically and socially inferior. In a Japanese social setting, those managers' recognition of their inferiority leads them to be more accepting of what outside observers sometimes see as unjust demands. Thus the ingrained recognition, acceptance, and use of hierarchy in Japanese society becomes an element in enabling Japanese-style long-term contracting and makes the system work.

Some firms are now considering or actually deconstructing parts of their *keiretsu* structures, but to extrapolate from this the demise of the system would be unjustified. The extreme distress of some corporations provides sufficient justification for dropping existing business relationships, but the more likely outcome will be for this period to be a one-time adjustment. Having corrected the set of inefficiencies and problems inherent in some of their relationships, firms are likely to build new long-term relationships, perhaps with some of the same suppliers. Hierarchy, reliance on personal relationships, and group orientation all remain core parts of social behavior. As long as this is the case, complete abandonment of the *keiretsu* system is unlikely.

Finance

Chapter 2 pointed out the heavy reliance on banking as a means of moving funds between savers and investors. Japan is not the only nation with a financial system that relies very heavily on banking. However, the enforced preference for banking is related to or reinforced by several social factors. Fashioning the system to emphasize banks was a deliberate choice of the government in the early postwar period. In so doing, though, the government was also drawing on social norms, establishing a system that would be comfortable and familiar to both household savers and corporate borrowers.

Savings accounts in banks offered households a low-risk form of investment with a known return. Bank deposits are the least risky means for households to save, even if the government is serious about enforcing the legal limit on the maximum size of deposits to be guaranteed by deposit insurance. Furthermore, the return on deposits is known; it may change from time to time, but the interest rate is public knowledge. In a three-year commercial bank savings deposit, the interest is set and the interest income known. For money invested in the bond or stock market, the return is quite variable. No investment bank can tell investors what their return will be (except in the unethical case of Nomura Securities and its VIP accounts in the 1980s, which guaranteed minimum stock portfolio returns for favored clients). The certainty of the return on the bank account is comforting, even if the *expected* return on bonds and stocks over prolonged periods of time is higher.

Risk-averse household behavior helps explain the decline in equities in household financial portfolios over time. A variety of explanations related to regulation might explain why households would put a higher share of their portfolios into bank accounts than is the case in the United States, but not why the share of bonds and equities would decline over time. Japanese households became far more affluent over time, which should have enabled them to meet minimum purchase-lot requirements and to deal with high, fixed commissions more easily than earlier in the postwar period. Instead, the trend has been toward greater reliance on bank accounts and, among banks, toward greater use of the Postal Savings system, the least risky of all possible investments. If this explanation is correct, households are unlikely to engage in a major shift of their financial portfolios as financial deregulation occurs. There may be enough new business for investment banks in the form of mutual fund sales to provide substantial profit opportunities for American financial institutions in Japan, but not enough to proclaim that household behavior has changed fundamentally.

With corporate borrowers the reliance on personal relations comes into play. The problem with bonds and stocks from a corporate perspective is that they involve heartless, impersonal markets. Bank loans, in contrast, involve one-on-one relationships with loan officers. This provides a social context in which to transact business. Corporate managers have an easier time relating to a system in which they will divulge corporate information to a finite set of bank managers with whom they have developed personal relationships than broadcasting intimate financial details—good and bad—to the broad public. Since these one-on-one relationships are lubricated in the accepted manner with meals, liquor, golf outings, and other entertainment, corporate managers have all the more reason to prefer bank loans to the impersonal bond and stock markets.

Bank loans also fit well with the notion of group orientation. Corporate managers would prefer to feel that they have a group relationship with the providers of capital. Banks provide that sense of stability and intimacy. A bank is likely to remain a lender to a corporation for an indefinite period, especially in the case of the main bank. The Japanese image of American stock and bond markets, in contrast, is that they comprise aggressive, fickle investors who will buy or sell out their holdings on a whim, without any long-term commitment to the goals and values of the firm. The impersonality and potentially short-term nature of these relationships is unsettling to managers. They want and value the warm sense of membership and inclusiveness that comes from a long-term business relationship with a bank.

Finally, reliance on banking is consistent with facades and the overall social preference for indirectness. In an environment of disparity between facades and reality, household investors have reason to believe that publicly available information on corporations is unreliable. This belief has been amply reinforced during the past decade by a spate of scandals revealing corporate efforts to conceal negative information—such as the revelation by Mitsubishi Motors in 2000 that it had been deliberately withholding information on product defects for thirty years, ever since the product recall law went into effect.[19] Bankers play a reassuring go-between role in such an environment. For households, banks obviate the need to research the risks attached to investments in individual companies. For borrowers, the banks are a shield from potentially embarrassing or difficult pressures from individual savers who might question corporate performance or goals. Thus corporations can maintain their public facades and still raise funds from a skeptical public through this indirect form of finance.

Vigorous bond and stock markets require large amounts of accurate financial and other corporate data made available publicly. Full disclosure of negative information is especially important in order for these markets to operate efficiently. These markets lack the warm personal relationships associated with banking; they represent an uncomfortable directness in dealing with providers of capital; and they cause unending embarrassment because of the necessity to be direct and honest in revealing bad news. Like individuals and other groups, corporations want to maintain a positive *tatemae* in public, avoiding revelation of problems. While increasing reliance on bond and stock markets may occur, the shift may not be buttressed by the necessary supporting institutional elements. Japan, for example, has virtually no viable domestic bond rating or risk assessment firms, and those that do exist date only to the 1980s. The only truly independent domestic firm, Mikuni and Company, has been subject to periodic harassment by the Ministry of Finance ever since its formation in the 1980s.[20] Furthermore, the foreign firms entering this market (principally Standard and Poor's, and Moody's) have faced intense media and government attention on their pronouncements because of the novelty and pain associated with negative ratings.

Presumably, a robust market for corporate information could develop. Just because an existing financial system conforms to many aspects of accepted social behavior does not mean that rules and regulations cannot be created by government to counter these tendencies. Indeed, recognizing the social tendencies to avoid disclosure, the Japanese government could react with strong rules and vigorous enforcement to overcome this problem. The new accounting practices implemented in 2001 presumably will bring better disclosure, but their impact is still somewhat uncertain. After all, why should the Japanese government move vigorously in this direction when it is motivated by the same social beliefs and sees a more open, direct financial system as counter to its own view of how the economy should operate?

The most likely outcome is a modest, partial shift in financial markets. Households will shift their portfolios toward equities and bonds, particularly in the form of mutual funds, but will not go as far as Americans. Corporations will issue more bonds, but will continue to rely more heavily on banks than their American counterparts, and the bulk of these bonds may continue to be purchased by the same banks from which they already borrow. Equity markets may well play an enhanced role in financing new high tech and e-commerce start-ups, but will not become a venue for contesting corporate control or providing corporate governance for established firms. Disclosure will improve, but the public will remain concerned that they are seeing corporate *tatemae*, a belief that will moderate the desire by individuals to participate in the stock market.

Corporate Governance

Chapter 2 noted the differences in corporate governance between American and Japanese firms. Even in the American context the shareholder-driven principal-agent model has not always typified actual behavior. In the past quarter century in the United States, though, a trend has set in, driven by the emergence of large shareholders (pension funds and mutual funds) who monitor corporations closely and exercise their voice as owners, plus a more vigorous market for corporate acquisitions and increased lawsuits by shareholders of the firm.[21]

In the Japanese context, the firm is far more than just a convenient economic construct to transform inputs into outputs. The firm has acquired attributes of family or other group organizations, as noted earlier. This creates a problem for American-style governance by the shareholders, since they are outsiders to the corporate group, delegitimizing their voice in a social sense. Except in clear cases of subsidiaries, shareholders are regarded as a source of funds but not a source of control. The colorful example of T. Boone Pickens's acquiring a large minority interest in Koito Corporation (a Toyota parts supplier) in the 1980s and then being denied a seat on the board of directors illustrates the point.

Banks (especially the "main" bank) and vertical *keiretsu* partners provide a theoretical substitute for shareholder oversight. Assigning *keiretsu* partners and banks this corporate governance role is consistent with the array of social factors discussed in this chapter. These overseers are part of the extended group of the corporation rather than true outsiders. Relations with them are personal and suitably lubricated in the manner of all personal relations. Hierarchy gives them authority to apply pressure, as the "parent" in *oyabun-kobun* relationships, because they either stand higher in the pecking order of a vertical *keiretsu* or have the higher social prestige of banks. When running properly, there is no reason why this version of corporate governance cannot function effectively. Management is willing to accept parent firms or banks as legitimate members of the corporate group, divulge the necessary corporate information to them, and respond to pressure for change when performance is inadequate.

Given the problem of facade versus reality, a corporate governance system relying on vertical *keiretsu* and banks might have been the only viable route. Only creditors able to build long-term group ties can get beyond the facade of company financial reports and develop a more accurate, detailed knowledge of what is going well or wrong at the corporation. As an important corollary to this point, such a corporate governance system may have been the only viable route given the government's unwillingness or reluctance to create or enforce a regulatory regime to counter the problem of *tatemae* or other aspects of social relations.

Chapter 3 pointed out the inherent problem of this nontransparent system of corporate governance. The system may never have worked as well as advertised, and certainly problems and scandals emerged during the 1990s. If the past system of corporate governance is no longer working properly, or was always flawed, how can it be changed? Repackaging corporate governance in a way that is more in line with American capitalism presents some problems. Assigning a greater role to shareholders raises fear among managers of pressure from individuals and groups considered outsiders who do not share the goals of the corporation or do not have the requisite detailed knowledge or loyalty to be comfortably granted a voice in corporate governance.

Worse, these outsiders focus on financial return (desiring to maximize the return on their investments in the firm), running counter to the multidimensional goals of corporate management. Maximizing the rate of return has never been a primary goal of management in Japan. Managers have been consumed by a focus on market share (and the hierarchical ranking of their firm in the industry) and product development, a focus that was made possible by the existence of trade barriers that limited competition at home from foreign firms. Being forced to focus more heavily on financial return by the market is viewed as interfering with these other goals. The contrast between Japanese beliefs and economic theory is fascinating. Theory says that the greatest efficiency comes from maximizing profit; the Japanese believe that maximizing profit interferes with corporate performance either by forcing an unnecessarily short-term time horizon or by diminishing the firm's freedom in putting financial resources into product development rather than shareholder dividends. While the Japanese media have been full of talk of corporations' changing their goals to focus on return on equity or return on assets in this new era, one doubts that actual returns will proceed as far as the U.S. level.[22]

Restrained Price Competition

Individual corporations are a form of social group, but so too are the groups of corporations that constitute industries. In many ways, corporate behavior within an industry is imbued with social overtones that conflict with simple economic theory. As a social group, an industry carries some obligation to protect or preserve its weak members. For the strongest members of the group to drive their competitive advantage to the point of bankrupting weak members is not desirable. Should egotistical strong firms act on their own self-interest, the government often intervenes to restore the norms of group behavior.

Hierarchy plays an important role in these relationships. Ideally the leading firm or firms in an industry should play a parent, *oyabun,* role and treat the others indulgently through *amae* relationships. The leaders may hold the presidency of the trade association, but they should use this role to advance industry policies of benefit to all.

When corporate members of an industry are mindful of their social obligations, the outcome is the reduced price competition examined in chapter 2. High prices provide an umbrella under which the most inefficient members of the industry can survive. Unburdened with strong shareholder pressures, the industry leaders can fritter away their high profits in this model by raising wages and salaries or spending more on new product development. Follower firms cannot engage in as much development but can play an imitation game, closely following the leaders in new products. With reduced price competition, enabled by protection from imports, an additional industry social benefit is reduced uncertainty. Individual firms are less likely to fail as long as the price umbrella remains intact. All members of the industry can feel relatively secure about their long-term viability.

Something has gone wrong with this sense of industry social obligation. When the chips were down in the 1990s, many firms looked out for their own individual interests—especially if they felt the sinking industrial ship had too few lifeboats for all to survive. Obviously, at some level of individual corporate distress the norms of group behavior and mutual obligations in a hierarchical setting give way to self-preservation. Consolidation, reorganization, bankruptcy, and new entrants have characterized a number of industries in the past several years.

What does this breakdown in social order reflect? Are corporations and industries moving toward a model of stronger competition driven purely by individual corporate profit goals? Is this just a temporary lapse of social order—like mob violence—to be restored once these unusual times have run their course? The answer is more of the latter than the former. Greater openness to international competition (including largely borderless e-commerce) may imply that intra-industry collusion will be unable to restrain price competition to the extent that it did in earlier years. Nevertheless, the tug of social norms for group behavior and hierarchical obligations has certainly not disappeared.

Industrial Policy

A final obvious element of the Japanese system that is firmly embedded in social norms is industrial policy. Put in the broadest terms, social behavior in Japan underwrites a strong role for government in influencing or shaping economic behavior in the private sector.

The most obvious social element involved here is hierarchy. Government officials, especially those on the top career path, come from the most prestigious departments of the most prestigious universities in Japan. In 1999, thirteen out of seventeen top posts (vice minister plus directors general) were occupied by graduates of the University of Tokyo, the most prestigious university in the nation. Ten of these thirteen officials were graduates of the law faculty, the most elite of the departments at the school.[23] At the Ministry of Finance (MOF) in the same year, the vice ministers (the administrative vice minister and the vice minister for international monetary affairs) plus all six of the directors general in the central office were University of Tokyo graduates. All but one was from the law faculty. Graduates of other universities hold director general positions only in the regional offices and some of the technical offices (such as customs inspection).[24] Even though the reputation of bureaucrats has been badly tarnished in the 1990s, they continue to hold a firm spot at the top of the social hierarchy. Many people are openly critical of the bureaucrats or even express contempt about their behavior or their stodgy thinking about the economy. However, these expressions do not necessarily translate into any substantial movement to alter the position or function of the bureaucracy and often represent no more than the normal carping about those in authority.

This status within the social hierarchy has been crucial for the functioning of industrial policy by creating expectations on both the government and corporate side. Government officials who are steeped in the ideology of the need to guide the economy are further convinced of the appropriateness of their role by their own sense of their position in the social hierarchy. Having attended the best schools and having passed the difficult entrance exam of a prestigious government ministry, they believe that others in the private sector should naturally look up to them and listen to their advice. On the private-sector side, those who must interact with government officials bring their own knowledge of—and acceptance of—their own lower status; they did not attend schools or departments that are as prestigious, nor did they pass the stiff entrance exam for the bureaucracy. This mutual acceptance of hierarchy creates a social atmosphere in which the private sector is generally far more tolerant of meddling by government officials than is the case in the United States.

Hierarchy does not imply that these government officials necessarily determine outcomes that are forced on a compliant industry. Just as often, the pressures for industrial policy initiatives have come from industry itself (not surprising since bureaucrats are often not experts on the industries they oversee). However, hierarchy still matters, because it puts bureaucrats in the position of prestige and symbolic power to bless the policy decisions or to mediate among industry factions when disagreement occurs.

At the extreme are examples where the government-business interface takes on the characteristics of *amae* in personal relationships. That is, in some cases industry expects and wants government guidance and behaves in a manner to invite favors, comfortable in the knowledge that the government will behave in a protective, maternalistic manner. There is no other way to describe the decades-long relationship between the government and the aerospace industry in Japan, a history exquisitely detailed by Richard Samuels.[25] In this industry, a small set of domestic firms has worked closely with MITI for decades, secure in the notion that the government will be "fair" to all participants in providing contracts and protecting them from foreign competition.

The same situation prevails in the construction industry, in a relationship that also includes politicians. The companies were permitted to engage in bid rigging and reciprocated by putting large legal and illegal donations into the pockets of politicians, as well as accepting large numbers of *amakudari* government officials.

A third example is finance, where government policy rigidly excluded newcomers, narrowly defined areas of business, and provided a comfortable profit level for all financial institutions. While some financial institutions resented bureaucratic interference, they knew that they led a very stable existence and generally accepted a flow of *amakudari* officials from the Ministry of Finance into their management ranks to cement the relationships. Since the mid-1970s changed economic conditions have put pressure on the existing structure of the financial sector, especially pressures from a rapid rise in government debt, slower growth in loan demand from traditional corporate borrowers, and the need to recycle current-account surpluses as net capital outflow. These pressures led to incremental deregulation steps through the rest of the 1970s and 1980s.[26] The economic shifts easily explain the regulatory changes, but most interesting are the carefully crafted agreements that attempted to balance benefits and costs for all financial institutions. At least until the mid-1990s, concepts such as group consciousness, *amae* by a paternalistic government, and strong government-private personal relationships reinforced by the practice of *amakudari* played a role in shaping deregulation. The huge bad debt problems and outright bankruptcy facing individual institutions or types of institutions have finally undermined these cozy relationships.

In the aerospace, construction, and finance industries, one of the benefits that accrue to firms from government involvement is a reduction of uncertainty. Any firm in any country would prefer to operate in an environment of great certainty about its profits and future existence. In Japan that desire appears to be much stronger, sufficiently strong to lead some firms to accept government guidance or mediation. That guidance may reduce the firm's chances of dramatic success in the form of profits or market share that comes at the expense of others in the industry, but it also reduces the chances of failure over the long run. Many firms appear to prefer to live with the assurance of existence than to have the opportunity to gamble on major gains. Government involvement cannot stave off harsh economic reality forever—as has been the case in the financial sector. However, its existence and the set of social beliefs and behavioral norms that mold its operation help the slowness of reform.

The government also has a role in the dynamics of industry behavior and reduced price competition. Firms in an industry may be capable of organizing themselves into a cartel or trade association for the purposes of constraining individual behavior, as discussed in the previous section. Despite the social logic of groups, the pull of individual profits or market share can inhibit successful group formation, perhaps like a social group that lacks older or wiser members to help pull everyone together. In this case the government plays a go-between role, providing a sense of indirectness. Firms within the industry can avoid direct confrontation over industry policy by using the government to mediate or shape the consensus. Economic logic dictates that firms should pursue their individual interests, but in a Japanese social setting, even aggressive firms that seem to fit the western mold can often be cajoled into complying to some extent with anticompetitive policies, especially when the government is pushing or mediating from behind the scenes. Even if firms oppose government involvement, the government's own notions of appropriate group behavior in industries will work toward forcing less egotistical behavior, given the high hierarchical standing of the government within this group dynamic. Some scholars studying industrial policy have pointed to examples of independent firms that refused to listen to government advice as proof that industrial policy was overblown and did not work.[27] Often resistance to industry and government pressure is only partial or is only temporary, however. Ultimately most senior executives at Japanese firms feel the tug of their domestic social setting and modify their behavior.

Most important, though, even the exceptions substantiate the general model of government business interaction. Just like the relationship between parents and children in a family, the government "parent" did not always force its will on reluctant or aggressive firms in the high growth era. However, private-sector firms had to work within, or struggle against, a world of government pressures, suggestions, interference, and influence. While the relationships are somewhat more ambiguous or more tenuous than thirty years ago, firms must still interact with a government that is a substantial player in influencing microeconomic developments.

Conclusion

The set of social conventions, routines, preferences, expectations, and rituals that shapes personal behavior also shapes economic institutions and their behavior. Continuing differences between Japanese and American social norms and behavior imply that systemic economic reform in Japan is unlikely to produce convergence on American economic patterns. This conclusion does not mean that structural reform will not occur, but it does mean that whatever change does occur must be compatible with the social context. That context remains sufficiently different from that of the United States to prevent convergence of the economic systems.

In the longer run, society itself changes. Postwar Japanese society is different in many ways from prewar society, and young people today behave differently from older generations. Speech patterns have lost some of the attention to hierarchy and gender that was so distinctive in the past. Terms like *giri* and *ninjō* (obligation versus human feeling) seem quaint to young people. Many of the fundamental features of society change only slowly.

The social features identified in this chapter may be constantly changing, but they represent dimensions of social behavior that continue to distinguish Japanese society rather sharply from American or western society.

In many ways, government can affect both social norms and the way in which economic institutions or behavior patterns relate to these norms. The Ministry of Education exerts a powerful role in shaping school curricula and teaching methods, which are important for instilling patterns of group consciousness, hierarchy, and other social attributes. The government also enforces or reinforces the social preference for indirectness in the economic realm by strictly limiting the number of lawyers, judges, and accountants. Government pushed finance toward the emphasis on banking during the war and early postwar period. Government encouraged collusive behavior to reduce price competition. Government tolerated lax accounting standards that increased the need for long-term personal relationships in monitoring corporate behavior.

Rather than reinforcing all the existing tendencies in Japanese society, the government could have taken a strong stand in the opposite direction, creating strong rules or regulations to counter inefficient or counterproductive economic aspects of social behavior. Government could, for example, vastly expand the number of accountants, lawyers, and judges while creating new, strict accounting rules with stiff penalties for violation. While new accounting rules are coming, and there is talk of expanding the number of lawyers, there is little evidence yet that these moves will have a real impact on corporate behavior. Despite the rhetoric of change and deregulation, the general pattern of government behavior in the 1990s has been to reinforce or protect what it perceives as traditional social values rather than to use government authority vigorously to offset those tendencies in the economic realm.

6

Weak Outcomes

Previous chapters have laid out the argument for systemic reform and the variety of factors that work against its accomplishment. This chapter considers the outcome of such reform. Since the mid-1990s some economic reform has proceeded in both the government and the private sector. Government has been engaging ostensibly in a process of both general economic deregulation and administrative reform to reduce and reorganize government. The private sector has engaged in corporate restructuring and consolidation, prompted by the poor performance of many firms. By the end of the decade, stories of reform and change abounded, providing an image of a nation embarked on a major regime shift. That some form of real change is occurring is obvious. However, the details of what has been happening belie much of the image of vigorous reform.

In many respects the process of government deregulation and administrative reform has been quite weak. Unlike the United States or some other western nations, deregulation and administrative reform have been left largely to the career bureaucracy itself. As one might suppose, the result has been a mild and slow process of change.

In the private sector, necessity is driving real change in corporate behavior, irrespective of what happens in government. Banks and other financial institutions have been saddled with enormous amounts of bad debt and are unlikely to escape without considerable restructuring. Many nonfinancial corporations have faced increased global competition and poor financial results over the past decade, causing them to rethink their structure, goals, and behavior. The "big bang" deregulation of financial markets appears to have pushed firms toward greater emphasis on rates of return and generally increased attention to the desires of shareholders. Nevertheless, the pressures for corporate change are weaker than they might appear and do not necessarily lead to convergence on American-style reliance on markets. Restructuring—resizing or reorganizing corporations in response to poor performance—should not be confused with reform of fundamental notions about corporate governance, labor practices, and market competition.

This chapter explores both government and private-sector reform processes and outcomes. The point here is not to deny that change is occurring. Despite the obstacles considered in previous chapters, something is happening. Under scrutiny, however, the process does not appear robust, and the eventual result will be disappointing.

Deregulation

Deregulation had become a buzzword by 1993 when Morihiro Hosokawa became prime minister. He initiated a process of broad economic deregulation that continues today. Over the years, the government has issued regular reports touting progress on removing or modifying existing economic regulations. However, the process by which deregulation has proceeded has been centered on the bureaucracy itself rather than on the broader consumer, business, political, or intellectual communities, in great contrast to the experience of the United States. The comparison is quite instructive.

Economic regulation in the United States dates to the late nineteenth century, when it began as a political response to the perceived failings of unfettered markets. By the end of the 1930s, explicit regulation governed finance, railroads, trucking, barges, airlines, electric power, natural gas, telecommunications, and some other industries. Additional health and safety regulation has been added to straight economic regulation over the years. By the 1970s, however, a strong counterreaction had begun, and it continues today.

The American process of deregulation emerged from an intellectual debate among economists and among private sector groups affected negatively by economic regulation. In place of the view that regulation was a necessary protection for consumers against the excesses of the market, a new notion emerged that regulation caused more problems than it solved. Both theoretical and empirical research suggested that regulation protected industry more than consumers, essentially legalizing tight cartel behavior to the disadvantage of consumers, and led to inefficiency and economic distortions. These changing views and the factual analysis behind them fed into a vigorous political process, led by both business and consumer interests, in the 1960s and 1970s. The outcome was new legislation in Congress, beginning with the Carter administration, to deregulate or restructure the regulatory framework for specific industries. Major legislative steps along the way have included the Airline Deregulation Act (1978), the Motor Carrier Reform Act (1980), the Staggers Rail Act (1980), the Cable Television Deregulation Act (1984), the Natural Gas Policy Act (1978), and the Telecommunications Act of 1996. Deregulation in the United States is not over, as the debate over the appropriate role of the government in the marketplace continues.

Deregulation in Japan has proceeded along very different lines. Consider first the very rationale for deregulation. The detailed industry-specific analysis of problems and solutions that has characterized American debate over appropriate models of industry regulation has been largely absent. In Japan deregulation has been an unfocused buzzword for those dissatisfied with the poor economic performance of the 1990s. A strong theme of irritation at the pettiness of regulatory behavior by government officials, equally unfocused on questions of specific industry distortions, also runs through the Japanese debate.

Second, the process in Japan has been largely administrative rather than legislative. With their rather vague focus on what deregulation was all about, the politicians turned to the bureaucracy and asked it to develop a deregulation agenda. Rather than dealing comprehensively with the regulatory framework for particular industries, the bureaucracy predictably focused on generating large numbers of individual regulations on which action was to occur.

Any process of deregulation controlled by career officials is inherently weak. Faced with a mandate to demonstrate progress through numbers of actions, any well-trained bureaucrat can discover a variety of small, inconsequential items to stick on the deregulation list that do not substantially change regulation in any meaningful sense. No bureaucracy dominated entirely by career officials can move very far in deregulation because the raison d'être of the competent officials depends on the existence of regulations.

In the early phases of discussion of deregulation, a committee composed of people outside government was proposed as the main body for driving the process. This proposal was pushed by the business sector and encouraged by the U.S. government. However, the eventual outcome was a committee left in a weak advisory capacity and with a secretariat supplied from the government bureaucracy. In contrast to the early 1980s administrative reform process, private-sector pressure was constrained, and bureaucrats retained a controlling position.

The contrast with the United States is striking. Some regulatory change in the United States has originated in the regulatory agencies themselves, aided by the ability of elected administrations (at both the federal and state level) to pick the commissioners—and in so doing to select outsiders (not retired bureaucrats) who might bring in new and innovative ideas. Similarly, for health, safety, and social regulations administered directly by federal departments, the ability of administrations to put numerous political appointees in place provides an opportunity to move the bureaucracy in new directions. With Japanese regulation centered on a career bureaucracy, and with only a marginal political presence in each ministry in the person of the minister and political vice minister, the possibility of innovation from within is greatly lessened. The career bureaucrats are certainly not totally inflexible, and changes do occur over time, but the system is less likely to move vigorously toward deregulation than the U.S. regulatory commissions or bureaucracy.

Some younger officials seem quite reformist in their views, and some with whom I have spoken seriously doubt the need for effectiveness of government intervention in markets. Two things should be kept in mind about these officials. First, "Young Turks" have always existed in the bureaucracy. Many of them become more conservative later in their careers. If they remain radicals, they are politely pushed out early in their careers to *amakudari* positions. Second, even if they are sincere, they do not make policy. Their real impact on deregulation will not be felt for many years, not until the conservative old guard at the top is retired, making room for them to rise to the positions of importance, at which point they will have similar-minded officials working under them.

More important, deregulation in Japan relied much less on legislative activity. Even in the somewhat more flexible bureaucratic system of the United States, the scope and speed of regulatory change was constrained by either past legal mandates or bureaucratic inflexibility. Therefore, the legislative process—buttressed by an informed political debate and detailed analysis originating outside the bureaucracy—was critical in moving deregulation forward. In Japan, very little of this has happened. Since the bureaucrats control much of the relevant information about the industries, the politicians have very limited staffs, and many of the knowledgeable academics serve on ministry advisory commissions, it is unlikely that an inde-

Table 6-1. *Chronology of Deregulation, 1993–2000*

October 1993.   The advisory commission on administrative reform advocates an economic deregulation "action plan" for 1994.

December 1993.   The Hiraiwa Commission, an advisory group reporting to the prime minister, recommends economic deregulation as part of its proposals for structural reform of the economy.

February 1994.   A cabinet meeting considering administrative reform endorses the notion of deregulation to be pursued over five years, 1995–99.

July 1994.   A cabinet decision on promoting economic recovery calls for a five-year deregulation agenda and specifies 279 items for consideration.

March 1995.   The government announces a preliminary list of regulatory items for consideration; it is approved by the cabinet by the end of the month.

April 1995.   The government announces an acceleration of the five-year deregulation plan to three years (1995–97).

December 1995.   The Deregulation Commission releases an interim report on progress on deregulation.

December 1996.   The Deregulation Commission releases a second interim report on progress on deregulation.

March 1997.   The final report on deregulation is released, announcing action on 2,793 separate regulatory items.

March 1998.   The government adopts a follow-on three year action program for the promotion of deregulation (1998–2000), proposing consideration of 917 regulatory items.

March 1999.   The Deregulation Promotion Commission reports action taken on 311 regulatory items.

March 2000.   The Deregulation Promotion Commission adds 351 items to the deregulation list of 1998.

Source: Ministry of Foreign Affairs, "Japan's Approach to Deregulation to the Present," www.mofa.go.jp/j_info/japan/regulate/approach9904.html (May 3, 2001); www.mofa.go.jp/j_info/japan/regulate/approach9904.html (May 3, 2001); "The Three-Year Programme for Promoting Deregulation as Revised, March 30, 1999; www.mofa.go.jp/j_info/japan/regulate/program9903.html (May 3, 2001); Hakusho (97-nenpan) [1997 Deregulation White Paper] (Tokyo: Ministry of Finance Printing Office, 1997), pp. 80–85; "Kisei Kanwasaku: Arata ni 351 Komoku Tusika" [Deregulation Plan: Adding 351 Items], Asahi Shimbun, April 1, 2000, p. 12; and Management and Coordination Agency, "Kisei Kanwa Suishin 3-kanen Keikaku," unpublished report approved by the cabinet, March 31, 1998.

pendent, politically driven effort can dislodge the bureaucrats from their dominance of the deregulation issue. Laws in Japan are also less specific than most American laws, giving bureaucrats rather wide latitude in creating or changing specific regulations or rules.

Table 6-1 shows a summary of the general deregulation process since the early 1990s. Periodic interim progress reports that engage in "bean counting" appear destined to continue for several more years. The accumulation of individual deregulatory actions can, of course, result eventually in meaningful change in the regulatory framework for particular industries. However, the overall picture is one of fitful, partial change that leaves the situation in most industries more fettered than is the case in the United States.

In the midst of this discouraging overall picture of deregulation, some pockets of substantial change have occurred. The infamous Large Scale Retail Store Law has been abolished, removing an obstacle to the expansion of large discount chain stores. Entry into electric power generation has been allowed, and pricing deregulated. Pricing and routes have been deregulated for domestic air travel. These represent genuine moves in the direction of reliance on market principles. Even in these cases, however, there are caveats in the details that constrain market competition. At the same time the Large Scale Retail Store Law was abolished, for example, prefectures and towns were encouraged to pass their own local laws that could restrict stores; these were disguised as regulations combating traffic congestion and protecting the environment. Meanwhile, new entry into the electric power industry has been minimal and price cuts modest.

Domestic airlines are a prime example of the uncertainty of progress. In the United States, the Airline Deregulation Act of 1978 eliminated all control over routes and fares, including the regulatory agency (the Civil Aeronautics Board). The one remaining problem in the U.S. market is access to gates at airports; a new or expanding airline can find at some airports (which are controlled locally, and not by the federal government) that it cannot obtain gates at which to load/unload passengers because they are owned by rivals.[1] Nevertheless, airline deregulation unleashed huge competitive pressures that led to major restructuring of the industry (including several bankruptcies and new entrants), lowered fares, vastly increased demand, and a new hub-and-spoke route strategy.

Japanese deregulation of airlines after 1993 gradually permitted greater flexibility in fares. Finally in early 2000 major revisions to the Civil Aeronautics Law—written by bureaucrats and passed by the Diet—came into effect, requiring the government to relinquish control over fares and routes.[2] This change will presumably move the situation in Japan closer to that of the United States. One recent study finds a large drop in average airline revenue per passenger-kilometer, starting from around 1992, presumably driven by the airlines' cutting fares in the newly deregulated market. For All Nippon

Airlines (ANA), the revenue drop was about 23 percent from 1993 to 1999, and for Japan Airlines (JAL) it was 29 percent from 1992 to 1999. Over this period, changes in regulation enabled broader and deeper discounts, and competition appears to have had the predictable impact.[3]

This price development is encouraging. However, two important caveats call into question how competition in the airline industry will evolve. First, the Ministry of Transportation (MOT) retains authority over licensing potential airlines and over landing slots and gates at airports. This fact leaves the MOT in a powerful regulatory position. It licensed two new airlines in 1998 out of six applicants, but granted each of them only enough slots for three round trips between a single city pair (Tokyo-Sapporo for AirDo and Tokyo-Fukuoka for Skymark). In 2000 the Ministry of Transportation gave each of these two airlines six additional slots (so that they could each add three more round trips). This allotment was part of a general increase in slots at Tokyo's Haneda Airport (due to completion of a new runway). However, the remaining sixty-eight slots (85 percent of the total) went to the three existing domestic airlines and were allocated among them on the basis of a complicated rating involving each firm's fares, safety, maintenance of flights to small local airports, and management efficiency.[4] In short, the entry of the new airlines was dependent on MOT licensing; their ability to expand remains totally dependent on MOT largesse; and even the existing airlines remain dependent on the MOT for slots.

Consider the competitive situation on the Tokyo-Sapporo route, the most heavily traveled air route in the country. The six round-trip flights permitted to AirDo in the fall of 2000 represented only 13 percent of the forty-five total daily round-trip flights, with JAL, ANA, and Japan Air Systems (JAS) each operating twelve to fourteen flights. All three airlines offer discount fares that match AirDo's fares (and even undercut its fares on their early morning and late night flights), though the standard fares are much higher.[5] With an administratively imposed limit on the number of flights, AirDo is effectively constrained from gaining market share through aggressive pricing and expansion of capacity. In fact, with low fares but not the economies in scale to drive average cost down, AirDo was in a precarious financial condition in the fall of 2000. Plans were under way for financial assistance from the Hokkaido prefectural government and local businesses.[6] AirDo did have a positive market effect by lowering fares, as the major airlines matched its discount prices for at least some of their customers, but the market outcome remains an administered one, and even the survival of the airline was in some doubt.

Second, the government is permitting the three dominant domestic car-
riers (JAL, ANA, and JAS) to engage in very cooperative behavior. In 2000, the
three announced they would begin a jointly operated shuttle service between
Tokyo and Osaka. On this route the airlines have been competing with trains,
but acting cooperatively (and without any competition from the two new airlines) to reduce price competition among the three.[7] Another cooperative
move involves an online ticketing site run by the three airlines. While this site
will offer various discounts, the prices available among the different airlines
turn out to be virtually identical.[8] These moves imply that the three dominant
domestic airlines are reacting to recent increases in price competition and
new entry by creating new forms of cooperation or collusion.

The major exception to the picture of weak general deregulation has been
the financial sector. The *process* of deregulation in this sector has been no different from the model of general deregulation, but the outcome appears to
be somewhat more robust. The difference lies in the stronger perception of
crisis and failure in the financial sector over the course of the 1990s due to
the emergence of huge bad debt problems and associated scandals stemming from the collapse of the speculative bubble in stock and real estate
prices. Rebuilding a healthy financial sector that would be less susceptible to
a repeat of the disastrous history of the 1980s and 1990s obviously required
a new regulatory framework. Even control-minded Ministry of Financial
officials could agree with this assessment.

Financial deregulation has been under way since the 1970s, spurred by the
need to accommodate the changed financial flows resulting from the decel-
eration of economic growth after the mid-1970s (mainly a lessened corporate demand for bank loans, an increased government need to float bonds,
and a need to accommodate an increased flow of capital overseas).[9] However, the recent spurt of deregulation stems from November 1996, when
Prime Minister Ryutaro Hashimoto called for a "big bang" deregulation of
the financial sector, borrowing the term from the "big bang" financial deregulation in Britain in the 1980s. Table 6-2 illustrates the main parts of the
reforms that were eventually included as part of the Hashimoto proposal.

The agenda for the big bang deregulations includes a variety of measures
affecting virtually all aspects of finance, which on the surface imply movement toward a much more market-oriented system that would rely less heavily on banking and more on securities. The list is actually considerably longer,
but many of the other items proposed were either quite minor or rather
vague. Changes in regulations concerning foreign exchange transactions,
removal of the holding company ban, and decontrol of brokerage commis-

Table 6-2. *Proposed "Big Bang" Financial Deregulation: Principal Components*

Foreign exchange. From April 1998, eliminates the limitation on foreign exchange business to licensed commercial banks; eases rules on nonfinancial firms' netting out exchange positions internally; permits firms to use foreign exchange in domestic transactions; eases limitation on individuals' maintaining foreign currency accounts abroad.

Brokerage commission. Deregulation of stock brokerage commissions, beginning with large-lot transactions (April 1998); eventually extended to all transactions.

Off-exchange trading. Eases rules concerning trading shares off-exchange.

Over-the-counter trading. Eases rules concerning the over-the-counter market with the intent of increasing the liquidity of the market.

Securities transaction tax. To be eliminated.

Financial holding companies. To be permitted, with certain restrictions on size and market share of the total entity and the individual companies held.

Asset-backed securities. To be legalized and encouraged.

Derivatives. Easing of rules, including those pertaining to trading on the exchanges and over the counter.

Insurance. Competition in price and product design to be allowed; separation between life and nonlife segments of the market removed; greater flexibility in marketing (permitting telemarketing, for example).

Segmentation. Through the financial holding company format and other means, the restriction between different forms of financial business will be lessened; commercial banks and nonbank financial firms will be permitted to issue bonds.

Accounting standards. Will move accounting practices closer to international standards, including requirements for reporting on a consolidated basis and use of current market values.

---

sions all occurred in 1998, with others spread out over the period through 2001. On the surface, the list of proposed changes was quite ambitious.

The overall thrust of financial deregulation has been to reduce fees and taxes on certain transactions, reduce rigid control over financial product design, further reduce remaining barriers on international capital flow, and reduce barriers among different kinds of financial institutions. The deregulation of commissions on equity transactions, dismantling a long-standing system of high, fixed commissions, is already injecting increased competition into the securities industry (including the advent of online trading) and will lead to substantial industry restructuring. Meanwhile, the proposed changes in accounting rules (registering assets at current market value and requiring broader consolidation of subsidiaries) will be a step in the right direction toward enforcing accurate corporate financial reporting. These changes have proved to be quite exciting for foreign financial institutions, which see extensive new opportunities to exercise their competitive advantages in the Japanese market. Faced with greater competition from abroad, presumably Japanese financial institutions will respond to deregulation by evolving—through both internal reform and mergers—into more efficient and robust organizations.

Regulatory change in the financial sector should be welcomed as a tangible case of positive change. Nevertheless, these reforms also involve several important caveats. First, deregulation pertaining to the financial sector per se may not have substantial broader ramifications for economic behavior throughout the economy. The reforms point in the direction of less reliance on banking in favor of equity and bonds (by lowering fees and regulatory barriers that had constrained both of these forms of finance). However, nothing in the changed regulatory framework necessarily points toward adoption of a stockholder-centered principal-agent model of corporate governance if bond and equity finance were to become more prominent. *Foreign* mutual funds and investment banks are already pushing on those Japanese corporations in which they have equity stakes, but this alone is unlikely to yield an altered model for corporate governance, because foreign financial institutions do not dominate the domestic flow of funds, even though their market position is larger than it used to be. Corporate governance is not changing very much.

Second, at least some of the big bang reforms have been seriously exaggerated. Consider, for example, the foreign exchange decontrol that occurred on April 1, 1998. Japan undertook major foreign exchange decontrol over the period from about 1976 to 1985, so what was left to be done? In reality, not much. Most foreign exchange transactions were not regulated in any meaningful way by the 1990s, so the new law and rules made little difference. Among the changes in 1998, restriction of foreign exchange transactions to authorized commercial banks was dropped, so that any company—financial or nonfinancial—could engage in foreign exchange. However, more than 160 banks were already authorized to engage in this business; it is unclear that expanding the number would inject more competition into the market. In addition, firms could net out foreign exchange transactions without even going to a bank, providing a modest efficiency gain for nonfinancial corporations, but presumably many of them were already doing so, because this was permissible with the approval of the MOF and obviously possible for any other firm willing to violate the rules.

Individuals were also allowed to hold foreign financial accounts in the 1998 deregulation of international transactions. Here is another puzzling development, since some Japanese already did exactly this. Nevertheless, would opening foreign accounts likely be the major path for individuals to invest abroad? Americans, who have not had any legal restrictions, hold only a minuscule amount (less than 0.1 percent) of their portfolios in foreign deposits; even allowing for nonreporting for tax cheating purposes, the amount is unlikely to be high.[10] Japanese individuals already had access to yen-denominated money market and mutual funds that were invested in foreign markets, and offerings of such funds (including by foreign financial institutions operating in Japan) increased in the late 1990s. Thus the freedom individuals obtained in 1998 brought only a very modest alteration in investment behavior. By March 2000 flow-of-funds data indicate that households were holding only 0.2 percent of their financial assets in the form of foreign securities.[11]

The big bang financial deregulations are causing consolidation or restructuring of the financial industry as a result of new competitive pressures. However, the splashiest development was the announcement of three huge mergers: one among Fuji Bank, Dai-Ichi Kangyo Bank, and the Industrial Bank of Japan; the second between Sumitomo Bank and Sakura Bank (itself the result of a merger several years ago between Mitsui Bank and Taiyo-Kobe Bank); and the third between Tokai Bank and Sanwa Bank. These mergers brought together several large banks into even larger bank combines. Why, in an environment of relaxation of rules restricting financial institutions to narrow niches, would banks in the same niche combine? Touted by the press as representing the impact of new competition spawned by the big bang, these mergers in reality only perpetuate the past, stodgy nature of these banks. The only discernible motive for the second of these mergers (Sakura-Sumitomo) was a copycat reaction to the first—as the president of Sumitomo Bank admitted.[12] To be sure, they will make moves into new areas—including marketing of mutual funds and insurance—but the mergers brought no new expertise in these areas to the combined organizations.

Equally puzzling was a decision of the Norinchukin Bank to stick firmly to its past. This huge bank is the central bank for the banking operations of the nationwide network of more than 3,000 agricultural cooperatives and their prefectural federations. While acknowledging that it would preside over a consolidation of local co-ops, the bank was unwilling or unable to realize that the whole concept of specialized agricultural co-op financial institutions was outmoded. Rather than thinking in terms of cultivating new markets, however, the bank emphasized in early 2000 its determination to reinforce its ties with its agricultural support base.[13]

Even the modest deregulation program that has characterized both financial and nonfinancial sectors since 1993 faced a backlash by late 1999. A large group of more than one hundred Liberal Democratic Party (LDP) members formed an informal antideregulation group in November 1999, called the Forum to Reconsider Deregulation. The new group was headed by Kabun Muto, who was the LDP's point man for administrative reform![14] Another formal LDP committee on financial issues (Kin'yū Mondai Chōsakai) expressed a need to "study" (a euphemism for "oppose") the applications of nonfinancial corporations for banking licenses (including Sony Corporation and retailer Ito Yokado).[15] Some specific policies related to deregulation and cleaning up the bad debt problem were also being delayed or watered down by the end of 1999.[16] Thus, in contrast to the United States or some other countries, the politicians were working to slow down or obstruct reform rather than prodding the bureaucracy to accelerate change.

Overall, the picture of deregulation by the end of 2000 was one of limited progress and political steps backward, but with pockets of more meaningful change. Domestic airfares had fallen. Large discount stores could advance if local jurisdictions did not move too aggressively to constrain them. In the financial sector the big bang deregulation measures were proceeding. These areas of success have caveats, however, and other areas show less progress. The government's slow and defensive stance in deregulating telecommunications (protecting the government majority-owned Nippon Telegraph and Telephone, NTT) is, for example, discouraging. Another decade of deregulation could yield an economy that operates largely in accordance with market forces, but a continued political backlash or emergence of informally tolerated cartel behavior that replaces regulation in industries such as domestic air travel could truncate or negate the gains.

Administrative Reform

Besides deregulation, the government has been engaged in discussion of administrative reform, designed to reorganize the government. Administrative reform has a much longer history, and it actually achieved some progress in the first half of the 1980s. At that time the private sector gained control of the process, with a prominent elder businessman heading the Administrative Reform Commission (known by its abbreviation of *Rincho* in Japanese) and with Keidanren (the federation of large business) supplying the secretariat—an achievement that contrasts with bureaucratic dominance of the 1990s secretariat of the Deregulation Commission.

The 1980s *Rincho* brought about privatization of three large government organizations: the Japan National Railways, NTT, and Japan Tobacco (with a monopoly on cigarette production and sales). Privatization was largely in name only; initially all shares of the new corporations were held by the government, and sale of shares to the public has proceeded very slowly, so the government remained the majority shareholder in 2000 in all of them. Nevertheless, it did lead to some deregulation and provided an excuse for more vigorous cost cutting (especially on the overstaffed railroad).

With this progress as prologue, a new administrative reform initiative began in 1996. This time reform yielded a comprehensive overhaul of government structure in 2001, as indicated in figure 6-1. The existing organization of the central government into twenty-three cabinet-level ministries and agencies has been chopped to twelve. Meanwhile some other affiliated government organizations (not shown in figure 6-1) underwent some consolidation in the 1998–2000 period.

What had been the prime minister's office expanded greatly, absorbing several other agencies and becoming a renamed cabinet office. The Management and Coordination Agency absorbed additional important functions (such as oversight of the relationship between the central and local governments) and the postal system, becoming the Ministry of Public Management, Home Affairs, Posts and Telecommunications (commonly known as the Ministry of General Affairs). The Ministry of Health and Welfare merged with the Ministry of Labor, becoming the Ministry of Health, Welfare, and Labor. The major ministries involved with public works all merged: the Ministry of Transportation, Ministry of Construction, Hokkaido Development Agency, and National Land Agency all were consolidated into the new Ministry of Land, Infrastructure, and Transportation. The major loser in this process was the Ministry of Posts and Telecommunications, which formally ceased to exist. Its postal services, broadcast regulatory functions, and telecommunications regulatory functions were transferred to the new General Affairs Ministry, while its industrial policy functions shifted to MITI, which, in turn, underwent a name change to Ministry of Economy, Trade, and Industry (METI).[17] The other loser is the Science and Technology Agency, which was split into two pieces, one going to the Ministry of Science and Education and the other to MITI. Thus MITI—or METI—also came out of this reorganization with expanded functions in both telecommunications and industrial research and development.

Figure 6-1. *Administrative Reform*

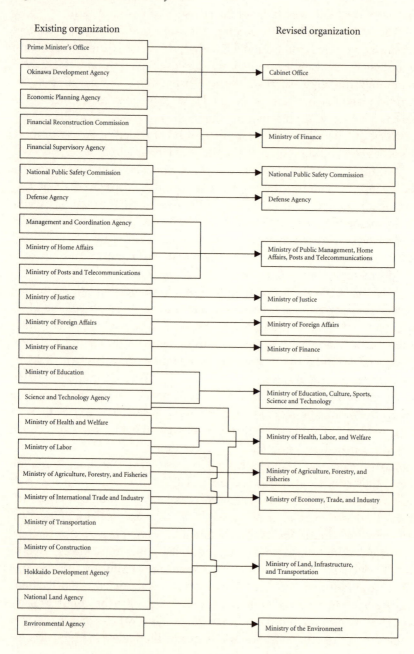

This plan was the outcome of an initial proposal from Prime Minister Ryutaro Hashimoto, who was widely perceived at the time as being eager to use administrative reform to enhance the power of elected politicians relative to the career bureaucracy. The series of scandals in the 1990s, plus the perception of bureaucratic policy mistakes, lent an aura of public discontent and a desire to reduce the power of the bureaucracy. After becoming prime minister, Hashimoto established the Administrative Reform Council (ARC) in November 1996, an advisory group that he chose to head himself. After a year of political wrangling, the ARC finalized the plan for administrative reform detailed in figure 6-1, which was then implemented in January 2001.[18]

The immediately obvious conclusion from this plan for administrative reform is that it is about reshuffling rather than reform. Some ministries lose (with MPT literally disappearing) and others gain. Personnel and offices will be relocated physically from one building to another, but will the functions of government be seriously altered? No. In general, this reform is nothing more than a rearrangement of the organizational diagram for government.

Even reshuffling could conceivably increase government efficiency by reducing debilitating interministerial fights over jurisdiction on particular policy issues. As the structure of the economy shifted and new industries emerged over the past several decades, bitter struggles erupted within the bureaucracy over which ministry would have jurisdiction. One way of looking at administrative reform, therefore, is as a settlement of these festering disputes. However, not all of the new combinations represent desirable efficiency gains. Consider, for example the new catchall Ministry of General Affairs. It absorbed the functions of the Management and Coordination Agency, the Ministry of Home Affairs (responsible for the relationship between the central and prefectural or local governments), and most of the functions of the Ministry of Posts and Telecommunications. This combination will actually lead to a discouraging anomaly. The Fair Trade Commission (formerly part of the Prime Minister's Office) now coexists within the same administrative framework as the telecommunications and broadcasting regulatory functions that had been in the Ministry of Posts and Telecommunications. Regulators and trustbusters under one roof make an odd combination, and a renewed diminution of power, autonomy, and vigor at the Fair Trade Commission (already modest) is the likely outcome.

For those combinations that do imply reduction in overlapping or contested jurisdictions, consider the possible political consequences. Bureaucratic power struggles opened the way for politicians to play a somewhat larger role in policymaking. Unable to settle their internal disputes, the bureaucrats had to turn to politicians to mediate. However, if the new reorganization reduces such conflicts, the bureaucracy could move back toward reducing its reliance on politicians as arbiters of policy outcomes. This result would be exactly the opposite of the purported rationale for administrative reform.

One reason politicians have had a limited effect on the bureaucracy has been that each ministry has had only two political appointees—the minister and political vice minister. With twenty-two cabinet posts, the old system involved forty-four political appointees. Additional slots added as part of administrative reform will raise the total to sixty despite the reduction in the number of ministries. The new system will have twelve ministers, twenty-two deputy ministers, and twenty-six state affairs officers. Thus the number of appointees expands from two to an average of five per ministry. Whether this increase will be sufficient to alter the relationship between the politicians and the bureaucracy remains to be seen.[19] Even five appointees per ministry is a far cry from the extent of political appointees in the U.S. government. While it is conceivable that the small group of appointees in each ministry could provide a new dynamic in ministerial policy formation, the more likely outcome is that they will be generally overwhelmed by the career bureaucracy.

The Ministry of International Trade and Industry is an example of possible reduction in political input. Apparently in a bid to escape the image of export promotion, the "International Trade" part of the ministry's name was dropped, and the agency became instead a ministry of industry and economy (*Keizai Sangyōsho*), even though the official name in English is Ministry of Economy, Trade, and Industry. The ministry's scope is considerably expanded. In addition to all of its former responsibilities (including international trade policy), it acquired some technology promotion functions from the Science and Technology Agency and some functions from the Ministry of Posts and Telecommunications (with which MITI had fought numerous jurisdictional battles in the past two decades). The new "super-MITI" will have greater capacity to settle policy issues internally without resorting to mediation by politicians to battle against other ministries.

The one area where politicians may gain an important increase in power over the bureaucracy is pork-barrel public works spending. The new Ministry of Land, Infrastructure, and Transportation combined the Ministry of Transportation, much of the Ministry of Construction, National Land

Agency, and Hokkaido Development Agency. The only missing element is the Okinawa Development Agency, which went into the new Cabinet Office. By putting all of these ministries and agencies that have had a piece of the action in public works projects under one roof, politicians now have a one-stop location for pork. The politicians who are appointed to serve as minister, deputy minister, and state affairs officers of this ministry will be even more important in the political firmament than in the past. These appointees may not necessarily be the politicians who wield the most power within the majority party on the pork barrel, but they will have formal authority over the purse strings, and holding these posts will be an essential step toward becoming a party pork-barrel leader.

What is true of administrative reform writ large is also true of some of the quasi-governmental agencies. The Japan Development Bank (JDB), for example, absorbed the Hokkaido-Tohoku Development Finance Public Corporation in 1999, becoming the Development Bank of Japan (DBJ). In addition, the Export Import Bank has merged with the Overseas Economic Cooperation Fund (the soft loan part of Japan's foreign aid). Merger has not resulted in any reduction in government's role, however. In fact the changes muddy functions and may jeopardize management.

The Japan Development Bank has prided itself over the past fifty years on its prudence, and it experienced no serious increase in bad loans in the 1990s, in stark contrast to the private sector banks. The Hokkaido Tohoku Development Fund, on the contrary, has had a reputation as a political slush fund and suffered in the 1990s from the failure of a number of its ill-advised development projects in these rural parts of Japan. Because the JDB has had to absorb (rather than lay off) the staff of the Hokkaido-Tohoku Development Fund, the resulting combined entity could well turn out to be more political, less cautious, and more susceptible to scandal. At the same time, the Japan Development Bank absorbed the loan portfolios of the Japan Environmental Corporation and the Japan Regional Development Corporation, two other rather suspect lending operations (with the so-called Environmental Corporation financing rural resort development). Furthermore, the merger of JDB and the Hokkaido-Tohoku Development Finance Corporation did not result in any discernible savings; the personnel count in 2000 was almost exactly the sum of employment at the two separate organizations in 1998.[20]

Even more discouraging is the fact that serious administrative reform should have abolished or privatized all these agencies. With well-developed private-sector financial institutions, why does Japan need a government-owned Japan Development Bank, Hokkaido-Tohoku Development Finance Corporation, Environmental Corporation, or Japan Regional Development Corporation? The theoretical reasoning for such a government-directed lending policy (the need for industrial policy in a developing nation where private markets might not allocate sufficient funds to the most important industries for development) no longer applies to Japan. The lack of any real rationale furthers the likelihood that the new institution will be susceptible to various forms of political influence, both aboveboard and illegal.

Equally murky changes are to occur at Postal Savings. The postal system offers both bank deposits and life insurance policies. With the formal breakup of the Ministry of Posts and Telecommunications (MPT), the postal system moved into the Ministry of General Affairs. Early talk about actually privatizing the postal system came to naught as plans for administrative reform proceeded. However, the MPT had fought for years to gain more autonomy over the investment of monies it collected in the form of postal savings deposits and postal life insurance premiums. By the 1990s, MPT was permitted to invest a portion of both sources of funds on its own rather than turning them over to the Ministry of Finance for lending through the Fiscal Investment and Loan Program, though technically the money is still turned over to the MOF and then lent back to the special quasi-independent agency established by MPT to invest these monies. Beginning in 2002, all the money being put into postal savings and postal life insurance accounts will be available for investment directly by Postal Savings rather than flowing to the FILP.

This change in authority appears to be a halfway step toward privatization. Rather than being forced to turn over funds for policy lending purposes, the postal system will be free to invest on the basis of securing the highest possible return—in theory. However, administrative reform placed the whole postal system into the new General Affairs Ministry, containing a number of functions that are quite political (such as management of the central-local government relationship). How independent and profit-driven will the new investment strategy of the postal system be? Serious doubts are in order.

More important, administrative reform completely failed on the larger issue. Why should an advanced industrial nation with well-developed private-sector financial institutions have a postal savings system at all? Because the government already has a post office in every town and village anyway, the marginal cost of running a financial institution in existing post offices is low, giving the government an unfair advantage in competing with private-sector banks. Regulation over the past half century has given the post office other advantages in attracting deposits, especially easy transfer of funds between branches all across the nation (something that was not possible at commercial banks in the 1960s), zero risk, and competitive deposit interest rates. The postal savings and postal life insurance systems have hung like a millstone around the neck of the private-sector financial industry. That millstone has become heavier as the postal savings system has gained as a share of total bank deposits over the past decade.

Rather than moving toward abolishing the whole system, the MPT (and presumably the new General Affairs Ministry) has endorsed a variety of mechanisms to strengthen the attractiveness of the whole system. Recent deals have included offering automatic monthly bill payments, tie-ins with major credit cards, and debit cards tying their ATM machines in with private-sector bankcards. These changes are driven by the postal bureaucracy itself; as an existing agency, it is loath to lose any part of its functions, and it has won a major bureaucratic victory by gaining control over use of its funds. Meanwhile, politicians are reluctant to privatize the postal system as a whole or to discard the savings and life insurance functions. Many post offices in Japan are actually operated by private citizens under license from the government. Both the licensing function and the fact that the postmasters know a great deal about the finances of local inhabitants make them very valuable to politicians. Therefore, the badly needed demise of both the postal savings system and postal life insurance is unlikely to materialize in the near future. The millstone will remain, impeding the overall reform of the financial sector.

The only other aspect of administrative reform that conceivably involves a change in the relationship of government to society occurred in 1998, when supervision of the financial sector was transferred from the Ministry of Finance to a new Financial Supervisory Agency (FSA), and control over nationalized banks and recapitalized banks passed to the new Financial Reconstruction Commission (FRC). This awkward separation ended in January 2001, when the two agencies merged (with the English name remaining the Financial Supervisory Agency). Splitting these functions out of the Ministry of Finance gave the appearance of a decline in the ministry's power. The appointment of Hakuo Yanagisawa to head the new FRC was also hailed as progress, since he was an outsider (a former prosecutor) who adopted an aggressive proreform attitude toward the financial sector that was at odds with the cautious, slow, weak, and opaque policies of the MOF.

This image of the FSA and the FRC as agencies independent of the MOF was not quite accurate. Most staff members are officials from the MOF. Up to a fairly high level in these organizations, the MOF can detail its career offi-cials for temporary positions and then retrieve them. It can also send offi-cials permanently through the *amakudari* process. At best, it will be many years before this new organization will have its own career staff that does not have any loyalty to the MOF. At worst, because of the MOF's ability to detail officials, the new organization may remain a virtual captive of the MOF once the initial aura of independence and action wears off.

Changes already in the chairmanship of the FRC reinforce doubts about its longer-term role. Yanagisawa himself lasted only a year as head of the FRC. Not surprisingly, his replacement was Michio Ochi, an LDP politician who began his career as an MOF official and who exhibited a typically cau-tious attitude about financial reform.[21] Ochi actually went too far in assur-ing bankers that the FRC would treat them generously, and he was forced to resign after a few months, but the point was made. His replacement, Sadakazu Tanigaki, was a six-term LDP member of the Diet with no dis-cernible background on finance until he was appointed as the parliamentary vice minister at the Ministry of Finance in July 1998. Tanigaki also lasted only a few months, replaced in June 2000 by Kimitake Kuze as part of a rou-tine cabinet shuffle.[22] Kuze lasted only one month, felled by revelations that he had accepted large illegal corporate donations during the 1990s. He was replaced by an eighty-one-year-old LDP politician and former MOF official, Hideyuki Aizawa, whose career at the MOF spanned the years 1942–74, the heyday of strong bureaucratic controls. During his political career Aizawa had been known as an opponent of financial deregulation.[23] Finally, Yanag-isawa was reappointed and once again spoke up strongly in late 2000 and early 2001 on resolving the bad debt problem, but his tenure was unlikely to last beyond the summer of 2001. These revolving appointments and the backgrounds of most of the appointees do not bode well for real reform.

Publicly, administrative reform has been touted as a major revision, alter-ing the postwar role of the government in line with the general direction of deregulation. In private, career officials laugh in embarrassment at the gap between image and reality. Most of their conversations turn on the details of which ministries and agencies gained or lost relative bureaucratic power, not on the broader question of the relationship of government to society. Over the next several years their personal energy will be absorbed in messy personnel questions concerning how to blend previously separate agencies and how to allocate promotions "fairly" among them. This broad effort at administrative reform will go down as yet another failure. Worse, it could lead to a stronger role for the bureaucracy in policymaking, and it could reinforce the focus of politicians on generating pork-barrel projects, for the reasons discussed above. This is not an encouraging prospect.

Continuing Government Role in the Economy

Directly contradicting the advertised thrust of deregulation and administrative reform, the economic role of the Japanese government has actually been increasing over the course of the 1990s. Meanwhile, traditional industrial policy initiatives continue unabated. The contrast between the public image of declining government involvement in the economy and the reality is startling.

At the heart of the government's industrial policy role has been the Fiscal Investment and Loan Program, described in detail in chapter 2. Key sources of funds for the FILP have been Postal Savings deposits and Postal Life Insurance premiums. Both of these sources exist in the midst of well-developed private markets for bank deposits and life insurance. Whereas there may have been a legitimate argument a century ago for government provision of savings deposits and life insurance, little rationale exists today. Nevertheless, the share of government in these markets is high and has been increasing. Figure 6-2 shows the share of Postal Savings and Postal Life Insurance relative to the total size of these markets.

In the heyday of industrial policy, Postal Savings accounts composed only some 14–16 percent of total savings deposits in the economy. That share rose to 28 percent by the early 1980s before subsiding to 24 percent during the "bubble" years. In the 1990s, however, the share of Postal Savings rose once again, to a record high of 32 percent of all savings deposits in banks by 1997. Thus the role of government in the domestic market for savings deposits has increased substantially over time.

In 2000 a decline in the high share of the Postal Savings System finally seemed possible. The maximum time deposit in the system is ten years. In 1990 interest rates had risen, as the government tightened monetary policy to stop the speculative bubble in the stock market and the real estate market. Money put into ten-year time deposits at that time locked in those higher interest rates (ranging from 5.0 to 6.3 percent). As those deposits came due in 2000–01, they would earn abysmally low interest rates (less than 1 percent). With financial deregulation bringing new mutual fund offerings (including both Japanese and foreign investment bank products) to the public, speculation rose that these maturing savings deposits would not be rolled over and instead would be drained off to other financial invest-

Figure 6-2. *Market Shares of Postal Savings and Postal Life Insurance,*
1965–96[a]

Percent

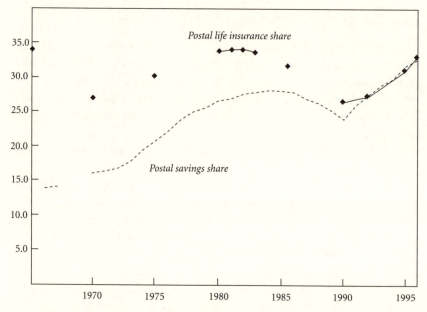

Sources: Data on Postal Life Insurance are calculated from Statistics Bureau, *Japan Statistical Yearbook 2001*, www.stat.go.jp/english/1431-13.htm, downloadable tables 13-18 (Principal Assets of Postal Life Insurance) and 13-41 (Policies in Force and Management of Assets of Life and Nonlife Insurance Companies), plus printed version of the same publication, 1995 edition, pp. 462 and 483, and 1984 edition , pp. 409 and 429. Data on Postal Savings are calculated from flow-of-funds tables and tables on Postal Savings accounts in Bank of Japan, *Economic Statistics Annual 1997*, pp. 190, 266–67, and similar tables in earlier years.

a. Data are for the end of each fiscal year, which is March 31 of the next calendar year.

b. For Postal Savings, the ratio represents the amount of deposits in Postal Savings to total time deposits and certificates of deposit. That is, the denominator does not include short-term demand deposits.

c. For Postal Life insurance, the ratio represents the total assets of the Postal Life Insurance system relative to total assets of life insurance companies plus the Postal Life Insurance system.

ments. Preliminary evidence suggests that this response by households has
been quite weak—most of the funds have been rolled over despite the low
interest rates. Some money has been drained out for payment of income
taxes, and some flowed out from deposits exceeding the maximum allowable
size, but most money that could be rolled over within the system has
remained.[24] From April to September of 2000, as the surge in these high-
interest accounts began to come due, the Postal Savings System was hanging
on to 51 to 53 percent of these funds. An additional 8 percent was going to

pay taxes, and 16 percent was subject to mandatory withdrawal because it exceeded the account limit. This left only about 22 percent that was voluntarily withdrawn from the system; much of that apparently was withdrawn for consumption rather than reinvestment in other savings vehicles.

A survey of households in the fall of 2000 largely confirmed the preference to remain with Postal Savings, since only 10 percent of respondents planned on moving their funds to other savings choices.[25] This choice is consistent with the evidence that households continue to prefer safe, low return bank deposits rather than riskier equity and bond investments. Postal Savings accounts offer rates that are only marginally below those of commercial banks and can end up higher in times of falling interest rates, since commercial banks have a maximum three-year deposit with a fixed interest rate. Postal Savings accounts also have zero risk since the government runs the system. Households are therefore likely to continue allocating a substantial share of their financial portfolios to them.[26]

Postal Life Insurance has also risen in parallel with Postal Savings. In the 1950s the share of Postal Life Insurance was even higher, but it dropped rapidly, presumably as the private-sector insurance industry matured. By 1970 its share was only 27 percent. In the 1980s and 1990s, the market share of Postal Life Insurance closely tracks that of Postal Savings (although the data in figure 6-2 are incomplete), rising from 26 percent in 1990 to 33 percent by 1996.

These shares are high. Imagine the political debate that would occur in the United States if the federal government ran postal savings and postal insurance plans that captured one-third of their respective markets. In Japan, the banking and insurance industries have complained over the years, but as discussed earlier, abolition of these programs is not on the political agenda.

The same is true of the total FILP program. Think of the FILP as those financial resources in the economy over which the government exercises direct control, lending them out for policy purposes. The FILP finances fixed investment in the economy—both public investment projects that generate revenue streams to repay the loans (such as highways and airports) and private (including residential housing and corporate plant and equipment investment). Figure 6-3 shows what has happened to the size of the FILP relative to gross domestic product (GDP) and total domestic investment.

In the 1970s the FILP was around 6 percent of GDP, but in the 1990s that level expanded to 10 percent. The share of the FILP to total gross fixed investment in the economy is much larger and has risen somewhat more dramatically. From 15 percent in 1972, it increased to more than 30 percent

Figure 6-3. *Relative Size of the Fiscal Investment and Loan Program, 1972–98*
Percent of GDP

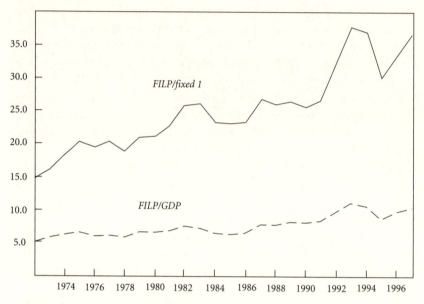

FILP/fixed 1

FILP/GDP

Source: GDP and the three parts of gross domestic investment are all from Japan Economic and Social Research Institute, "GDE at Current Prices," www.esri.cao.go.jp/en/sna/qe004-2/gdemenue.html (May 3, 2001); FILP data are from Bank of Japan, *Economic Statistics Annual 1997*, p. 289; 1992, p. 267; 1987, p. 230; 1981, p. 218.

in most of the 1990s. Another way to look at the same relationship is through flow-of-funds data. These data show that outstanding loans provided by government financial institutions were 35 percent of total outstanding loans in the economy as of the end of calendar year 2000, up from 24 percent in March 1989.[27] Thus at the same time the government talks about reducing its economic role, the resources over which it has direct command have actually expanded as a share of the economy. This is hardly the picture of a government that is withdrawing from the marketplace.

The role of the FILP is particularly strong in the area of housing investment. The largest single recipient of loans from the FILP in recent years has been the Housing Loan Corporation (HLC), a government organization that plays a substantial role in housing finance. The HLC has had a major role in financing mortgages, as shown in figure 6-4. In 1997, the HLC provided 38 percent of all new mortgage loans, somewhat higher than the 33 percent it provided in 1980 and considerably higher than the 23 percent it provided in 1990. The HLC was responsible for 43 percent of total out-

Figure 6-4. *Percentage of Mortgages Held by the Housing Loan Corporation, Selected Years, 1980–97*

Percent

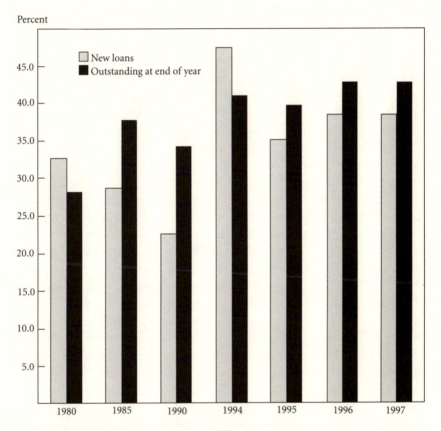

Source: Bank of Japan, *Economic Statistics Annual 1997*, pp. 771–72.

standing mortgages in 1997, also up very sharply from 28 percent in 1980. Even accepting the problems in private-sector financial institutions, this is a startlingly high share for the government in financing real estate, and the trend has been upward.

In theory, discussion of the FILP became moot in 2001 because the government has formally ended the forced flow of Postal Savings and Postal Life Insurance funds into the FILP. However, the implications for the nature of the FILP are modest at best. The initial plan was for the FILP to compensate by issuing FILP bonds, and the government-affiliated organizations that have borrowed from the FILP would be authorized to issue "FILP agency bonds." The overall FILP financing will continue to exist as an annual budget submitted to the Diet. Decisions on financing within the budget will be based on a new system of cost-benefit analysis (which has been totally unused until the present), but how much difference this will make remains to be seen.[28]

The changes in the FILP presumably bring Japanese practice closer to that of the United States, forcing some proposed revenue-producing public projects to undergo a market test and to produce hard evidence of their benefit to the public. This is a step in the right direction. However, the end result will not be so radical. By late 2000, strong doubts were emerging about the extent to which the FILP agency bonds would be used. Large FILP fund recipients, such as the Development Bank of Japan, complained that raising money at market rates would jeopardize the organization's mandate to make "low-cost" loans, which of course, is precisely the point of holding such organizations to a market test.[29] When the government announced the planned FILP agency bond issues for fiscal 2001, the news confirmed the doubts. Only fifteen organizations (of the sixty-nine FILP fund recipients other than local governments listed in table 2-3) would issue bonds, and the amount would be only ¥866 billion ($8.1 billion), a mere 2 percent of total FILP financing.[30] This weak outcome was the apparent result of internal debates over principle (over the appropriateness of market financing for "policy" project finance) and the realization that many FILP fund recipients were in sufficiently poor financial condition that markets would be unlikely to purchase their bonds at all. More than half of these government-related organizations were reported to be operating at a loss in 1999—even with their subsidized financing from the FILP.[31] The institutional change from the past method for FILP financing certainly opened the door for forcing government-related organizations to meet market-determined standards, but that door did not open very far.

The failure to rely much on FILP agency bonds means that the bulk of FILP financing will occur in the form of central government–issued FILP bonds, with the proceeds handed out to the various organizations in the same nontransparent manner as in the past. Equally important, the emerging market for FILP and FILP agency bonds could easily be skewed by the government's stepping in to make purchases if the public is reluctant to buy them. Keep in mind that the central government already does this for local government bonds. The Postal Savings, Postal Life Insurance, and public pension systems will undoubtedly come under pressure to buy these bonds even though they will have nominal freedom to invest their funds as they wish.

Finally, cost-benefit analysis has had a problematic history in the hands of American agencies such as the U.S. Corps of Engineers. One can just imagine what creative Japanese bureaucrats can do with cost-benefit analysis. As a small bit of discouraging evidence, a 1999 Ministry of Finance summary explanation of what the FILP is and why it is so important features a photograph of the trans–Tokyo Bay tunnel-bridge project, one of the worst, unjustifiable, white elephants built in the 1990s. It has exorbitant tolls, and its traffic levels are well below expectations, implying that it will never justify its cost.[32] This project dates back to proposals in 1959—part of a grandiose scheme for Tokyo Bay development that would have filled in much of the bay. While much of this scheme was subsequently canceled, the tunnel-bridge, connecting industrial Kawasaki with a largely rural area of southern Chiba Prefecture on the Boso Peninsula, miraculously survived to be built in the 1990s. Had 10 percent annual economic growth continued from the 1960s to the 1990s, perhaps the project could have been justified, but the combination of slow economic development and large improvements in the highways skirting the perimeter of the bay made this an unjustifiable project.[33]

In addition to direct lending, government further increased its economic role by providing massive loan guarantees to small business in the second half of the 1990s. Believing that small business faced a credit crunch as banks tried to repair their weak balance sheets, the government expanded loan guarantees to entice banks to continue lending. In 1998 the government's loan guarantee program for small business supplied some ¥30 trillion ($248 billion at 1998 exchange rates), but in August of 1998, the government authorized an additional ¥20 trillion ($165 billion), and added another ¥10 trillion ($88 billion) in late 1999. By doubling the level of loan guarantees to small business, the government's guarantees protected close to 20 percent of all private-sector loans to small business.[34]

Arguably the government was correct. As banks tried to repair their balance sheets in the late 1990s, they might have unfairly turned away from small borrowers on the presumption of riskiness without serious credit analysis. However, the fact that small businesses tend to support the LDP suggests that the motivation was political rather than economic. In fact, provision of credit guarantees to small borrowers may have impeded the restructuring of the economy that the recession of 1997–98 should have been causing.

At the end of the 1990s, the government even became a part owner of private-sector banks. To recapitalize the weakened banking system, the government injected ¥9.5 trillion ($79 billion) into the capital bases of leading banks (in two separate tranches in 1998 and 1999). In theory, this capital infusion did not bring the government any formal ownership voice because the capital was in the form of subordinated debt and preferred (nonvoting) shares. In reality, however, this new ownership position provided the government with a strong voice in bank affairs. The government reserved the right to convert its preferred shares to common stock should banks fail to adhere to government instructions on bank restructuring. According to one estimate, conversion of shares in some leading banks would make the government the majority shareholder.[35] Less formally, all banks receiving capital infusions from the government were well aware of their benefactor, whether or not that benefactor had voting rights. Any bank would ignore signals from the government at its peril since the government could always decide to withdraw its support.

Among the signals that these recapitalized banks had to heed was a quota for loans to medium and small sized firms. A prudent government concerned about restoring weak banks to a more secure position might have insisted on strict guidelines for cracking down on risky loans. The Japanese government did exactly the opposite—pressing banks to continue or expand their loans to small business. While the government may have had a legitimate concern that small business would bear a disproportionate and unjustifiably high share of the burden of the banks' efforts to repair their balance sheets, the policy encouraged banks to loan, regardless of risk, just to meet the mandated total. In fiscal 1998 the banks missed their targets, but in fiscal 1999 the recapitalized banks were told to increase their loans to small businesses by ¥3 trillion ($28 billion) and actually exceeded the target. Only one of the fifteen banks fell short.[36] It is discouraging that the government was using its increased voice over banks to prop up politically popular lending to small business rather than pressing for rapid balance sheet improvement or strict accounting for and disposal of nonperforming loans. It also illustrates the dangers in increased government influence over banking.

In this particular case of bank recapitalization, presumably the increased government role was necessary and positive. The banks needed to be recapitalized to prevent widespread failures, and their failure to reform and clean up their nonperforming loans in the earlier 1990s implied a need for a more forceful government hand in bringing about necessary action. Nevertheless, the fact remains that the resolution of the banking crisis in Japan left the government with a heightened rather than a lessened role in regulating, supervising, or informally influencing private-sector financial institutions.

Traditional industrial policy outside the financial sector was also continuing at the end of the 1990s. Chapter two discussed the variety of tools the government has used over the past half century to prod, cajole, and encourage private-sector industries and firms to move in desired directions. The formal tools available to government have diminished, and the coherence of policy goals (once focused single-mindedly on industrial development) has dissipated. Nonetheless, the determination of the government to play an activist role in shaping or at least influencing private-sector outcomes remains intact. Consider the following partial list of plans and projects the government was pushing in the late 1990s.

—In August 2000 MITI announced a major new cooperative government-business-university semiconductor research and development project under the banner of restoring Japan as "the Kingdom of Semiconductors" through a five-year plan explicitly modeled on the government's well-known VLSI project of the 1970s. That plan had developed the production technology for 64-K DRAM chips and was instrumental in increasing the global market share of Japanese semiconductor manufacturers. Motivation for the project came from the slipping global market share of Japanese semiconductor manufacturers at the expense of American and Asian firms. The project was to be budgeted at ¥100 billion ($945 million at 2000 exchange rates).[37]

—Also in August 2000 an information strategy conference reporting to the prime minister announced its intent to produce a five-year plan within two months outlining steps to overtake the United States as a high-speed Internet country. The plan encompassed construction of a high-speed Internet backbone, promotion of e-commerce, promotion of e-government, and development of human resources. Some aspects of the plan call for deregulation (especially e-commerce), but others rely on a traditional concept of government promotion, including subsidies to lay fiber-optic cable to homes.[38]

—In 1999 MITI pursued a major new industrial revitalization initiative, including a new industrial promotion law—the Law on Special Measures for Industrial Revitalization. This law makes selected industries eligible for help in focusing on their core businesses (quite likely decreasing competition in some industries under the rubric of encouraging firms to drop out of their noncore businesses), making labor and capital adjustments, and developing new products to meet specific industry productivity targets. While the purpose of the law is to support the competitiveness of the private sector, the traditional concept of private sector–government cooperation (*kanmin kyōchō*) lies behind the effort.[39] Some observers noted that the new legislation would increase the role of government in guiding the economy.[40]

—In early 1999 the Diet passed a new law enabling MITI to promote start-up businesses with subsidies, debt guarantees, exceptions to limits on stock options, and even equity investments by MITI's Structural Improvement Fund. The law also includes subsidies and debt guarantees for research and development by medium and small firms.[41]

—In the spring of 1999 a MITI study group (a *kenkyūkai*—an advisory body with heavy industry representation) recommended a major restructuring of the heavy electrical equipment manufacturing industry, citing decreasing demand at home and intensified competition abroad. MITI was asked to support the industry through such measures as increased foreign aid (for electric power plants in developing countries to which Japanese firms would then have an inside track in supplying equipment).[42]

—In 1999 the ministries of International Trade and Industry, Agriculture, Education, and Health and Welfare, plus the Science and Technology Agency put together a new "national strategy" plan to catch up with the United States and Europe in biotechnology. The project included accelerating the timetable for the Japanese portion of the human genome project (to comply with the American acceleration of the whole international project); its aegis extended also to promotion of a variety of other genetics projects deemed of potential commercial value. The explicit goal was to accelerate the commercialization of biotechnology and enhance the international competitiveness of the Japanese industry.[43]

—In 1997 the Diet passed a new law dealing with nursing care for the elderly. A new tax to finance its provisions remained politically controversial in 2000, and the starting date of the tax was postponed. However, the important feature of the law was to create a new, powerful regulatory and financial role for the Ministry of Health and Welfare, which would control disbursement of subsidies to the nursing care industry.

—In late 1998, MITI released a traditional industry policy report on the textile industry, providing a government view on how the industry should evolve and suggesting a variety of technology and other possible government support measures.[44]

—In 1999 the National Land Agency created new industrial zones in Tokyo and Osaka exempt from certain land use restraints, hoping to foster new industrial plant investments.[45]

—In 1998 MITI announced a project to develop an eighty-passenger jetliner, slightly downsizing a previous plan to develop a one hundred–

passenger plane, dubbed the YSX project. Boeing had participated in the earlier project but it withdrew, prompting MITI to proceed on a smaller plane without Boeing's input.[46] Related to this project, MITI began a joint R&D project with the private sector to develop better carbon-fiber materials for aircraft fuselages, continuing a trend of support for commercial R&D well beyond the precommercial, experimental stage.[47]

—In late 1998 MITI announced a seven-year plan to help Japanese firms reduce the manufacturing costs for commercial satellites to help them compete with American and European firms. The thrust of the plan was a series of joint research projects to reduce the cost of some two hundred satellite components.[48]

—In the summer of 1999 MITI and the Ministry of Posts and Telecommunications, the Ministry of Construction, and the National Police Agency announced a project to develop technology for intelligent transportation systems with a group of one hundred participating corporations. The explicit aim of the project was to enable Japanese technology to become the international standard in this industry, enhancing the global market share and profits of Japanese firms. In the spirit of government-business cooperation, Soichiro Toyoda (chairman of Toyota Motor Corporation and head of Keidanren) was named to head the consortium.[49]

—In late 1999 (and again in the fall of 2000) the government included in the supplemental budget a variety of subsidies and direct spending measures on infrastructure to "catch up" in information technology. These included subsidies to cable television companies for digital broadcasting investments, public-private investment in developing digitalized geographic information, and subsidies for small-firm research on Internet-related topics.[50]

—At the end of 1999 MITI announced a special three-year plan to help small businesses with "informationalization," that is, to keep up with the anticipated rapid spread of e-commerce and other information-technology developments. In the first year, the proposed MITI budget for this was ¥650 billion ($6 billion at the existing exchange rates).[51]

—The Ministry of Agriculture issued a new call in its 1999 white paper for food self-sufficiency, proposing a new, higher target and paving the way for a variety of possible promotional programs for domestic farmers and food processors.[52]

—The Ministry of Posts and Telecommunications announced a plan in early 2000 to promote e-commerce software development by offering a year's free T-1 Internet connections to one hundred selected software developers.[53] These firms were housed in a building in the trendy Shibuya district of Tokyo, and both this project and other government subsidies for start-up firms were touted as creating "Bit Valley" (a takeoff on Silicon Valley) in Shibuya.[54]

—MITI and the Ministry of Transportation announced in early 2000 a plan to build an Internet-based system to match truckers with return loads in order to increase truck utilization rates by reducing empty back-hauls. Some one hundred firms were to participate in the government-funded project.[55]

Had enough? This list is only a sampling of the many ways in which the government continued to engage in traditional industrial policy at the end of the 1990s. Some of the specific examples above may not result in major government promotion programs, and one may question the relevance of some proposals to the future development of the economy, such as the continued effort of the Ministry of Agriculture to promote domestic food production or that of the Ministry of Finance to force banks to lend to small businesses. Others may be dismissed as representing nothing more than what happens in the United States or other countries. What does matter is the obvious continuing bureaucratic impulse to be involved in guiding, shaping, prodding, encouraging, and cajoling the economy to move in what a small group of bureaucrats deem an appropriate direction. At the same time, the private-sector impulse to manipulate the government's willingness to engage in industrial policy also continued; the participants in some of these schemes are likely the originators, since they stand to reap financial and competitive benefits.

Often this impulse produces policies that do go beyond both the model and the practice in the United States, providing rather specific benefits for targeted industries. Sometimes the objective, as in the cases of semiconductors and biotechnology, is the traditional and explicit goal of enhancing the competitiveness of Japanese firms vis-à-vis Americans and Europeans. This continued vigorous policy activity belies the plethora of public relations statements about deregulation and reduction in the role of government.

Most of these actions have not been controversial. With a rapidly aging society, subsidies to promote nursing care for the elderly, for example, are hardly a surprising or unusual development. However, no one seems to be speaking up in Japan about the inappropriateness of the government's decision in the mid-1990s to subsidize the laying of fiber optic cable to the home when the nation's well-developed telecommunications industry is quite capable of making decisions about such investments on a profit basis. On the contrary, the head of technology at Hitachi Corporation wrote a major op-ed piece in late 1999 calling for what eventually became the 2000 cooperative government–private sector scheme to regain global competitive power in semiconductors.[56] A poll in 1999 by one major newspaper found 45 percent of respondents' favoring some form of government financing—including special tax measures, loan guarantees, and direct lending—to promote venture capital businesses.[57] In the summer of 1999, the lobbying organization for big business, Keidanren, called for government-business cooperation on developing new technologies to revive the economy (focused on digital information technologies, geriatric care technologies, and environmental protection technologies).[58] This is the very same Keidanren that had been advocating deregulation and administrative reform through the 1990s—supposedly to lessen the role of the government in the economy. The irony of this contrast was undoubtedly not evident to the leaders of Keidanren. In the summer of 1999 another major newspaper wrote in approving terms about broadening government-business cooperation's playing a role in reviving the economy by subsidizing start-up firms.[59] For a nation whose government has been touting deregulation, the term government-business cooperation (*kanmin kyōchō*) pops up in government documents and media stories with amazing frequency.

Meanwhile, the personal connections in the form of *amakudari*, which facilitate the flow of communication and influence between government and the private sector, continue unabated. Government officials continue to retire at a relatively early age, and they continue to need post-retirement positions. Rules lengthening the period of time before a retired bureaucrat can move into an industry with which he was involved directly during his final years of government service were lengthened in the late 1990s, but this was only a minor change.[60] As one example of continuing practices, in early 2000 a major newspaper noted that the defense industry had absorbed 756 *amakudari* officials over the previous decade from the Defense Agency and Self-Defense Forces, including forty to sixty at each of the six top contractors.[61] Another media story in early 2000 complained of the flow of *amakudari* from the National Police Agency into plush jobs in the private sector—documenting the landing spots of 165 former officials currently employed in *amakudari* jobs.[62] The bureaucratic scandals of the 1990s tarnished the reputation of bureaucrats, but the machinery of *amakudari* clanks on.

One modest step finally occurred in 1999 that could potentially affect *amakudari*. The Diet passed a law permitting bureaucrats to remain employed beyond age sixty—but only on annual contracts at half pay and no fringe benefits. Even with this change, a new maximum age of sixty-five for final full retirement went into effect.[63] This change might affect bureaucrats who are not on the top career track, reducing their annual flow into private-sector jobs. However, the half-pay deal is not particularly attractive, and many will still want or need jobs at age sixty-five. More important, the change will not affect the top career officials, who abide by a system of "voluntary" early retirement if they are not promoted as the management pyramid narrows, so that the ranks of each age cohort are whittled down, leaving at most one lucky winner for the administrative vice minister position. Therefore, the new law will have only a very modest impact on the overall practice of *amakudari*. Elimination of this practice would require a combination of a retirement age (from full pay) of about seventy, better retirement benefits, an end to official ministry involvement in finding jobs for their retiring officials, and a halt to the forced retirements of top-track bureaucrats as their colleagues are promoted to higher posts.

Thus, despite the rhetoric about deregulation, reliance on markets, and entrepreneurship, the reality has been a real role for government that is increasing as a share of economic activity through its FILP and other actions. At the same time, government's continuing role in industrial policy and its interference in industries and markets has not elicited much criticism because so many in society take it for granted. Any economist who believes in the efficiency of markets must be dismayed by the reality of Japanese government behavior. One is tempted to shout out, "Let the market do it!"

Private-Sector Restructuring

The remaining element of systemic reform has been the effort of the private sector itself. By the end of the 1990s, the notion arose that even if the government failed to move vigorously on administrative reform or deregulation, private-sector corporations would change the overall economic system by altering their own behavior. For corporations the bottom line has always been profits. Even if Japanese firms did not maximize or even emphasize profits over the past fifty years, at least they had to earn a positive profit over the long run. As in any society, firms that lose money eventually get into trouble and restructure or cease to exist. Eventually they cannot meet their loan payments, or they cannot even meet their payroll commitments. Firms go out of existence, they are absorbed by others, or they successfully restructure and reform their operations.

The collapse of asset prices pushed some firms into default on their loans, primarily firms in real estate development or those in other industries that had strayed from their main business to invest in equities and real estate. Manufacturing firms also faced increased international competition, especially in the 1994–96 period, when the yen rose rapidly against the dollar. Although firms delayed their response to these problems, by the end of the decade, many firms appeared to be taking action.

One indicator of the delay and eventual action comes from employment data. Even though the economy was close to stagnant, and firms were left with excess employment by the sudden downshift from the high growth of the "bubble" years, employment continued to grow in the first half of the 1990s. From 1992 through 1996 total employment in the economy grew at a 0.4 percent annual rate. Only from 1997 did total employment begin to fall, as firms belatedly coped with their excess staffing. By January 2000 total employment had fallen 3 percent from the 1997 average.[64]

Reducing employment is a simple response to poor profitability, but it does not necessarily indicate reform of the way in which companies do business. Most announcements by Japanese corporations concerning labor adjustment involved no overt layoffs. All firms can reduce employment through attrition by constraining hires of new school graduates, and many have done so. They might also induce older employees to accept early retirement packages, and sometimes the voluntary nature of these retirement choices is suspect. Nevertheless, outright firing of staff (such as closing a factory and terminating all the employees there) remains rare.

Most announcements of planned cuts in labor force have been well within the range of attrition. Even with lifetime employment, normal annual separation rates imply that a firm should be able to reduce its labor force by several percent a year if new hires are held to zero. Data on separations show an average 14 percent annual separation rate for all corporations.[65] Presumably separation rates at large firms practicing lifetime employment are lower, but even they should be able to generate separation rates of 4–5 percent annually. Separation among those male employees with lifetime employment may run as low as 3 percent, assuming a thirty-five-year career, but the firm's average is pushed higher by the presence of women and temporary employees.

Recent major cutback announcements are certainly within this range. NKK, the troubled number-two integrated steel maker, planned a 4,000-person cut in early 2000, to be spread over three years and amounting to an annual 4 percent reduction in staff.[66] Japan Tobacco, the partially government–owned cigarette giant, announced reductions that amounted to 2.5

percent a year for domestic employees (and 5 percent a year for foreign workers) for three years.[67] In fiscal 1999 the top ten banks were reported to have accelerated labor downsizing, but their labor force reduction for the year averaged 4.7 percent, also spread over three years. Of the ten, only Sakura Bank had a staff reduction (8.6 percent) that may have exceeded attrition limits.[68] Except for those unfortunate Japanese employees identified as misfits or dead wood at such times, and subjected to an unendurable barrage of psychological pressure to quit, staff reductions are not at all equivalent to American-style layoffs.

As a recent study of this issue by economist Douglas Ostrom notes, none of the Japanese restructuring comes close to the magnitude of the American labor force downsizing effected by Ford or IBM in the 1980s or AT&T in the 1990s. Indeed, he concludes that Japanese manufacturing firms have undertaken less vigorous downsizing in the 1997–99 period than they did during the previous downturn in industrial output during the 1985–87 period. In both time periods manufacturing employment dropped less than industrial output, indicating that firms are reluctant to reduce their work force when output declines, as one would expect with lifetime employment, but the disparity between declining output and the more mild decline in employment was more pronounced in the 1990s than in the 1980s.[69] This analysis supports the conclusion that lifetime employment continues. Firms moving to new labor practices characterized by greater flexibility of employment and reduced implicit long-term commitments to core workers should have produced less of a disparity between the drop in output and employment adjustment rather than more.

Reductions through attrition do not necessarily imply an end to lifetime employment. With some older employees under pressure to accept early retirement, these workers feel the commitment has been weakened. However, there was no discernible move away from the preference toward hiring new school graduates rather than midcareer people. Undoubtedly those unlucky few who have actually been laid off by their firms in midcareer will eventually find new jobs. However, an individual's probability at midcareer of finding a job at a large firm with comparable pay or using his acquired skills is much lower than in the United States. The plight of these people makes good media stories, but remains atypical because most firms have relied on attrition. These stories of woe also confirm the continued existence of lifetime employment by emphasizing how thin the market is for midcareer job changers.

Beyond simple downsizing, were Japanese corporations altering their behavior? Were distinctive characteristics of reliance on bank loans, a preference for *keiretsu* ties, or other aspects of corporate governance changing? The data imply that not much has changed; cracks have appeared in some of the distinctive aspects of corporate behavior, but most of the traditional patterns remain in place.

Reliance on Bank Loans

Were Japanese firms shifting away from banks toward the bond market to raise funds? Data through March 2000 indicate that this was not happening. Figures 6-5a and 6-5b provide data on corporate liabilities from 1990 to 2000, representing the stock of liabilities on March 31 of each year. As a share of total liabilities, bank loans have remained very stable—55 percent in 1990 and slightly higher, 59 percent, in 2000. Bank loans are not a higher share of liabilities because Japanese corporations rely heavily on trade credit as a means of financing; trade credit represented 22 percent of liabilities in 2000. Since trade credit represents nonfinancial corporations' lending funds among themselves, it is not a net source of funds to the corporate sector as a whole and perhaps should be excluded from liabilities. However, as figure 6-5b shows, this exclusion makes no difference; dependence on bank loans remained a stable share of liabilities, fluctuating narrowly between 73 and 76 percent of the total.

Paralleling the stability in reliance on bank loans, corporations' use of nonequity securities (short-term commercial paper and corporate bonds) has also been quite stable. As a share of total liabilities, these securities fluctuated between 8 percent and 10 percent. As a share of liabilities exclusive of trade credit, securities fluctuated narrowly, between 11.0 and 12.6 percent. To be sure, the composition of these securities changed somewhat. One could get the impression that Japanese corporations were becoming more dependent on bonds because issues of *domestic* bonds were up. Outstanding issues of domestic corporate bonds rose from ¥2.2 trillion in 1990 to ¥5.8 trillion by 2000—almost tripling in a decade. Offsetting this rise was a substantial drop in bonds issued *overseas*—from ¥3.5 trillion in 1990 (actually larger than domestic bonds) to only ¥0.8 trillion by 2000.[70] Overall, corporations did not rely more heavily on bonds, but simply brought their bond issues home as domestic interest rates fell and the peculiar regulatory framework of the 1980s, which had actually favored overseas bond issues, eroded.

Next, consider corporate cross-shareholding. As a broad phenomenon, corporations do appear to have sold some of the shares that they had held for years to cement their business relationships. One estimate shows overall cross-shareholding falling from a peak of about 55 percent of total corpo-

Figure 6-5a. *Percentage of Total Corporate Liabilities, 1990–2000 (March 31)*

Percent

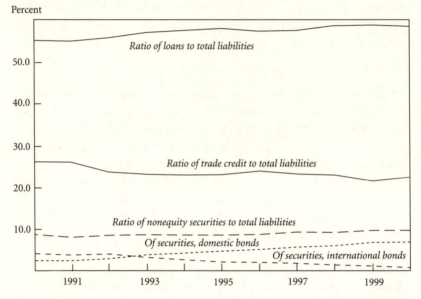

Figure 6-5b. *Percentage of Corporate Liabilities, Exclusive of Trade Credit,*
1990–2000 (March 31)

Percent

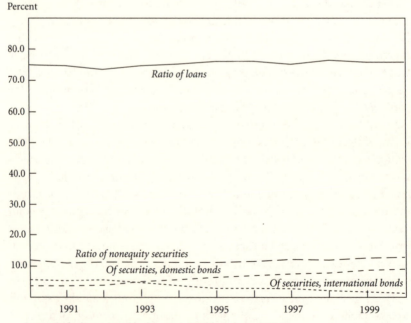

Sources: Bank of Japan data tables, "Corporate FOF," for each year, 1989–99.

rate shares in the late 1980s to only 40 percent by 1999—bringing the ratio back to where it was in the mid-1960s.[71] However, the pace of the decline was fading, and doubts arose as to whether the trend would continue. Clearly some firms needed to sell some of their share holdings to provide cash as their financial situation deteriorated. The drop in overall cross-shareholding is a noticeable shift in corporate behavior. Nevertheless, even with the decade-long reduction, 40 percent of all corporate equity remained locked up in such holdings.

Other evidence suggests even less change in corporate shareholding patterns—especially the ties with the six major horizontal *keiretsu* discussed in chapter 2. Moving into 2000, the boundaries of these groups were blurring as some mergers of firms across *keiretsu* lines began to occur. Nevertheless, cross-shareholding and bank loan data indicate no dramatic attenuation of ties within these groups, as shown in figures 6-6a and 6-6b.

As a share of total equity outstanding, the proportion held within these groups (figure 6-6a) has shifted over time, but there is little evidence of any acceleration in the late 1990s. Intracorporate equity ties in all the groups were down modestly from the 1980s to the mid-1990s; Sumitomo is the only group with a clear trend toward attenuation. However, from 1996 to 1999 these groups generally exhibited little change. Mitsui intragroup shareholdings remained steady; Mitsubishi and Sanwa holdings fell less than 1 percentage point; and those of the Fuyo and Dai-Ichi groups actually rose. Only the Sumitomo group continued its slide, with a reduction in cross-shareholding of more than 1 percentage point.

How can these data on continuing equity ties be reconciled with the evidence of a decline in the proportion of total corporate equity held in long-term cross-shareholdings? To the extent that banks or nonfinancial corporations are selling long-held shares, they must be selling shares they held in firms that were not part of their horizontal *keiretsu* groups. Banks, for example, might be selling shares in companies to which they lend without being in a main bank relationship. Nonfinancial corporations might be reducing their shareholdings as part of the relationship they have with their parts suppliers or other business dealings. In these cases, the cross-shareholding was often largely symbolic, and companies could decide that the symbolism is no longer necessary as part of the package of actions that cement long-term vertical *keiretsu* relationships.

A similar picture emerges from the loan data in figure 6-6b. Reliance on loans from the banks belonging to each *keiretsu* had fallen from the late 1970s to 1990. However, these shares remained rather stable in the 1990s.

Figure 6-6a. Keiretsu *Cross-Shareholding Ties, Selected Years, 1978–99 (March 31)*

Figure 6-6b. Keiretsu *Loan Ties, Selected Years, 1978–99 (March 31)*

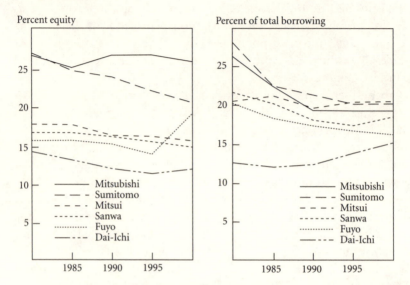

Percent equity

Percent of total borrowing

Mitsubishi
Sumitomo
Mitsui
Sanwa
Fuyo
Dai-Ichi

Source: Edward J. Lincoln, *Troubled Times* (Brookings, 1999), p. 186; Toyo Keizai, Kigyo Keiretsu Soran, 2000, pp. 30–39.

Dependence on the group's banks continued to decline marginally in the Fuyo Group (from 17.4 percent in 1990 to 16.3 percent in 1999) and Sumitomo Group (from 21.5 percent to 19.4 percent), but the others were either stable or higher in 1999 compared with 1990. In the Dai-Ichi group, historically the loosest group of the six, dependence on the group bank has been slowly increasing since the mid-1980s. These data on loans, therefore, do not suggest that *keiretsu* lending ties are unwinding.

Keiretsu Ties

This picture of what has happened to the ties within the existing horizontal *keiretsu* is now challenged by new bank mergers that cut across *keiretsu* boundaries. These mergers, occurring as banks struggle to survive in a more deregulated world, might seem to imply an end to the *keiretsu* concept. However, the Japanese media have already begun to assume the emergence of a new *keiretsu* configuration, collapsing the former six large *keiretsu* into four larger groups. Figure 6-7 shows the outlines of how this reconfiguration is occurring.

Figure 6-7. *Reconfiguration of* Keiretsu *Groups*

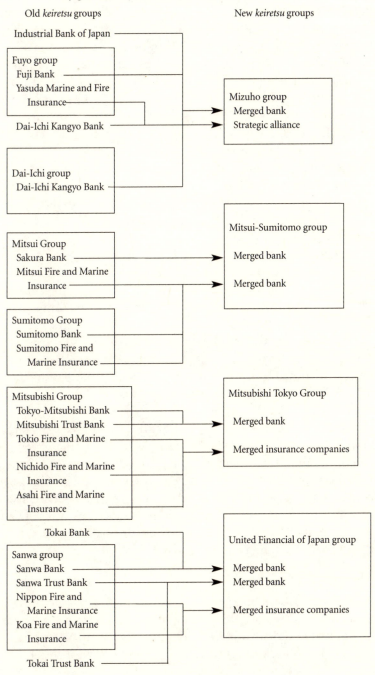

Old *keiretsu* groups

Industrial Bank of Japan

Fuyo group
  Fuji Bank
  Yasuda Marine and Fire
    Insurance

Dai-Ichi Kangyo Bank

Dai-Ichi group
  Dai-Ichi Kangyo Bank

Mitsui Group
  Sakura Bank
  Mitsui Fire and Marine
    Insurance

Sumitomo Group
  Sumitomo Bank
  Sumitomo Fire and
    Marine Insurance

Mitsubishi Group
  Tokyo-Mitsubishi Bank
  Mitsubishi Trust Bank
  Tokio Fire and Marine
    Insurance
  Nichido Fire and Marine
    Insurance
  Asahi Fire and Marine
    Insurance

Tokai Bank

Sanwa group
  Sanwa Bank
  Sanwa Trust Bank
  Nippon Fire and
    Marine Insurance
  Koa Fire and Marine
    Insurance

Tokai Trust Bank

New *keiretsu* groups

Mizuho group
  Merged bank
  Strategic alliance

Mitsui-Sumitomo group
  Merged bank
  Merged bank

Mitsubishi Tokyo Group
  Merged bank
  Merged insurance companies

United Financial of Japan group
  Merged bank
  Merged bank
  Merged insurance companies

The most dramatic development is the three-way merger among the Fuji Bank, Dai-Ichi Kangyo Bank, and Industrial Bank of Japan (IBJ) to form the Mizuho group. This merger brought the Fuyo Group together with the Dai-Ichi Group and adds to it IBJ, a bank that was not part of a formal *keiretsu* (having evolved out of a government financial institution that was privatized after the war) but had its own set of companies for which it served as a main bank. Reinforcing the sense of a new group, Dai-Ichi Life Insurance, with strategic ties to IBJ, formed a strategic alliance (a vague term that connotes a cooperative partnership short of merger) with Yasuda Fire and Marine Insurance of the Fuyo Group.

The existing Sumitomo and Mitsui groups came together through the merger of their respective banks. Reinforcing this development, Mitsui Fire and Marine Insurance merged with Sumitomo Fire and Marine. So far, the respective life insurance companies that are part of the two groups have not announced any move.

The Mitsubishi Group did not combine with another group, though the merger of the Mitsubishi Bank and Tokyo Bank (a large non-*keiretsu* bank) in 1996 was a precursor to the current moves. The Tokyo-Mitsubishi Bank acquired Mitsubishi Trust Bank, a move enabled by deregulation and one that increases the bank's size in response to the other mergers.

Sanwa Bank merged with the Tokai Bank, bringing the Sanwa group together with a non-*keiretsu* bank to form United Financial of Japan (UFJ). Reinforcing this move, Nippon Fire and Marine plus Koa Fire and Marine, both of which had an association with the Sanwa group, merged. Sanwa Trust Bank, Tokai Trust, and Toyo Trust merged.

The reconfiguration of the horizontal *keiretsu* has focused so far on banks and insurance companies. Whether this new combination of four large financial groups will prompt mergers and acquisitions among the respective nonfinancial firms that have been part of the groups is somewhat unclear. However, in the fall of 2000, NKK and Kawasaki Steel announced a merger (through a holding company to be established by 2003); NKK belongs to the Fuyo Group, and Kawasaki to the Dai-Ichi Group, so their merger is consistent with the ties forming the Mizuho Group.[72]

Accounting Rules

Next consider accounting rules as an element of corporate change. Lax accounting rules have enabled firms in the past to hide important developments from the outside world (including from their own shareholders). The practice of recording assets at purchase value rather than at current market value introduced a strong element of unreality into corporate accounts, because many firms held land or equity that had been purchased decades ago and still appeared on the books at its original price. More important, corporations were required to provide a consolidated financial report that included only those subsidiaries in which the firm held more than a 50 percent stake. This requirement opened the way for companies to establish minority-owned subsidiaries in which they could park some of their more problematical business dealings, without having to disclose the negative information concealed in these subsidiaries to their shareholders. Revised accounting rules slated to go into effect by 2002 are supposed to fix both of these problems. Firms are to record assets at market price, and the 50 percent rule will change to one of "effective control" so that minority-owned subsidiaries will be included. These changes are supposed to remedy the ills of the past.[73]

The new accounting rules, however, remain far from perfect. Of particular concern is the new subsidiary rule. In actuality, the new rule is more vague than the old one. The reporting corporations themselves will decide under the new rule which subsidiaries they effectively control without majority ownership and thereby need to be consolidated in their financial reports. Outside accountants can only evaluate on the basis of the data they receive from the reporting corporation. If the corporation fails to disclose to the auditors other subsidiaries that a careful, impartial analyst might believe should be included, the auditors have no means of knowing what they have been denied. Shareholder lawsuits provide a theoretical deterrent should the shareholders eventually find out that the firm hid losses in a subsidiary that should have been consolidated in the accounts. However, shareholder suits depend on two critical factors: actual bankruptcy of the firm (leading to a thorough audit of the company's remains, as was the case with suits filed against the Long-Term Credit Bank and Nippon Credit Bank) and a set of lawyers and courts to handle the suits. If a company merely underperforms, rather than actually going bankrupt, the new system, like the old, allows corporations to conceal critical information from shareholders and creditors for long periods. Unless the government authorizes a dramatic increase in the number of lawyers and judges, a deluge of lawsuits initiated by private shareholders will clog the legal system. Japan is infamous for the rigid, low limits placed on the number of lawyers and judges trained and accredited each year. A series of lawsuits has been filed against some firms, involving mainly the former managers of the bankrupt Long-Term Credit Bank and Nippon Credit Bank, but the very long time that will elapse before those cases are settled will have a chilling effect on lawsuits as a viable form of shareholder protection against management malfeasance.

To be sure, the new consolidation rule will bring a one-time consolidation of subsidiaries, and some corporations have already announced lower consolidated profits as a consequence. The real test will be what happens over the next decade or two, as firms consider creation of new, unconsolidated subsidiaries to hide new problems. Reform of accounting rules, therefore, is a modest step toward greater transparency, but one that could be undermined by the vagueness of the new consolidation rule.

Mergers and Acquisitions

Undeniably, activity has picked up in mergers and acquisitions. In 1999 there were 630 mergers or acquisitions involving two domestic firms, 137 cases of foreign firms' acquiring Japanese firms, and 215 cases of Japanese firms' acquiring foreign firms.[74] The acquisitions within Japan are up from earlier years. During the years from 1989 through 1997, an annual average of only 289 mergers or acquisitions between domestic firms occurred, and an average of only 39 acquisitions of domestic firms by foreign firms. At the same time, Japanese acquisitions of foreign firms are down from an average 260 a year and down much more from the burst of overseas acquisitions during the "bubble" of the 1980s, when the number exceeded 400 a year in 1989 and 1990.[75] These data at least suggest that the market for corporate control is becoming more fluid. In early 2000 an investment banker opined in an article in the *Wall Street Journal* that the unwinding of cross-shareholdings among Japanese firms could result in contests for corporate control in the stock market.[76]

What does this activity really signify? In some cases, mergers and acquisitions may resemble activity in the United States, an effort by corporations to reconfigure themselves in accordance with the way they see markets evolving. Some visible mergers, though, bear little resemblance to this model. Consider the large merger among the Industrial Bank of Japan, Fuji Bank, and Dai-Ichi Kangyo Bank, forming the new Mizuho group. All three banks are large commercial banks, though in the past the Industrial Bank of Japan specialized in longer-term loans. Their merger, therefore, represents a combination of three companies in the same business, not a rearrangement of corporate pieces to fit a changing market. Furthermore, this is a merger among equals, and the process of blending the personnel of the three will be enormously difficult. The pressures to be "fair" in doling out positions in the combined bank among personnel from the three will be so strong that it will act as a strong brake on any efforts to achieve cost savings or to adopt a new business model. Personnel issues will absorb so much of management's time that a focus on how to reposition the bank to survive in a changing financial environment will be diminished at best. About all this merger has accomplished is the creation of a bank so large ($1.3 trillion in assets) that the government could never consider allowing it to go bankrupt.[77]

Similar caution should be applied to interpreting the current upturn in foreign acquisitions of Japanese firms. The data are encouraging, since the extreme difficulty of acquiring existing firms in Japan has been a major stumbling block for any foreign firm attempting to enter the Japanese market in the past sixty years.[78] Just a few years ago, for example, no one would have thought that Renault or any other foreign auto manufacturer would be able to buy Nissan Motors, the second largest auto firm in Japan. That acquisition has occurred, but it deserves a more detailed look. Renault does not own Nissan; it has a 37 percent minority stake. That stake makes Renault the largest of any shareholder, but it does not have a majority share. Renault's share is enough to give it veto rights on certain basic corporate decisions, such as declaring bankruptcy or floating new shares. Nevertheless, veto rights on some decisions are a far cry from having a 51 percent controlling interest, as numerous foreign firms involved in joint ventures in which they had only a 49 percent stake have learned to their chagrin over the past several decades. Because Nissan was literally on the brink of bankruptcy, partial foreign ownership was a preferred outcome for management, its creditors, and the government. Because avoidance of bankruptcy, even with the new capital infusion from Renault, required fairly radical restructuring of the firm, it was convenient for existing Nissan management to push the burden for forcing change onto foreigners.

What is happening here is a quintessential example of *gaiatsu* (foreign pressure) being used to accomplish domestic purposes. At the moment Renault has a strong hand in reshaping Nissan because of the firm's critical financial situation. However, should the operation prove successful, Renault could well find in the future that its 37 percent stake is far short of majority control. Japanese society has a long history of periodic willingness to learn directly from foreigners, but an equally long tradition of excluding them or minimizing their role once the lessons have been absorbed. This tale of caution applies to any foreign firms that are purchasing large minority stakes in Japanese firms. All of the foreign acquisitions in the Japanese auto industry, for example, involve minority ownership: Ford-Mazda, Chrysler-Benz–Mitsubishi Motors, General Motors–Fuji Heavy, and General Motors–Isuzu.

Corporate Governance

To be sure, the rise of inward direct investment, plus the larger presence of foreign institutional investors holding sizable portfolio investments in some Japanese firms, implies a role for foreigners in corporate governance beyond what they had just a few years ago. They bring with them a hard-nosed approach to pushing the firms in which they invest toward better performance. As visible as their role has become, however, the reality is that Japanese corporate behavior will depend fundamentally on what Japanese choose to do, not on what foreigners press them to do. Indeed, the foreign pressure for performance will eventually result in resentment and resistance. Signs of that resentment were already showing before the end of 1999. The government permitted sale of the carcass of the nationalized Long-Term Credit Bank to American-owned Ripplewood Holdings, largely because there were no credible offers from Japanese firms, but then it very pointedly rejected an American bid for Nippon Credit Bank and accepted a lower Japanese bid for nationalistic reasons.[79] Even MITI jumped into the discussion of changing business behavior norms, issuing a report in the summer of 1999 arguing that the American business model is not the only one—on the basis of a MITI study mission to Germany and Israel. The study noted approvingly, for example, the role of the Israeli government in incubating start-up firms.[80]

Other popular evidence for changing corporate behavior comes from the decision of some corporations to reduce the size of their corporate boards. In a well-publicized move, Sony Corporation cut its board in 1999 from thirty-eight members to ten. Some other corporations have carried out reductions of similar magnitude.[81] Viewed from abroad, this change may appear to imply a change in the nature of corporate governance. The *New York Times*, for example, noted that with this move Sony seemed to be adopting American management concepts.[82] Certainly a smaller board may reach decisions more easily. Size, however, was never the critical issue. What matters is that Japanese corporate boards were almost entirely composed of the career managers of the firms themselves. Reducing the size of the board without changing the composition to include outsiders who represent the interests of the shareholders does nothing to alter the nature of corporate governance. Indeed, a prominent Japanese business magazine made exactly this point in 2000. It argued that while the Sony board change looked like Americanization, it actually remained purely Japanese. By 2000 the board had expanded slightly, to twelve members, of whom only three were from outside the Sony group. The rest are either Sony executives or executives of Sony affiliated firms.[83] In reality, little changed.

As a small bit of evidence of the relative lack of change in corporate governance, consider the role of the shareholders meeting. Historically, these meetings have been extremely short, with most corporations holding them on the same day to prevent holders of portfolios from attending meetings for more than one company. They have also been marred by the presence of *sokaiya*. In 1999, 2,227 firms continued the tradition of holding their meetings on June 29. The only evidence of change was that in at least some of these meetings, an actual dialogue between management and shareholders occurred.[84] At least the National Police Agency (NPA) was able to report that the number of *sokaiya* in 2000 was down to about 400 (from a peak of 1,700 in 1983), though one wonders why there are any left if the NPA had such accurate knowledge of who these illegal operators are.[85]

Rates of Return

Beginning in 1999 the terms "return on assets" and "return on equity" became quite popular.[86] In the high-growth years, when Japanese firms could combine new, productive technology with inexpensive labor, corporate profits were high. In recent years, however, return on assets and return on equity have fallen to low levels. One recent study found that the total return on business capital (gross operating profit as a ratio of nonresidential fixed capital) was about the same in Japan and the United States until the early 1980s. After that time profit levels were higher in the United States, and the gap widened sharply in the 1990s. By the late 1990s the return to capital was more than 50 percent higher in the United States than in Japan.[87] At the end of the 1990s the return on assets in the corporate sector was only about 2 to 3 percent. Even a doubling of that rate to 4 percent would bring Japanese firms back only to where they were in the 1980s.[88] Firms would be able to claim they had changed their behavior to be more like western firms by putting more emphasis on profits, but without driving profits to western levels.

In summary, there is no denying that something interesting has been happening in the corporate sector in Japan, driven by fear of bankruptcy. Firms have reduced employment, and some have become willing targets for acquisition. This is a positive change from companies' seeming inability to focus on their problems and deal with them realistically during most of the 1990s. This belated flurry of corporate restructuring, though, is likely to fall far short of a revolution in labor practices, corporate financing, or corporate governance. Optimists may feel that the genie cannot be put back in the bottle, but Japan has a long tradition of doing exactly that. Obviously, the system will not revert entirely to the assumptions and behavior of the past half century, but Japanese firms remain distinctive in comparison with their American counterparts a decade from now.

Conclusion

Reform in Japan appeared to be finally making progress by the end of the 1990s. Deregulation had been under way since 1994; a new round of administrative reform occurred in January 2001; and the corporate sector was engaging in real restructuring. Appearances, however, can be deceiving. Deregulation remained a relatively weak process; it made progress in some industries, but the overall picture was one of halting, incomplete progress. Administrative reform was largely a fraud, involving a reshuffling of ministries without altering the relationship of government to society. Corporate restructuring was real, but by no means represented a revolution in corporate governance or behavior. Meanwhile, the government continued to involve itself in the economy in ways quite familiar in the past half century and in some ways actually increased its role.

Overall, the process of reform has been quite weak and mild. Bureaucrats themselves have controlled much of the process of deregulation and administrative reform. Industrial policy initiatives and the rising role of government finance in the private sector indicate a continued commitment to the principles of government guidance or involvement in the economy. Corporations have been sincere about cutting costs through attrition in labor, but they have shown little interest in real reform of governance and behavior. The Japanese may feel they are undergoing a revolution, compared with the relative inaction of the past two decades as problems were building, and they are right to perceive an acceleration of change. What is happening in Japan looks rather exciting compared with the recent past. However, what appears to be significant change within a Japanese frame of comparison does not appear so radical when viewed from abroad.

7

Implications for American Policy

A quarter century ago a number of nations began unwinding government involvement in the economy. Government-owned corporations have been privatized. Management of market outcomes through regulation or manipulation has eased or been abandoned. In the United States the process of deregulation is a continuing story.

The Japanese government has been the quintessential activist, interventionist government. Relatively few sectors have been subject to direct government ownership, but the government has interfered indirectly in markets, hoping to achieve its design of what was best for economic development. For over a century, industrialization aimed at catching up with the advanced industrial nations was an explicit national goal. Fearing that markets would fail to allocate investment and output in a manner that would accomplish that goal, the government carved out a role for itself, a role that peaked in the first three decades of the postwar period. The result was the "Japanese economic model" outlined in chapter 2, an interconnected set of features whose institutions and behavior patterns were substantially different from those of the United States or other advanced nations.

That model suited the special needs of a rapidly industrializing country. Who can argue with 9 percent average annual real economic growth for a quarter of a century? Whether this economic system was a necessary element of Japan's economic success story will probably remain forever a controversial question. At the very least, however, the system was consistent with rapid growth and development.

The century-long era of catching up with the global industrial leaders was largely over by the mid-1970s. At that point, efforts to dismantle or reformulate the architecture of the economic system should have begun. To be sure, some changes did occur over the next two decades, but the pace of reform was modest at best and often simply a fraudulent image to cover the government's continuing regulation and intervention in the economy. Many formal controls were discontinued, but they were often replaced with informal mechanisms of government-business consultation that had much the same effect. Continuation of growth higher than that in other industrial nations from the mid-1970s to the beginning of the 1990s also enhanced belief among government officials, businessmen, and Japanese academics that their distinctive system was actually superior to those of western nations and did not need to change. To some outside observers, however, by the 1990s the nature of the economic system seemed rather badly out of line with the needs of a mature industrial nation.

Now the Japanese have been through almost a decade of economic stress. The relative stagnation of the economy since 1992, the emergence of a massive number of nonperforming loans, and the eruption of numerous economic scandals were a depressing experience for a nation used to rapid economic growth. Although much of the relatively poor economic performance could be ascribed to macroeconomic variables, the 1990s unsurprisingly spawned vigorous debate over systemic reform.

Some signs of change finally appeared in the late 1990s. After a decades-long dearth of activity in this area, a flurry of high-tech start-up firms is appearing, especially in the information technology sector. The Large Scale Retail Store Law, which impeded restructuring of the retail sector for a quarter of a century, was repealed in 1999. Domestic airline fares were deregulated in 2000. The "big bang" deregulation of the financial sector was proceeding. Merger and acquisition activity accelerated, including a sharp increase in acquisitions by foreign firms.

Optimists can point to such examples and read into them a picture of a society that is finally facing up to a fundamental restructuring of the economic system. In this view, change may be belated, but is finally occurring; the dam has finally burst. The direction of change is to reduce the overt role of government in markets and inject new flexibility into the behavior of corporations and households. At least, so it would seem.

Despite the surface appearances, the direction of change and its eventual effect on the overarching architecture and behavior of the economic system are modest, to say the least. The pace of formal reform has accelerated when compared with the near stasis of the past quarter century, but it is not so dramatic when compared with the trends in many other countries around the world. Furthermore, the surface changes do not necessarily lead to a more market-reliant system that is closer to the current norms of the American economy.

The flurry of start-up firms looks impressive, but only in comparison with the earlier dearth; the numbers are not large, and many of these new firms fared poorly when they went public in 2000. The Large Scale Retail Store Law is gone, but it has been replaced with government encouragement of local initiatives that may turn out to be just as restrictive in the future. Airline fares have been deregulated, but the industry is still far from a competitive model, since the government controls entry and allocation of landing slots at key airports. The financial sector "big bang" deregulations have proceeded, but with little effect on the flow of funds in the economy. Acquisitions by foreigners have increased, but they have risen from a very small base and are largely restricted to purchase of failing firms.

This study has argued that multiple factors are responsible for the slow and limited reform of the economic system. The very strong growth of most of the past fifty years engendered a strong belief in the value and superiority of the system, a belief that has been only partially dislodged by the troubles of the 1990s. The fact that the existing system comprises interlocking features implies that alteration of any single element is difficult. The rather mild nature of economic distress over the course of the 1990s compounds the problem of reform. People and corporations may be anxious about the future, but actual job loss and bankruptcy have not been sufficiently widespread to produce a strong political movement in favor of more radical or thorough reform. The recession of 1997–98 was serious, and the banking sector teetered on the edge of catastrophic collapse, but a more expansionary fiscal policy and a government bailout for banks staved off crisis without generating reform. Without a more serious crisis, the many vested interests in the existing system have had little reason to give up their perquisites. Too many people have a stake in the benefits accruing from the existing economic system to endorse radical change. They may prefer to see reform in those parts of the system that do not affect them personally, but coalition building can be difficult if they do not want to give up their own privileges. Finally, lack of clarity about how to change the system is understandable given the general conformity of current institutions and behavior patterns to broader social norms.

This constellation of factors has not totally prevented change, but it does explain why reform did not begin in earnest in the 1970s and why it took more than a half decade of stagnation to get the process initiated. Even now these factors imply a slow, moderate, and ultimately constrained process of endorsing greater reliance on markets. Chapter 6 outlined what has been happening in government and the private sector. Some deregulation has occurred, and a few industries are now operating in a less regulated environment with lower prices stemming from real price competition. Progress has been uneven and generally slow, however, and even in deregulated industries, informal collusion could easily replace regulation. Meanwhile, other measures of government involvement in the economy show little sign of abating—the government's financial role through the Fiscal Investment and Loan Program (FILP) has actually expanded, and the proclivity to devise industrial policy schemes to promote favored industries continues. Private sector restructuring, driven by the poor financial condition of many companies, has gotten under way, but more fundamental reform of corporate behavior is problematic. Reliance on bank loans in corporate finance has not diminished, patterns of corporate governance have not changed much, and even the horizontal *keiretsu* may continue in somewhat modified and consolidated form.

The central prediction of this study, therefore, is that the current economic system will evolve to something different from that of the past half century, but that the system will continue to constrain market behavior more than is the case in the United States or increasingly in Europe. The Japanese economy is unlikely to become a paragon of reliance on unfettered markets for labor, corporate control, finance, or overall allocation of resources in the economy. Current changes will move the Japanese model modestly in the general direction of greater reliance on markets than has been the case in the past half century, but the shift will be partial and incomplete. To be sure, the U.S. economy is hardly a laissez-faire economy either, but the current American system is, and will remain, closer to an unfettered market ideal than will be the case in Japan.

This prediction matters because Japan sorely needs changes in corporate governance, changes in labor markets, and greater reliance on markets for finance and goods and services to guide the economy back to economic health. Only markets can provide the necessary economic signals to allocate and reallocate productive resources in an uncertain world, and only corporations with robust corporate governance can respond appropriately to those signals.

The critical question will be whether the modest reforms in Japan will be sufficient to revitalize the economy. The corporate downsizing that is a critical part of revitalization is proceeding, and to that extent, change will underwrite a cyclical economic recovery. However, even if corporate restructuring combined with heavy macroeconomic stimulus restores the economy to modest economic growth, that recovery will be stronger and more robust if broad structural reform occurs. Weak reform implies a system that will grow more slowly than necessary and will be more susceptible to recurring recession or crisis. In this scenario, annual economic growth would be on the order of zero to one percent over the first decade of the twenty-first century.

Weak economic recovery accompanied by modest reform that avoids a depression but leaves the economy underperforming is the most likely outcome. What about the more positive and more pessimistic possibilities? An optimistic outcome is less likely, though still possible. Current reforms could turn out to be sufficient to unleash new competition and growth, especially in the information technology sector. Ultimately, no one knows how much deregulation and reform are necessary to revitalize markets and overall economic growth. Even optimistic scenarios, however, call for rather low growth because of the falling labor force and aging population. The Economic Strategy Council, an advisory group reporting to the prime minister, predicted in early 1999 that the economy could grow at 2.3 percent if structural reforms were carried out.[1] A year later the Industrial Structure Council, an advisory body to the Ministry of International Trade and Industry (MITI), decided that 2 percent growth was "within reach," given further economic reforms.[2]

The analysis of the previous chapters, however, implies that the optimistic scenario is unlikely. Politicians would have to be motivated by disgruntled voters to tackle the bureaucracy's hold on the reform process, and there are few signs that this will happen. For example, a brief revolt within the Liberal Democratic Party in the fall of 2000, led by senior party member Koichi Kato and those in the party favoring more reform, failed, leaving the proponents of the status quo firmly in charge. Vested interests would have to feel that their own benefits from the current system were either lost already or that they would benefit more from a radical reconfiguration of the system, but there are no signs of such public attitudes. The social features identified in chapter 6 could turn out to be less important to people than they have been in the past, leading them to embrace riskier high-return personal financial portfolios, greater personal uncertainty in more fluid labor markets stripped of lifetime employment, or less reliance on personal relationships and their associated wining and dining in business dealings. However, there are few signs of changing norms of social behavior, other than occasional government advisory commission reports exhorting society to behave differently. Concepts of personal freedom and independence were a key theme in pronouncements of the Prime Minister's Economic Council—an advisory group—in 1999.[3] Virtually none of the current signs in Japanese society, political behavior, or economic behavior support a scenario of more radical change.

The one unknown factor that could drive a more optimistic scenario is the emerging technology revolution. Rapid growth of this sector, plus the application of new information technology to other sectors, could provide a new engine for economic growth and higher productivity growth. Much will depend on the progress of deregulation in the telecommunications sector, where high fees have slowed the spread of household Internet use. Other fees and red tape have hobbled the spread of cable television. Progress has occurred, but slowly and often only as the result of protracted U.S.-Japan negotiations. In addition, no one knows the extent to which vested interests, entrenched business practices, or long-term business relationships will give way to more impersonal Internet transactions. *Keiretsu* (both vertical and horizontal), personal relationship–based business ties, reliance on traditional bank finance, and other aspects of the system *could* be swept away by a new paradigm based on information technology (IT). However, adherence to current institutions and practices could equally delay or weaken the impact of the IT revolution so that the economy does not reap its full potential benefits. Japanese society has been quite adaptable to previous waves of technology, suggesting it will do well in responding to the possibilities of this one. Nonetheless, the challenges posed to existing economic patterns are sizable, and progress may well be slower than desirable. Thus the potential positive impact of the IT revolution on pulling the economy out of the malaise of the past decade remains uncertain.

The pessimistic downside scenario is also less likely than the central conclusion of an underperforming economy, but the probability of economic disaster is certainly greater than zero and should be considered more likely than the optimistic scenario. Failure to clean out the existing problems—bad debt in the banking sector, excess manufacturing capacity, underfunded pension plans, and bankrupt corporations—could result in a more severe economic downturn in the future. A system that continues to rely heavily on banking, has weak corporate governance, has a government still meddling with market outcomes, and remains burdened with existing debt problems will be vulnerable to renewed recession or even a more severe economic crisis. Actors in the economic system may be sufficiently chastened by recent problems to behave more responsibly for a time. However, the nontransparent nature of much of the system, coupled with losses resulting from the problems of the 1990s, could lead to irresponsible behavior—essentially gambling on risky schemes to earn enough to overcome past losses. The probability is great that the government will make poor decisions, pushing industrial policy plans that are inappropriate for a mature economy, while propping up agriculture, construction, and other inefficient sectors.

Meanwhile, over the next decade, demography creates its own problems, with a shrinking and aging population leading toward a social security and pension fund crisis. A poorly performing economy will not be in good shape to cope with this looming problem. Demography could also exacerbate opposition to systemic change and sap corporate vitality. Young people adept at the new information technologies and less wedded to the existing economic system are a rapidly shrinking group of the population. The absolute number of people in the twenty to twenty-four-year-old age cohort will shrink an astounding 35 percent over the next twenty years.[4] Society in general, and decisions about economic reform in particular, will be dominated by older people who are inherently more conservative about change and who have stronger vested interests in the current system. Starved for bright young employees, especially as they use attrition to downsize, corporations may stumble in responding to new technologies. A slow response to the new business models embodied in the information technology revolution could leave most Japanese firms out in the cold as global business restructures, causing further erosion of their global market shares in industries ranging from steel and semiconductors to finance and hotel management.

Demographic change also implies that real estate prices will continue to fall as the number of households needing housing begins to shrink. If firms face eroding market shares, and real estate slips further in value, banks could face renewed problems from losses on nonperforming loans. Interest rates lowered to cope with economic weakness could expand the dilemma of underfunded pension funds. Eruption of another round of bad debts and unfunded pension obligations in an environment of a shrinking, aging population, and weakened corporations could result in a devastating downturn in the economy. With its debt already at 130 percent of gross domestic product (GDP) by the end of 2000, the government will face some difficulty over the next decade in expanding the deficit to cope with recession.

A severe downturn in the Japanese economy would have negative implications for the U.S. economy. The direct trade impact would be relatively small. Japan is the third largest export market for the United States (after Canada and Mexico), but it absorbs only about 9 percent of American exports.[5] Overall, therefore, a major contraction in Japan's GDP and imports would have only a small direct effect on American exports. Similarly, economic contraction would make Japan a less desirable location for direct investment, but Japan is the location of only 4 percent of American foreign direct investment.[6] The more serious possibility is disruption of international capital markets. Some Japanese investors might have to repatriate their investments to meet debts at home. Meanwhile, deterioration of the domestic economy could cause other investors to send their money abroad, producing capital flight. Even if these offsetting tendencies both prove correct, the result could be gyrations in international financial markets, because the sums are large. At the end of fiscal year 1999, Japanese investors held ¥308 trillion ($2.7 trillion) in overseas assets.[7] Therefore, substantial shifts in this large stock of investments one way or the other could have a disruptive effect on global financial markets.

At the margin, the dark downside scenario seems somewhat more probable than the optimistic scenario of resurgence. Neither is more likely than the middle prediction of "muddling through" with less growth than possible while avoiding disaster. One can think of this outcome as the *o-mikoshi* view of the economy. Local Shinto festivals often involve carrying a portable shrine, called an *o-mikoshi*, through the streets of the neighborhood, on the shoulders of a couple dozen or more people. With employees of neighborhood shops in a suitably lubricated condition taking turns with the carrying, the heavy shrine tends to lurch somewhat drunkenly from side to side of the street, threatening to go crashing through the bystanders or streetside windows and doors. Miraculously, this never seems to happen, with the procession veering off in a safe direction at the very last second. With a long tradition of pragmatism, Japanese society should slide through its economic troubles like the local *o-mikoshi* procession, responding to crisis with new policies that prevent the economy's descent into a true depression at the very last minute before disaster.

What happens to the Japanese economy is of primary interest to the Japanese themselves. Employment and unemployment, rising or stagnant income levels, wealth and poverty, are outcomes that affect all Japanese deeply. What happens in the Japanese economy also affects both Japanese and American foreign policy.

Implications for Bilateral Economic Relations

The most obvious conclusion for American economic policy toward Japan is that planning should proceed on the assumption of only modest Japanese reform and continued disappointing economic performance.

While the U.S. government can hope to nudge Japan in a more favorable direction, as discussed below, the starting point should be to recognize that the most likely outcome is continued weakness, and to be prepared to cope with the economic problems that will arise. Japan will not be an engine of growth for Asia or the world. Weak domestic performance is likely to lead to continued low domestic interest rates and net capital outflows from Japan to the rest of the world. A defensive government will continue to fight a determined delaying action on dismantling trade barriers. Moreover, recurring financial problems or crises are likely to punctuate the next decade. The U.S. Treasury Department, for example, needs to monitor closely developments in Japan to be prepared for recurring financial crises and the possible impact of such crises on American or global capital markets.

While the U.S. government will face some policy challenges in coping with this outcome, ironically the American corporate sector will encounter new opportunities. From the standpoint of American financial institutions, for example, the problems of their Japanese counterparts offer business opportunities. American institutions have been very active advancing into Japan (including some highly visible acquisitions that would have been impossible just a few years ago) and displacing Japanese institutions in international markets. This newfound opportunity has blunted an area of past negotiation and frustration for the U.S. government. As of 2000 foreign financial institutions appear to be relatively satisfied with the conditions of market entry and participation in Japan, and their technical skills—in portfolio management, handling stock and bond offerings, and in mergers and acquisitions—should give them a competitive advantage in the context of the "big bang" financial sector reforms. The same has been true to some extent in the nonfinancial sector, with new investment opportunities arising in the auto sector and elsewhere as a result of the extreme distress of some Japanese corporations.

These business opportunities are more than just a benefit for foreign firms. Japan benefits from the introduction of foreign technology and the pressure that foreign firms mount on regulatory issues once they are ensconced inside the Japanese economy. The overall impact of these foreign influences should not be exaggerated; even in finance the importance of foreign financial institutions in the total flow of funds within the economy is small. At least at the margin, however, they have a positive effect in moving the economy in the direction of less regulation and greater reliance on markets.

However, the central prediction of only modest systemic reform implies that foreign financial institutions and nonfinancial corporations could easily bump up against new problems or frustrations in the next several years. Having sold a handful of visibly large institutions to foreign owners, the window of opportunity for acquisitions may be closing. Foreign institutions may well discover that reform does not extend as far as they hoped in permitting them to operate on the basis of their comparative advantage.

Even with the silver lining of increased opportunities for foreign firms, therefore, clearly American interests lie with more robust reform efforts and a return of the economy to a higher rate of economic growth. If systemic reform were to proceed with vigor, the implications for Japan's economic relations with the outside world, and the United States in particular, would be quite positive. A reform process that underwrites a healthy growing economy produces an outcome that sucks in more imports and more inward direct investment—including from American-owned firms. Foreign firms in Japan account for somewhere between 2.4 and 6 percent of total domestic corporate sales, while foreign firms in the United States account for 12.4 percent of sales. If foreign firms' presence in Japan expanded to equal that U.S. level, the total value of cumulative American direct investment in Japan could expand from its 1997 level of $36 billion to anywhere from $75 billion to $186 billion.[8] Thus a growing Japan contributes to global economic opportunities and growth, even if modestly. Because a growing Japan is beneficial to both American and global economic interests, the U.S. government has pressed the Japanese government on both its macroeconomic policy stance and systemic reform over the past decade.

What can the U.S. government do that would help invigorate reform? Should the United States have an active agenda of pressing Japan on systemic economic reforms—supplying *gaiatsu* to encourage a faster or more thorough pace of change? Yes. The U.S. government should focus on an agenda that concentrates primarily on trade issues (that is, regulatory or reform issues that have a direct bearing on the ability of American firms to compete in Japan) and maintain a low-key dialogue on broader economic reform. This answer, however, comes with cautions and limitations.

First, the United States lacks the kind of leverage with Japan that characterized International Monetary Fund (IMF) pressure on other Asian countries in the wake of the 1997 financial crisis. Those countries were dependent on foreign investment funds and were in imminent danger of running out of foreign exchange to service those debts. Japan, on the other hand, is the world's largest net creditor. Therefore, the U.S. government has no major economic pressure point to use to bring about compliance with policy requests. If there is any leverage at all, it is much more subtle. Should Japan fail to reform, then Japanese firms could fall farther behind in global competition, especially in financial markets. If the Japanese government does not want that longer-term outcome, then it behooves the government to listen to outside advice. The Japanese government does appear to be somewhat concerned about Japanese firms' falling behind their key global competitors in areas such as finance or electronics, but the extent to which that concern motivates the government to be receptive to outside advice or pressure for change is mixed.

Second, pressing Japan for reform certainly fits a long tradition of American *gaiatsu* toward Japan, but the exercise of this pressure easily creates an image of American arrogance (especially if clumsily done) and creates resentment among those in Japan against whom it is directed. Aficionados of *gaiatsu* argue that it can work when the U.S. government cultivates domestic groups in Japan that support the American position. If they work together, building on preexisting pressures for change, this approach can succeed.[9] However, even when the process has some support among Japanese groups, the media can easily portray the process as one in which the Americans are exerting unfair, overbearing pressure. This is especially true on many of the issues involved in systemic economic reform, which concern domestic issues that are not normally part of international negotiation. As discussed in chapter 5, many interest groups are likely to react in this negative manner; for every group favoring change in Japan, another is opposed to it. Even an American administration that tries to finesse the tactics of *gaiatsu*, therefore, could easily find itself stuck in a game of mounting tension and unfavorable media attention in Japan. Furthermore, the era of *gaiatsu* may be drawing to a close as a younger generation of Japanese officials and politicians—people who did not experience defeat and occupation and who harbor a more negative attitude toward American pressure—moves into positions of importance.

There is no harm in pursuing a low-key dialogue with the Japanese government on system economic reform, but the above cautions imply that this strategy will not yield large dividends. Without leverage, American advice or pressure must rely on piggy-backing on existing Japanese willingness to pursue change. Given the opposition on many aspects of reform, the low-key and coalition-building approach will stall, and most American officials will balk at returning the level of tension and negative media attention to the level that prevailed in 1993–95.

In addition, applying bilateral pressure on Japan on some of the reform issues involved takes the U.S. government onto troubling political ground.

Many Japanese will wonder what right the United States has to press Japan on issues such as the functioning of labor markets, the details of corporate governance, or regulation of real estate markets. Japan is, after all, a large and proud sovereign nation, and being told by another government that various features of its domestic economic system must be changed understandably creates resentment. Therefore, finding mechanisms for delivering the reform message other than through bilateral government-to-government talks or negotiations would be helpful.

In some cases, tension over pressing Japan for reform might be ameliorated by moving some of these issues to a multilateral forum—using either the World Trade Organization (WTO) or private-sector groups to push concepts such as best-practice in corporate governance or transparent accounting standards. The notion of global standards has been popular in Japan in the past several years, so government or private-sector dialogues that focus on producing such standards would at least get rhetorical support in Japan. Again, there is no harm in pursuing these options, though whether such broad initiatives succeed or whether American interests would want to participate (if American standards exceed those of most other nations, as is the case in accounting) is uncertain. Whether creation and acceptance of theoretical standards would actually yield altered behavior will depend not on multilateral discussion but on a domestic decision by Japanese government and business.

This message of a low-key approach on systemic reform issues needs one caveat. In times of impending economic crisis a stronger, less diplomatic *gaiatsu* approach will be necessary, from which U.S. officials should not shy away. As was the case in 1998, when the banking sector was sliding toward mass insolvency with no credible government rescue, the U.S. government needs to apply swift and open pressure to drive the government to better policies. The international consequences of serious economic collapse are sufficiently serious for the United States and other nations to warrant a less diplomatic approach.

Some reform issues are closely linked to traditional trade issues. Foreign firms often feel that their ability to compete in Japan is constrained by domestic regulations. Financial market regulations and telephone interconnection fees are examples of regulations that put foreign firms at a disadvantage, but that also relate to the broader question of moving Japan toward greater reliance on markets. In many cases, trade issues involve problems of the disparity between Japanese government commitments in previous bilateral or multilateral trade negotiations and actual behavior in the market, with unexpected regulatory barriers cropping up that negate presumed benefits from lowering trade barriers. Therefore, the U.S. government should continue to pursue an active trade policy toward Japan that continues to chip away at those regulations that have a direct effect on American firms.

Among the trade issues that are worth pursuing are those that have larger implications for further reform. The financial sector is an obvious example. A larger presence of foreign financial institutions brings competitive pressures to bear that force Japanese counterparts to adapt. In addition, if vigorous reform and changes in financial market behavior were to lessen the role of banks and increase the role of security markets, it could have a positive effect on the corporate governance of nonfinancial firms. That tantalizing prospect makes financial sector trade issues worth pursuing, even if the probability of major success in generating this favorable outcome is modest. A similar argument could be made for negotiations concerning direct investment—regulatory changes that encourage further foreign direct investment into Japan. In all areas, not just finance, a more favorable market for inward foreign direct investment could enhance the role of foreign firms in the economy, thereby enlarging their competitive pressures on domestic firms and enhancing their voice in pressing for further reform with the Japanese government.

The American government approach to Japan, therefore, comprises three elements: an underlying acceptance of the high probability of a very incomplete reform process, probably having a negative effect on economic performance; an active trade agenda, focusing on issues of broader significance for reforming the economy; and a quiet dialogue on other reform issues. Ultimately, systemic reform of the economy must emerge from a domestic debate in Japan, and American influence will come only at the edge of that debate despite the long tradition of *gaiatsu* in Japanese policymaking (and perhaps because that tradition is now fading). The main message here, therefore, is one of modest expectations. The U.S. government has some opportunities to influence outcomes at the margin, and American firms have some opportunity to bring new ideas and technology, but reform will be governed mainly by domestic Japanese interests, and the outcome is likely to be disappointing.

Diplomatic-Political Relations

During the 1980s the continued superior performance of the Japanese economy lent a new sense of self-confidence to Japanese policy elites, who enunciated a determination to play more of a leadership role in regional and global affairs. The U.S. government welcomed this trend, using words like "partnership" in bilateral summit statements and endorsing Japan's bid for a permanent seat on the UN Security Council. Having spent the postwar period up to that point keeping a very low profile in international discussions or debates, this potential change fit with American foreign policy goals, even if it implied that the government did not always conveniently support U.S. positions.[10]

Much of the self-confidence that provided a platform to contemplate a more active participation in global affairs has now evaporated. The economy has performed poorly, and the distinctive economic model that government leaders took such pride in advertising to others around the world has been tarnished. Some developing countries had been attracted by both the success and the strong government role of the "Japanese model," but that attraction has cooled in the past several years. This sobering experience and the probability of only moderate reform of the model holds several implications for Japanese government involvement in global affairs.

First, Japan's role in global trade negotiations will continue to be an area of concern. For at least the past two decades, American officials have wished that Japan would play a more positive role in multilateral trade negotiations. The ambivalent and modest movement on reform will leave Japan in a defensive and obstructionist role in the multilateral setting. The very notion of moderating the pace of change at home, even if reforms do proceed in the desired direction, leaves the government in opposition to more radical changes toward open trade and investment. Japanese industries, and the government behind them, will continue to worry that aggressive foreign firms want to exploit changes in access faster and farther than the domestic consensus will tolerate. The fact that the Japanese government behaved in a largely obstructionist manner in 1999 during the aborted effort to begin a new round of WTO negotiations should not be a surprise. Progress in multilateral negotiations is certainly possible, but within the same framework as in the past—with difficult negotiations on matters related to Japan in which grudging concessions are made only after prolonged and frustrating negotiations.

Second, Japan and the United States will continue to have differing attitudes toward global macroeconomic and financial issues. For the past decade and a half, U.S. government leaders have spoken of a bilateral partnership on major global economic issues and have cajoled the Japanese government to play a larger leadership role in global affairs. The Japanese government is more vocal in international settings than it used to be, but often the voice is one that favors controls and other forms of government intervention in markets, putting it considerably at odds with American policy positions. Rather than joining in a multilateral move toward reinforcing a rules-based system for more open global financial markets, for example, the Japanese government has sided with those who favor capital controls and slow integration of developing countries into global finance—a choice that reflects the reluctance to embrace true reform at home. When the Japanese government proposed an Asian monetary fund in 1997, the underlying rationale had much to do with assisting Asian economies to resist IMF pressures to reform their economies. Having lost that international policy battle, the Japanese government then nominated recently "retired" vice minister for international monetary affairs Eisuke Sakakibara to replace Michel Camdessus as executive director at the IMF. Sakakibara is well known for his distrust of markets; he was one of the principal spokesmen for the "Japanese model" in the 1980s and even in 2000 was writing that the curtain was coming down on what he termed "market fundamentalism."[11] U.S. policymakers must recognize that these rather fundamental policy differences will continue; Japan is not fully embracing markets at home and will work against American policy initiatives in this direction at the IMF and in other multilateral settings.

Third, domestic economic problems—macroeconomic, structural, and systemic—imply that the government will have fewer funds to throw at international issues. Over the next decade, in response to the current large fiscal deficits, the high and rising level of cumulative government debt, and the coming rapid decline in the social security fund, the government will face a much more serious need to reduce its discretionary government deficit. Having used fiscal stimulus to pump up the economy, the government will be increasingly reluctant to continue increases in spending, especially since raising taxes as part of a strategy to reduce the government deficit will be unpopular politically.

In this more severe fiscal environment, international contributions will not be exempt from budget cuts. The situation was different during the 1970s and 1980s as Japan rapidly expanded its contributions to the United Nations, World Bank, International Monetary Fund, other multilateral institutions, and its own bilateral foreign aid. Now, however, the volume of foreign aid and financial support for crises such as East Timor or the Gulf War may diminish. In the wake of the Asian financial crisis, the government created a $30 billion package of loans and guarantees to assist Asian countries, but much of that money appears to have been more relevant to bailing out Japanese financial institutions that had nonperforming loans in Asian countries.

Japan will certainly remain an important financial contributor to multi-national institutions, but the government's reputation for "checkbook diplomacy" will fade, as international goodwill must compete against domestic spending programs in this more constrained fiscal environment. Weak reform and poor economic performance could also alter the public perception of foreign aid and other international spending. In the past the public appeared to accept foreign aid as an obligation and symbol of advanced-nation status. In a less vibrant economic context the public may wonder why the government is spending money to help other nations when there are problems to solve at home.

Fourth, domestic considerations will play a larger role in shaping international policy stances. After a decade of criticism of the narrow commercial aims of its foreign aid program in the 1980s, the Japanese government had moved toward less de facto tied aid and a more genuine interest in supporting projects (such as coral reef protection) that had no direct commercial benefit to Japanese industry. Now economic problems at home are tipping the balance back in the other direction. One example is the call for promoting foreign aid projects to help the domestic manufacturers of heavy electrical equipment to sell more to electric power generating plants being built in developing countries (discussed in chapter 6). Another example is the Ministry of Agriculture's call for using food aid as a carrot to obtain support from developing countries for Japan's protectionist stance on agricultural trade barriers in the WTO. This trend is likely to continue. To be sure, all nations act out of self-interest, but those facing serious economic problems at home are more likely to skew their international policies toward benefiting domestic economic interests.

Fewer financial resources and a more economically self-interested approach to foreign policy do not mean that the Japanese government will retreat from regional or global discussion of international problems. The generation of officials and politicians who experienced war, defeat, and occupation and thereby chose a very low profile in international affairs in the shadow of the United States is fading from the scene. The current and future generations are less reticent about speaking up and pushing their own policy agenda, at least on economic issues. It is unfortunate that they are rising to positions of importance at a time when the economy has performed poorly and the reform process has not proceeded very far. Their sense of national pride will lead them to continue to advocate a "Japanese" or "Asian" economic model, at least among Asian nations, as a reaction to American economic triumphalism even though Japanese performance has been disappointing. They may have fewer financial resources to throw at promoting their positions, but their ideas or policy initiatives in an international setting will resonate with some to the discomfiture of American officials.

In these ways, the lack of economic reform and the resulting poor economic performance of the Japanese economy will create challenges and problems for American international economic and diplomatic policy. Had reform moved forward more vigorously, Japan would have more common interests with the United States and would be in a position to contribute more generously to international problems. However, the lack of real reform and the disappointing economic performance will make Japan a less generous partner with a continued determination to push alternatives to the American creed of free markets.

Security

What might happen to security policy as a consequence of "muddling through" on systemic reform is the most difficult area to predict. American policy toward Japan over the past two decades has emphasized getting Japan to play a larger role in the bilateral security alliance. As the anguish over the nation's disastrous experience with militarism faded, Japan has done more, increasing defense expenditures and participating in a tentative manner in UN peacekeeping operations. However, the economic environment now presents problems for further changes in Japan's security role.

The most likely outcome is simply that Japan will continue to be a minor player in global security affairs despite its increasing assertiveness on international economic issues. With its own economy performing poorly, and self-absorbed in managing even modest reform, the policy elite will not be focusing on resolving the security problems of the world. Only those security issues on the nation's doorstep—the Korean peninsula and China—will generate much real attention, and even here the tendency will be to play only a minor role as the major nations dominate the action and decision-making. Many issues (such as turmoil in the Middle East) seem more remote to Japanese interests than international economic issues. Exchange rate regimes, IMF policy toward developing countries in Asia, or agriculture negotiations in the WTO matter directly to Japanese economic interests, but whether nations in the Middle East can get along peacefully with one another does not, as long as Japan can obtain oil. Not feeling as strong a sense of direct interest in these issues, the Japanese government is less likely to have strong policy views (other than a desire for uninvolvement), leaving it on the fringe of policy discussions among major powers.

Coming budget constraints also affect Japan's security role. In the more severe fiscal environment described above, defense spending could fare poorly. With the government loath to reduce spending on industrial policy objectives, expenditures for defense could become increasingly vulnerable. Defense spending has long had an industrial policy element to it, with defense contracting used to promote the growth and technological advance of the aerospace industry. More broadly, the defense budget may be difficult to defend against budget items of more direct impact on the economy. As with general foreign policy, the public, politicians, and bureaucrats may question the value of spending money on defense or sending peacekeeping forces abroad rather than on education, healthcare, or public works at home.

Within overall defense spending, support for American bases in Japan could be especially vulnerable. The debate that began in 2000 over base support will be only the beginning of a prolonged discussion over the budget allocation dilemma. With constrained fiscal resources, do Japanese politicians and bureaucrats desire to spend the money supporting U.S. bases (even though most of the money actually flows to Japanese contractors and workers) or directly on Japan's Self Defense Forces? The answer to this question should be obvious, so there will be a struggle between the sense of obligation to be supportive of the Americans in the context of the bilateral security treaty and the natural desire to spend the money on Japan's own forces.

One can imagine a darker scenario. In the "muddle through" scenario of mild systemic reform, both the policy elite and the public could feel quite frustrated with the nation's performance. The sense of national direction, which was so clear during the century of "catching up" with the West, is lost. Meanwhile, a sense of envy, resentment, and inferiority relative to the United States, Europe, or even China could well build up. In this environment, defense policies could turn far more nationalistic. During the late 1980s Japanese enthusiasm about the economic superiority of their nation compensated in part for the long-standing sense of inferiority on defense matters. With that enthusiasm gone, those who advocate being a "normal" nation with a larger and more independent military capability could find a stronger voice within Japanese politics, if troubling developments in the Asian region were to provide a rationale for a stronger defense policy. The Japanese government could go much further than simply reducing financial support for American bases by ending the local basing of U.S. military forces altogether, as the Philippine government did in the 1980s. The constitution could be revised in a manner that declares the unilateral right to maintain and use military force. The fact that this route would be detrimental to Japan's security needs is immaterial; this scenario is predicated on simple nationalism to restore a sense of importance in the world, given the inability to declare superiority on the economic front.

Within this scenario, the fiscal constraint issue could possibly be turned on its head. Recognizing public displeasure over corruption and inefficiency of public works spending, but fearing the employment consequences of sharply reducing such make-work spending, the government could turn to a military spending build-up as an alternative to public works. Military spending would be sold as enhancing national security (in the face of an unreliable American ally), thereby providing a public good, versus the public harm of corrupt civilian public works spending. This darker scenario is not a likely outcome, but it cannot be entirely ignored as a possibility.

These two scenarios are quite different, and which one materializes will depend a great deal on the nature of security issues that arise and how the United States responds to them. Crises geographically remote from Japan reinforce the probability that Japan will remain a minor player. A crisis close to Japan, in which the Japanese feel that the United States has behaved in a manner detrimental to their interests, though, would encourage the nation to slide in the direction of loosening the bonds of the bilateral security relationship and strengthening its independent military capabilities.

American policy has emphasized a slow and steady approach toward increasing the role of the Japanese military within the context of the bilateral security treaty, while maintaining U.S. bases and troop levels within Japan. That strategy will be difficult to achieve—either the Japanese will fail to step up to American expectations, or they will bristle at being tied to an ally they do not trust. At best the U.S. government will have to cajole Japan into supporting American security initiatives around the world and face continued disputes over host-nation financial support for the bases. At worst, the alliance will unravel because of a more independent-minded, nationalistic Japanese government. The time has come to give serious thought to more fundamental changes before they occur in a less controlled manner. Acceptance of less financial support for the bases and a reduction of U.S. troop presence or closure of some bases could be an acceptable bilateral outcome—acceptable to both revised U.S. strategic thinking and the Japanese economic and political environment.

Conclusion

A decade ago the Japanese economy was flying high, generating 5 percent growth that was the envy of the rest of the advanced economies. Producing that enviable growth was an economic system that differed in a number of important ways from others, with less reliance on open markets for goods, services, and finance than was the case in the United States and less government ownership or public welfare than in Europe. Rising from the ashes of the Second World War to become one of the most affluent nations of the world and then continuing to grow faster than other advanced economies gave the Japanese much to be proud of. The distinctive economic system also gave them a ready explanation for their success. They told developing countries to emulate the Japanese model. They looked at the higher unemployment, "rust-belt" distress, and proclivity for violent crime as symbols of the failure of the American reliance on a less constrained capitalism.

Today those views have been severely shaken. Collapse of the stock market and real estate bubbles that artificially pumped up economic performance in the late 1980s resulted in a decade of near stagnation. A plethora of scandals involving politicians, businessmen, and even the supposedly selfless bureaucrats undermined faith in the existing system. Since the ascendancy of Prime Minister Morihiro Hosokawa in 1993, reform has been in the air. Deregulation, government administrative reform, and corporate restructuring have all been key domestic policy issues. Prime Minister Hosokawa and his political coalition lasted less than one year, but the LDP-led coalitions that have followed have continued the reform theme.

On the surface, reform appears to be proceeding. Deregulation has introduced competition into domestic airline fares and retail gasoline pricing. Administrative reform led to a major reorganization of government ministries. Corporate restructuring has brought needed downsizing, a wave of mergers and acquisitions, and pledges to improve profitability. The stasis of the 1980s, when reform should have been under way but was not, appears to have been broken.

But is it? The central message of this study is that the factors inhibiting or slowing reform remain formidable. The outcomes, while positive, are decidedly modest. The existing system did have a number of features that seemed desirable or superior to American practices, leading to uneasiness about discarding them. These features were part of an interlocking whole, making change more difficult. Support for reform was further tempered by the mild nature of the economic downturn of the 1990s; an average 1 percent growth meant that people were better off at the end of the decade than at the beginning. That mild stagnation meant that the many segments of society with a vested interest in the existing system could feel that their interests were still valuable and should not be carelessly abandoned in hopes of a better performance. Finally, the compatibility of the existing system with broader social norms complicated reforms and would have to be factored into whatever new system would emerge.

The outcome has been a halting, mild course of economic reform with some pockets of greater success. By and large, this arthritis patient is still relying on aspirin for the pain while avoiding the painful but beneficial hip replacement. The big unknown is whether this meager amount of reform will be sufficient to underwrite a healthy resumption of growth or will leave the economy vulnerable to renewed recession and financial crisis. This study concludes that a "muddle through" scenario, in which the economy manages to avoid disaster but fails to reach its potential, is the most likely. Like Great Britain after the 1890s, the economy could go on for decades of disappointing growth.

In 2000 talk abounded of a Japanese economic recovery built on corporate restructuring, emergence of a high-growth information technology sector, and several years of government fiscal pump priming. After scattered quarters of negative growth in 1997–98 and two more in the second half of 1999, the first two quarters of 2000 were positive. Nevertheless, conviction that recovery was finally under way subsided again when the third quarter turned negative, and forecasts for 2001 were revised downward. By the spring of 2001 the situation had worsened further, with the economy headed back into recession. The economy may well recover to a positive growth path by 2002, but the "muddle through" reform scenario will leave the economy underperforming and susceptible to periodic financial crises and serious recessions.

The broader political and security implications of an underperforming Japan are not encouraging. Despite a gradual trend toward greater participation and assertiveness by the Japanese government in international economic issues, the poor performance of the economy and the inability to transform the economy could lead to constraints on fiscal resources to finance Japan's involvement in global affairs and continuation or exacerbation of a narrowly defined economic self-interest.

These problems will affect the government's participation in regional and global trade negotiations, diplomatic, and security affairs. At the extreme, continued muddled reform at home could lead to a harsher nationalism.

Coping with these possibilities will present challenges for American policymakers. First they must recognize the reality of incomplete reform and the high probability of weak economic growth combined with recurring financial crises. Tools available to the U.S. government to push Japan toward better outcomes are limited since Japan is a major creditor nation. Officials can push trade issues and engage in quiet dialogue on other reform issues, but the outcomes will be modest. Stronger *gaiatsu* is possible, but its effectiveness may be fading even when some domestic Japanese groups have similar policy goals, and intruding into some reform areas would leave the U.S. susceptible to criticism for unjustifiable domestic intrusion.

Security and diplomatic issues will also be a challenge. Japan is not moving smoothly into a global partnership with the United States. The goal of enhancing Japan's security role within the context of the bilateral security treaty is laudable. Nevertheless, difficulties will arise either from the domestic battle over fiscal support for security rather than other budget items or from a sharper nationalism that chafes at perceptions of being locked into a confining relationship with the United States. The worse Japan's economic performance, the more severe these problems will be.

All of these conclusions could be wrong. Japan has been a surprising country, confounding foreign views of its possibilities since it opened up to foreign trade almost 150 years ago. If reform is more vigorous and provides a more favorable setting for new industries to advance and old ones to become more efficient, then a decade of strong growth similar to that of the United States in the past decade is possible. If this were to occur, the policy implications would be quite different. Economic relations would be easier and markets for foreign firms more open. Evolution of the security relationship toward more active and full participation by the Japanese would be a more viable possibility. A more confident Japanese government would also play a more productive role in overall regional and global economic affairs. One can hope for the best, but the bottom line of this study is: do not hold your breath waiting for this outcome, and do not be disappointed if reform stumbles and the economy sputters.

Notes

Chapter One

1. Paul Gigot, "The Great Japan Debate Is Over. Guess Who Won?" *Wall Street Journal*, January 31, 1997, p. A18.

2. Keizo Obuchi, "Japan's Quiet Reforms," *New York Times*, April 29, 1999, p. A29.

3. See the diametrically opposed viewpoints paired in *Foreign Affairs*. Representing the optimistic view is M. Diana Helweg, "Japan: A Rising Sun?" Representing the pessimistic view, of little change, is Aurelia George Mulgan, "Japan: A Setting Sun?" *Foreign Affairs*, vol. 79, July/August 2000, pp. 26–52.

4. For a comprehensive survey of the intellectual and policy trends that have reduced the economic role of government, see the study by Daniel Yergin and Joseph Stanislaw, *The Commanding Heights: The Battle between Government and the Marketplace That Is Remaking the Modern World* (Simon and Schuster, 1998).

5. Japan Economic and Social Research Institute, www.esri.go.jp/en/sna/qe004/gde-menue.html [May 3, 2001], "Figures in Each Component Annual Figures."

6. "Furanchyaizu no Mirai" [The Future of Franchising], *Nikkei Bijinesu*, issue 992, May 24, 1999, p. 23.

7. Statistics Bureau, *Japan Statistical Yearbook 1998*, p. 388, www.stat.go.jp/english/1431-10.htm, table 10-22 [March 3,2001]; "Japan's Cell Phones Surge, Top 60 Million in July," *Reuters*, August 8, 2000.

Chapter Two

1. Bai Gao, "Arisawa Hiromi and His Theory for a Managed Economy," *Journal of Japanese Studies*, vol. 20 (Winter 1994), pp. 115–53.

2. For an elegant presentation of one economic model of the game played between regulators and the regulated, see Klaus Wallner, "Implicit Contracts between Regulator and Firms: The Case of Japanese Casualty Insurance," Columbia University, May 1997.

3. Bank of Japan, *Economic Statistics Annual 1997*, pp. 55, 347.

4. For the definitive study of the *zaibatsu*, their breakup in the Occupation, and reassembly into the postwar *keiretsu*, see Eleanor Hadley, *Antitrust In Japan* (Princeton University Press, 1970).

5. Richard E. Cares, "Industrial Organization," in Hugh Patrick and Henry Rosovsky, eds., *Asia's New Giant: How the Japanese Economy Works* (Brookings, 1976), pp. 502–03.

6. For an excellent, detailed exposition of the *keiretsu* and the reasons for their existence, see Michael L. Gerlach, *Alliance Capitalism: The Social Organization of Japanese Business* (University of California Press, 1992), esp. pp. 1–38, 246–62.

7. For a more technical theoretical discussion of some of these aspects of Japanese corporate governance, see Masahiko Aoki, *Information, Incentives, and Bargaining in the Japanese Economy* (Cambridge University Press, 1988), especially pp. 99–149. Aoki, however, believes shareholders have a larger role than is portrayed here.

8. Toyo Keizai, *Kigyō Keiretsu Sōran '99* (Tokyo: Toyo Keizai Shimposha, 1999), p. 393.

9. Mark J. Scher, *Japanese Interfirm Networks and Their Main Banks* (St. Martin's Press, 1997), especially pp. 55–73.

10. For examples of this genre, see Eisuka Sakakibara, *Beyond Capitalism: The Japanese Model of Market Economics* (Washington: Economic Strategy Institute, 1993); or Hajime Karatsu, *Tough Words for American Industry* (Cambridge, Mass.: Productivity Press, 1986).

11. This theory of the firm originated with an article by Ronald H. Coase, "The Nature of the Firm," *Economica*, vol. 4 (November 1937), pp. 386–405.

12. The theory of long-term contracting is generally associated with Oliver E. Williamson. See, for example, his *Markets and Hierarchies: Analysis and Antitrust Implications* (New York: Free Press, 1975); or his *The Economic Institutions of Capitalism: Firms, Markets, Relational Contracting* (Macmillan, 1985).

13. The following paragraphs on the benefits of vertical *keiretsu* draw on Michael J. Smitka, *Competitive Ties: Subcontracting in the Japanese Automotive Industry* (Columbia University Press, 1991), especially pp. 135–74; and Aoki, *Information Incentives and Bargaining in the Japanese Economy*, pp. 208–23.

14. See, for example, Ikko Shimizu, *Keiretsu*, trans. in Tamae K. Prindle, ed., *The Dark Side of Japanese Business: Three "Industry Novels"* (Armonk, N.Y.: M.E. Sharpe, 1996). This novel also became a popular drama serialized on television.

15. See David Halbertsam, *The Reckoning* (William Morrow and Co., 1986), pp. 716–17; Halberstam emphasizes the difference in American and Japanese parts purchasing systems and the strong positive effect of Japanese *keiretsu* on quality of finished automobiles.

16. Kōsei Torihiki Iinkai [Japan Fair Trade Commission], *Kōsei Torihiki Iinkai Nenji Hōkoku, Heisei 9-nenpan* [Annual Report of the Fair Trade Commission, 1997] (Tokyo,

1997), appendix, pp. 84–85.

17. Mark Tilton, *Restrained Trade: Cartels in Japan's Basic Materials Industries* (Cornell University Press, 1996).

18. Kōsei Torihiki Iinkai, *Kōsei torihiki Iinkai Nenji Hōkoku*, p. 239.

19. U.S. Department of Justice, *Compendium of Federal Justice Statistics, 1996* (November 1998); available at www.ojp.usdoj.gov/bjs/pub/pdf/cfjs96.pdf [March 8, 2001]), p. 42.

20. Federal Trade Commission, *Annual Report of the Federal Trade Commission for Fiscal Year Ended September 30, 1997*, www.ftc.gov/os/ar97/competition.htm, p. 7. The FTC initiated thirty-eight investigations, of which ten proceeded to full-phase investigative action. In three cases the FTC accepted consent agreements for public comment, and on three others it finalized consent agreements (after public comment).

21. Data generated by inquiry to the Judicial Statistical Inquiry Form, Federal District Court Civil Cases (teddy.law.cornell.edu:8090/questcv2.htm).

22. MITI, *Tsūshō Sangyōshō Meikan* [The Ministry of International Trade and Industry Directory] (Tokyo: Jihyosha, 1999), pp. 355–428.

23. See Ulrike Schaede, *Cooperative Capitalism: Self Regulation, Trade Associations, and the Antimonopoly Law* (Oxford University Press, 2000).

24. For a fuller discussion of price differences between Japan and other countries, see Edward J. Lincoln, *Troubled Times: U.S.-Japan Trade Relations in the 1990s* (Brookings, 1999), pp. 66–73.

25. Organization for Economic Cooperation and Development (OECD), *Main Economic Indicators* (Paris, 1999), pp. 21–22.

26. Industrial Policy Bureau, Ministry of International Trade and Industry, *Survey on Foreign and Domestic Price Differentials for Industrial Intermediate Input*, June 6, 1999, www.meti.go.jp/english/report/data/gIP9907e.html [March 9, 2001].

27. Kozo Yamamura, "Success That Soured: Administrative Guidance and Cartels in Japan," in Kozo Yamamura, ed., *Policy and Trade Issues of the Japanese Economy* (University of Washington Press, 1982), pp. 77–112.

28. See Takatoshi Ito, *The Japanese Economy* (MIT Press, 1992), pp. 209–58, for an excellent overview of lifetime employment and other features of Japanese labor markets.

29. Kazuo Koike, *The Economics of Work in Japan* (Tokyo: LTCB Library Foundation, 1995), p. 147.

30. Ito, *Japanese Economy*, p. 223. Ito gives an excellent exposition of the basic features of lifetime employment and how it compares with the U.S. practice, pp. 214–26.

31. On access to Japanese markets and how it has changed over time, see Edward J. Lincoln, *Japan's Unequal Trade* (Brookings, 1990), and *Troubled Times*.

32. For one analysis emphasizing the benefits of this form of intervention, see Chalmers Johnson, *Japan's Public Policy Corporations* (American Enterprise Institute, 1978).

33. Calculated from flow-of-funds data for fiscal year 1998; Bank of Japan, available at www.boj.or.jp/en/down/siryo/dsiryo99.htm, zip file flowpre.zip.

34. See, for example, Kent Calder, "Elites in an Equalizing Role: Ex-Bureaucrats as Coordinators and Intermediaries in the Japanese Government-Business Relationship,"

Comparative Politics, vol. 21 (July 1989), pp. 379–403; and Ulrike Schaede, "The 'Old Boy' Network and Government-Business Relationships in Japan," *Journal of Japanese Studies*, vol. 21 (Summer 1995), pp. 293–317.

35. Group 2001, "Kisei Kanwa to Iu Akumu" [The Nightmare of Deregulation], *Bungei Shunju*, vol. 72 (August 1994), pp. 134–46; and "Kisei Kanwa to Iu Akumu II" [The Nightmare of Deregulation, Part II], *Bungei Shunju*, vol. 72 (November 1994), pp. 318–30.

36. Eisuke Sakakibara, "Reforming Japan: The Once and Future Boom," *The Economist*, March 22, 1997, p. 89.

37. Eisuke Sakakibara, "Mr. Yen Looking Back / 'Cybercapitalism' World Needs Map," *Daily Yomiuri*, January 28, 2000, p. 6.

38. Tadao Suzuki, "Kisei Kanwa ga Anzen o Obiyakasu" [Deregulation Threatens Safety], *Nikkei Business*, September 18, 2000, p. 199. Suzuki is the CEO of Mercian Wine Company and serves as vice chair of Nikkeiren, an influential group of corporate presidents.

39. Takamatsu Sawa, "The Crystal Balls Grow Opaque," *Japan Times*, October 9, 2000, p. 14.

Chapter Three

1. For an analysis of the problems of the 1990s that relies on macroeconomic explanations, see Adam S. Posen, *Restoring Japan's Economic Growth* (Washington: Institute for International Economics, 1998).

2. See, for example, Aurelia George Mulgan, "Japan: A Setting Sun?" *Foreign Affairs*, vol. 79 (July/August 2000), pp. 40–52; Brian Woodall, *Japan under Construction: Corruption, Politics, and Public Works* (University of California Press, 1996); or Jacob M. Schlesinger, *Shadow Shogun: The Rise and Fall of Japan's Postwar Political Machine* (Simon and Schuster, 1997).

3. For a detailed discussion of the causes of the slowdown in the Japanese economy in the 1970s, see Edward J. Lincoln, *Japan: Facing Economic Maturity* (Brookings, 1988), pp. 14–68.

4. The U.S. growth rate in the 1974 to 1991 period is based on Organization for Economic Cooperation and Development, *Historical Statistics 1960–1987* (Paris, 1989), p. 44; and U.S. Census Bureau, *Statistical Abstract of the United States: 1997* (Government Printing Office, 1997), p. 449.

5. For an analysis of the macroeconomic problems of the 1996–98 period, see Edward J. Lincoln, "Japan's Financial Mess," *Foreign Affairs*, vol. 77, no. 3 (May/June 1998), pp. 57–66.

6. Ministry of Health, Labour and Welfare, "Final Report of Monthly Labour Survey," August 2000, www.mhlw.go.jp/english/database/db-1/1208fr/nk1208re.html [March 14, 2001]; and Japan Statistics Bureau and Statistics Center, Labor Force Survey, January 30, 2001, http://jin.jcic.or.jp/stat/stats/09LAB21.html.

7. "FSA Tally of All Shaky Loans, at ¥87.5 trillion, Is a Stunner," *Japan Digest*, July 10,

1998, p. 2. The "shaky" loans are so-called category two and three loans; the additional bad loan figure represents category four loans reported by the Federation of Bankers.

8. See Posen, *Restoring Japan's Economic Growth.*

9. See "The Weekly Post Special 3: TEP Obtain Confidential Document from Nomura Security Fraud Case," *Weekly Post*, July 14, 1997; or "Investigation Must Reveal VIP Accounts," *Weekly Post*, September 22, 1997. Because of the scandalous nature of this issue and the names of prominent bureaucrats and politicians who are presumably on the VIP lists, reporting has been left mainly to the sensationalist weekly magazines.

10. "Osaka Tea House Mistress Onoue Gets 12 Years for Her Extravagant Fraud," *Japan Digest*, March 3, 1998, pp. 1–2.

11. This was also true of the *jūsen*; "HLAC Plans to Sue Four Banks That Got *Jusen* to Make Risky Loans," *Japan Digest*, January 26, 1998, p. 1, notes, "The banks typically 'introduced' to the *jūsen* borrowers that the banks themselves couldn't touch, and in at least one case did so with clearly fraudulent intent."

12. "Prosecutors Charge 2 MOF Officials with Accepting Bribes," *Nikkei Net*, January 27, 1998. The amount, ¥5 million (roughly $40,000) in meals and golf outings over an unspecified amount of time, does not seem particularly high.

13. "Banks Took MOF Inspectors to Dutch Red Light District, Vegas Casinos," *Japan Digest*, January 30, 1998.

14. "Prosecutors Raid Finance Ministry Securities and Banking Bureaus," *Japan Digest*, March 9, 1998.

15. "BOJ Exec Allegedly Gave Bankers Advance Word on Money Market Operations," *Japan Digest*, March 9, 1998.

16. Japanese per capita GDP calculated from GDP and population tables in the electronic version of Japan Statistical Association, *Japan Statistical Yearbook 2000*; www.stat.go.jp/english/1431-02htm (this is the PDF version of table 2-1B, "Growth of Population, 1920–1998); and Social Research Institute, www.esri.go.jp/en/sna/qe004/gde-menue.htm [March 30, 2001], downloadable table, "The First Preliminary Estimates of National Expenditure Apr.-Jul. 2000" (September 11, 2000). The population table has data through 1999; 1999 population was estimated by adding the 1996–97 population growth (0.25 percent) to the 1998 population total.

17. www.oecd.org/publications/figures/2000/english/gross_domestic_product_1999.pdf [April 19, 2001].

18. Auto registration growth is calculated from data in Japan Automobile Manufacturers Association (JAMA), *Automobile Statistics of Japan 1998*; population data and household formation from data in Japan Statistical Association, *Japan Statistical Yearbook 1998*.

19. For an analysis of the shift in government priorities, see Lincoln, *Japan: Facing Economic Maturity*, pp. 47–52.

20. Steel consumption data are from the International Steel Institute (ISSI), www.worldsteel.org/trends_indicators/figures_21.html; GDP data at market and PPP exchange rates are from Organization for Economic Cooperation and Development,

OECD in Figures, www.oecd.org/publications/figures/2000/english/gross_domestic_product_1999.pdf [April 9, 2001].

21. U.S. Census Bureau, *Statistical Abstract of the United States: 1998*, p. 452 (for U.S. GDP); U.S Department of Commerce, *Survey of Current Business*, January 2000, pp. 39, 56; Japan Statistical Association, *Japan Statistical Yearbook 1998*, pp. 156–59.

22. Calculated from data from U.S. Census Bureau, Department of Commerce, *Economic Census 1997* CD-ROM database (gasoline stations are NAIC Industry 447); and Japan Statistical Association, *Japan Statistical Yearbook 1998*, p. 705; domestic supply of gasoline, *Japan Statistical Yearbook* online, table 7-14, "Production, Sales and Inventory of Petroleum Products," www.stat.go.jp/english/1431-07.htm—domestic supply of gasoline [May 3, 2001]. Ministry of International Trade and Industry, *Waga Kuni no Shōgyō-1988* (Tokyo: Tsūsan Tōkei Kyōkai, 1998), p. 118 (for employment per station); and "Japan Oil Distributors to Shrink Gas-Station Networks," Nikkei Net, June 3, 1998 (for 1998 figure on number of gas stations); *Statistical Abstract of the United States 1998*, p. 642 (for U.S. vehicle miles); *Japan Statistical Yearbook*, online version—www.stat.go.jp/english/1431-10.htm, downloadable table 10-5, "Motor Vehicles Owned by Kind" [May 3, 2001]. In 1997 the United States had 90,000 gas stations, and there were 2,360 billion vehicle miles. In 1998 Japan had 59,615 gas stations and produced 454 billion vehicle miles. Therefore, each U.S. gas station kept vehicles running 26 million miles, while in Japan only 7.6 million miles, 29 percent as much. This implies that each station pumped only 29 percent as much gasoline, making the generous assumption of equal miles per gallon for vehicles in each country (if Japan's smaller vehicles produce more miles per gallon, this would imply even less gasoline pumped per station in Japan relative to stations in the United States).

23. Richard J. Samuels, *The Business of the Japanese State: Energy Markets in Comparative and Historical Perspective* (Cornell University Press, 1987), p. 224.

24. Kyūyojo I-Manten Sakugen" [Cutting Gas Stations by Ten Thousand], *Nihon Keizai Shimbun*, June 3, 1998, p. 11.

25. Michael Zielenziger, "Japanese Are Pumped over Self-Service Gas," *San Jose Mercury News*, June 17, 1998.

26. For a recent analysis of this situation, see Mulgan, "Japan: A Setting Sun?" especially pp. 45–50.

27. Schlesinger, *Shadow Shogun*.

28. On the ratio of revenue sharing to total local government revenue, see Hiromitso Ishi, *The Japanese Tax System* (Oxford University Press, 1989), pp. 240, 242 (the ratio was 30 percent in 1987). Data for 1995 are from Ministry of Finance, *Zaisei Tōkei 1997* (Tokyo: Ministry of Finance Printing Office, 1997), p. 337; and Japan Statistical Association, *Japan Statistical Yearbook 1998*, p. 518. For holdings of local government bonds, see Bank of Japan flow-of-funds data, available at www.boj.or.jp/en/down/siryo/dsiryo00.htm, downloadable files, "Flow of Funds Accounts for the Fiscal Year 1998," file sj98fy.zip.

29. For example, a bid-rigging scandal in Hokkaido involved Diet representatives and Ministry of Agriculture officials. "Hokkaido Bares All on Bid Rigging," *Daily Yomiuri*, March 29, 2000, p. 2.

30. Norihiko Shirouzu, "Nissan's Revival Relies on Operating Chief's Agility," *Wall Street Journal*, October 18, 1999, p. A37.

31. Phred Dvorak, "The Trials of a Reformed Japanese Bank," *Wall Street Journal*, March 27, 2001, p. A14.

32. "MOF's Matsuno Reportedly Told Yamaichi to Hide Its Losses off the Books," *Japan Digest*, January 30, 1998, p. 2.

33. "Three Ex-Yamaichi Executives Arrested over Loss Cover-Up," Nikkei Net, March 5, 1998.

34. Amy Shiratori, "Ministry Penalizes Nomura, Dai-Ichi," *Asahi News*, July 31, 1997; "X-Yamaichi Chief Arrested," *Asahi News*, October 2, 1997; "Sokaiya Wrote to Store Chief," *Asahi News*, October 23, 1997; "Prosecutors Aim for Ex-Nikko Execs," *Asahi News*, October 30, 1997; "Daiwa Exec Approved Trading for Sokaiya, *Daily Yomiuri*, November 6, 1997; "Mitsubishi Estate, Hitachi Execs Are Arrested in Sokaiya Payoffs," *Japan Digest*, vol. 8 (November 26, 1997); and "Mitsubishi Hit by New Scandal," *Asahi News*, February 5, 1998.

35. For an excellent review of these theoretical developments and their application to the financial sector from the 1950s through the 1980, see Peter L. Bernstein, *Against the Gods: The Remarkable Story of Risk* (New York: John Wiley & Sons, 1996).

36. Mark Scher, *Japanese Interfirm Networks and Their Main Banks* (St. Martin's Press, 1997), pp. 55–101.

37. Eugene R. Dattel, *The Sun That Never Rose: The Inside Story of Japan's Failed Attempt at Global Financial Dominance* (Chicago: Probus, 1994).

38. Ibid.

Chapter Four

1. Mancur Olson, *The Rise and Decline of Nations: Economic Growth, Stagflation, and Social Rigidities* (Yale University Press, 1982).

2. For an analysis along these lines, see Richard Katz, *Japan: The System That Soured* (Armonk, N.Y.: M.E. Sharpe, 1998), pp. 165–234.

3. For an analysis of the change in attitudes and politics in Great Britain, see Daniel Yergin and Joseph Stanislaw, *The Commanding Heights: The Battle between Government and the Marketplace That Is Remaking the Modern World* (Simon and Schuster, 1998), pp. 92–124.

4. Japanese data are from Statistics Bureau, *Japan Statistical Yearbook 1998* (Tokyo, 1997), p. 570; U.S. data are from U.S. Census Bureau, *Statistical Abstract of the United States: 1998* (Government Printing Office, 1998), p. 464. Note that in both cases, food expenditures include restaurant meals.

5. Organization for Economic Cooperation and Development, *Agricultural Policies in OECD Countries* (Paris, 1999), pp. 19, 124, 166–68.

6. The correlations are calculated from data on population land area, construction sector employment, and public works contracts by prefecture in Statistics Bureau, *Japan Statistical Yearbook 1998*, pp. 17, 48, 184–85, 334.

7. Ibid., pp. 184–85. The nine prefectures are Niigata, Akita, Shimane, Iwate, Hokkaido, Fukushima, Yamagata, Aomori, and Oita.

8. Ministry of Agriculture, Forestry, and Fisheries, "Statistical Research on the Farm Economy Survey" (1998), www.maff.go.jp/esokuhou/kei199924.pdf [April 30, 2001].

9. U.S. Census Bureau, *Statistical Abstract of the United States 1997*, p. 439; and Statistics Bureau, *Japan Statistical Yearbook 1998*, p. 129.

10. The U.S. data on the share of employment in government are from U.S. Census Bureau, *Statistical Abstract of the United States: 1998*, p. 422.

11. Ibid., p. 421.

12. Bank of Japan, *Economic Statistics Annual 1977*, pp. 277–78.

13. Statistics Bureau, *Japan Statistical Yearbook 1998*, p. 332; U.S. Census Bureau, *Statistical Abstract of the United States: 1998*, p. 714. Japanese data are for 1995, and U.S. data for 1997.

14. David Flath and Tatsuhiko Nairu, "Is Japan's Retail Sector Truly Distinctive," Working Paper 72, Center on Japanese Economy and Business, Graduate School of Business, Columbia University, November 1992.

15. U.S. percentages calculated from data in U.S. Census Bureau, *Statistical Abstract of the United States: 1998*, pp. 421, 548.

16. Flath and Nairu, "Is Japan's Retail Sector Truly Distinctive."

17. On the department store law, see M. Y. Yoshino, *The Japanese Marketing System: Adaptions and Innovations* (MIT Press, 1971), p. 204.

18. Employment data are from Statistics Bureau, *Japan Statistical Yearbook 1984*, p. 86; *Japan Statistical Yearbook 1998*, p. 74; and U.S. Census Bureau, *Statistical Abstract of the United States: 1998*, p. 422.

19. U.S. Census Bureau, *Statistical Abstract of the United States: 1998*, p. 166.

20. Employment data are from Statistics Bureau, *Japan Statistical Yearbook 2000*; www.stat.go.jp/english/zuyou/b0304000.xls [March 15, 2001], table 3-4, "Employed Persons by Industry and Occupation."

21. Data are from Ministry of International Trade and Industry (MITI), *Chūshō Kigyō Hakusho, Heise: 8-Nenpan* [1996 Medium-Small Business White Paper], statistical supplement, p. 7; and MITI, *Chūshō Kigyō Hakusho 2000-Nenpan* [2000 Medium and Small Business White Paper], statistical supplement, p. 13.

22. Data are calculated from Statistics Bureau, *Japan Statistical Yearbook 2000*, www.stat.go.jp/english/1413-17.htm [May 3, 2001], downloadable table 17-14, "Ordinary Households by Year of Last Move, Type of Previous Residence of Main Earner, Kind of Household, and Tenure of Dwelling."

23. U.S. acquisition rate calculated from data in U.S. Census Bureau, *Statistical Abstract of the United States: 1998*, pp. 720, 722.

Chapter Five

1. Yasusuke Murakami and Thomas P. Rohlen, "Social-Exchange Aspects of the Japan-

ese Political Economy: Culture, Efficiency, and Change," in Shumpei Kumon and Henry Rosovsky, eds., *The Political Economy of Japan*, vol. 3: *Cultural and Social Dynamics* (Stanford University Press, 1992), p. 77.

2. Include in this list Ruth Benedict, *The Chrysanthemum and the Sword: Patterns of Japanese Culture* (World Publishing, 1946); Takeo Doi, *The Anatomy of Dependence* (Tokyo: Kodansha International, 1973); Chie Nakane, *Japanese Society* (University of California Press, 1970); Takie Sugiyama Lebra and William P. Lebra, eds., *Japanese Culture and Behavior: Selected Readings* (University of Hawaii Press, 1974); and, in a lighter journalistic vein, Robert Whiting, *The Chrysanthemum and the Bat: Baseball Samurai Style* (Dodd, Mead, 1977).

3. Ronald Dore, *Japanese Factory, British Factory: The Origins of National Diversity in Industrial Relations* (University of California Press, 1973), and his *Taking Japan Seriously: A Confucian Perspective on Leading Economic Issues* (Stanford University Press, 1987) are examples of this attempt to ascribe economic success to various social aspects, such as the dynamics of group behavior.

4. For example, see "Telecommunications: In Japan, Teens Gab, Gab, Gab—Cell Phones Fad Links 'Pen' Pals in Faceless Talk," *Wall Street Journal*, July 6, 1999, p. A17. Cell phone usage by teenagers is touted as an example of a new individuality.

5. In the interest of brevity, I cannot describe the complete array of caveats and qualifications that might apply in delineating the distinctions between Japan and the United States, but I hope the reader will not take umbrage at excessively broad or naive stereotypes.

6. For an excellent set of analyses on the role of early education in fashioning Japanese social behavior, see the symposium, "Social Control and Early Socialization," *Journal of Japanese Studies*, vol. 15 (Winter 1989), pp. 5–40, especially the introductory essay by Thomas P. Rohlen, "Order in Japanese Society: Attachment, Authority, and Routine."

7. Francis Fukuyama, *Trust: The Social Virtues and the Creation of Prosperity* (London: Penguin, 1995), pp. 23–32, 49–57, 149–207.

8. This attribute is important enough to have spawned an entire analytical book. See Takeo Doi, *The Anatomy of Dependence* (Tokyo: Kodansha International, 1971).

9. For an exposition on *oyabun-kokun* relationships, see Tadashi Fukutake, *The Japanese Social Structure: Its Evolution in the Modern Century* (University of Tokyo Press, 1982), pp. 49–56.

10. Rodney Clark, *The Japanese Company* (Yale University Press, 1979), especially pp. 95–97.

11. Rohlen, "Order in Japanese Society," p. 21.

12. John Owen Haley, *Authority without Power: Law and the Japanese Paradox* (Oxford University Press, 1991), pp. 106–08.

13. *Report of Corporate Legal Study Group (Kigyo Hosei Kenkyukai) for Research on Economic Activity and the Judicial System*, May 9, 2000, http://www.meti.go.jp/ english/report/data/gCorpMaine.html [April 30, 2001].

14. Koji Taira, *Economic Development and the Labor Market in Japan* (Columbia University Press, 1970), pp. 98–164.

15. See for example, Masahiko Aoki, *Information, Incentives, and Bargaining in the Japanese Economy* (Cambridge University Press, 1988), p. 50.

16. For a discussion of corporate training programs, see Thomas P. Rohlen, "Sponsorship of Cultural Continuity in Japan: A Company Training Program," in Lebra and Lebra, eds., *Japanese Culture and Behavior*, pp. 333–41.

17. Ministry of Labor, www2.mhlw.go.jp/info/hakusyo/josei/990126/ 990126_04_j_zu1-4.html [May 2, 2001] and www2.mhlw.go.jp/kisya/daijin/20000808_01_d/20000808_01_d_hyou2.html [May 2, 2001].

18. Mike Zielenziger, "Nissan to Put Finishing Touches on Brand Strategy, CEO Says," *San Jose Mercury News*, November 19, 1999.

19. "MMC Hid Customer Complaints for 30 Years," *Daily Yomiuri*, August 16, 2000.

20. Stefan Wagstyl, "Ratings Maverick Makes His Mark," *Financial Times*, March 23, 1989, p. 40.

21. On American corporate governance, see, for example, Margaret M. Blair, *Ownership and Control: Rethinking Corporate Governance for the Twenty-First Century* (Brookings, 1995).

22. See, for example, "ROE Jōi ni 'Shinsangumi,'" [The "Collection of New Participants" in the Upper Ranks of ROE], *Nihon Keizai Shimbun*, 3d section, p. SB1, June 30, 1999.

23. *Tsūsan Sangyōsho Meikan, 1999-Nenpan* [MITI Directory, 1999 Edition] (Tokyo: Jihyōsha, 1999), pp. 3–298.

24. *Okurasho Meikan, 1999-Nenpan* [Ministry of Finance Directory, 1999 edition] (Tokyo: Jihy_sha 1999), pp. 3–265.

25. Richard J. Samuels, *"Rich Nation Strong Army": National Security and Technological Transformation of Japan* (Cornell University Press, 1994).

26. See Edward J. Lincoln, *Japan Facing Economic Maturity* (Brookings, 1987), pp. 130–210.

27. For example, Kent Calder makes much of the 1950s example of Kawasaki Steel's building a major new plant in opposition to government pressures. See Kent E. Calder, *Strategic Capitalism: Private Business and Public Purpose in Japanese Industrial Finance* (Princeton University Press, 1993), pp. 183–95.

Chapter Six

1. Steven A. Morrison and Clifford Winston, "The Remaining Role of Government Policy in the Deregulated Airline Industry," draft paper, February 2000.

2. Akemi Nakamura, "Deregulation Likely to Send Air Fares into Nosedive," *Japan Times*, February 1, 2000.

3. Arthur Alexander, "Japan's Aviation Industry: Deregulation Advances on Broad Front," *JEI Report*, no. 21A, May 26, 2000, pp. 6–8.

4. "Additional Slots at Haneda Sought for Skymark, AirDo," *Japan Times*, February 29, 2000.

5. Flights and fares based on the October 2000 schedules published by AirDo, JAL, ANA, and JAS.

6. "Hokkaido Government, Business Plan to Help AirDo out of Trouble," *Japan Digest*, September 15, 2000, p. 5.

7. "Japan's Major Airlines Begin Tokyo-Osaka Shuttle Service," *Japan Times*, July 2, 2000; and "JAL, ANA, JAS Share Counters at Haneda, Kansai Airports," *Japan Times*, September 21, 2000.

8. "Kōkū 3-sha no Kyōtsū Saito, Kakaku mo 'Kyōtsū'" [The Unified Site for the Three Airlines, Unified Pricing as Well], *Nikkei Business*, August 4, 2000, p. 8.

9. Edward J. Lincoln, *Japan Facing Economic Maturity* (Brookings, 1988), pp. 169–210.

10. U.S. Census Bureau, *Statistical Abstract of the United States: 1997* (Government Printing Office), p. 511.

11. Calculated from data in Bank of Japan, flow of funds charts, asset and liability chart, and Excel spreadsheet downloaded from Bank of Japan website, www.boj.or.jp/en/down/siryo/dsiryo00.htm [March 20, 2001].

12. "Merger Prompted by Other Banks' Tie-Ups," *Daily Yomiuri*, October 15, 1999, p. 14.

13. Terumitsu Otsu, "Big Bang: Norinchukin Bank Adapts to Big Bang in Its Own Way," *Daily Yomiuri*, February 8, 2000.

14. John Neuffer, "Behind the Screen: Japan's Lawmakers Backpedal on Reforms," www.thestreet.com/comment/screen/855701.html [March 20, 2001, January 9, 2000; and John Neuffer, "Behind the Screen: Japan's GDP Slowdown Renews Obuchi's License to Spend," www.thestreet.com/comment/screen/837226.htm [March 20, 2001], December 12, 1999.

15. "Ginkogyō e no Igyūshu Sannyū: Jimin Chōsakai mo Giron" [Entry of Other Businesses into Banking: LDP Study Group Will Also Debate], *Nihon Keizai Shimbun*, February 5, 2000, p. 5.

16. Gillian Tett and Michiyo Nakamoto, "Reform Runs into Sands of Electoral Expediency," *Financial Times*, January 14, 2000, p. 15.

17. "MITI to Become METI," Daily Yomiuri Online, September 10, 2000, p. 5. This official English name is not an exact translation of the ministry's new name in Japanese, which would be Ministry of the Economy and Industry.

18. For details on the process of producing the plan for administrative reform, see Ko Mishima, "The Changing Relationship between Japan's LDP and the Bureaucracy," *Asian Survey*, vol. 38, no. 10 (October 1998), pp. 968–85.

19. Aurelia George Mulgan, "Japan's Political Leadership Deficit," *Australian Journal of Political Science*, vol. 35 (July 2000), p. 198.

20. In 2000, the new Development Bank of Japan employed 1,387 people; in 1998, the JDB employed 1,102 people and the Hokkaido Tohoku Development Finance Corporation 287 (for a combined total of 1,389). Data are from "Development Bank of Japan: Profile," www.jdb.go.jp/about/profile01_e.html [April 26, 2001]; "Welcome to North East Finance of Japan," www.iijnet.or.jp/NEF/english/index-e.htm [November 11, 2000]; and Japan Development Bank, Annual Report, 1998, p. 2.

21. "Japan Replaces Leader of Bank Overhaul Agency," *New York Times*, October 6, 1999, p. C4.

22. "Mori Selects New Cabinet," *Japan Times Online*, http://www.japantimes.co.jp/cgi-bin/getarticle.pl5?nn20000705a1.htm [March 30, 2001].

23. Peter Landers, "Appointment Roils Japan Markets," *Wall Street Journal*, August 1, 2000, p. A17; "Aizawa's Appointment to FRC May Spell Bad News for Financial Reform," *Japan Digest*, vol. 11, no. 137 (August 1, 2000).

24. Bill Prindle, "Japan's Post Office Keeps Deposits Many Hoped Would Go to Stocks," *Wall Street Journal*, May 1, 2000, p. A24; and Shigeru Asai, "Iyoiyo 'Yūchokin manē Tairyō Shōkan,'" [The Rising 'Repayment of Large Amounts of Postal Savings Money'], *Nikkei Business*, September 18, 2000, p. 155. In the two years beginning in April 2000, ¥106 trillion in ten-year accounts mature, of which ¥25 trillion must be withdrawn because they will exceed the ¥10 million limit on individual accounts.

25. "Yūcho no Manki shikin Azukekae wa 1-wari" [Shift in Maturing Savings Funds 10 Percent], *Nihon Keizai Shimbun*, September 21, 2000, p. 5.

26. For an analysis that reaches a similar conclusion on the likelihood of household savings' continuing to flow to Postal Savings, see Arthur Alexander, "Where Will Japan's Maturing Postal Savings Go?" *JEI Report*, no. 15A, April 14, 2000.

27. Bank of Japan, *Economic Statistics Annual 1989*, pp. 221–22; www.boj.or.jp/en/siryo/siryo_f.htm (downloadable zip file "Flow of Funds Accounts for the Calendar Year 2000 [Preliminary]," sj00cy.zip.

28. Details of the proposed changes to the FILP are contained in "Fundamental Reform of the Fiscal Investment and Loan Program (FILP)," www.mof.go.jp/english/zaito/zae054a.htm; and "Summary of the Discussion Concerning Fundamental Reform of the Fiscal Investment and Loan Program (Working Groups in Subcommittee of Fund Operation Council)," www.mof.go.jp/zaito/zae054b.htm [March 21, 2001]; and www.mof.go.jp/english/zaito/zae055.htm [March 21, 2001].

29. Yumiko Miyai, "Loan Program Reform Doubts Surface," *Daily Yomiuri*, June 6, 2000, p. 7.

30. "Zaitō Kikan Saihatsu wa Jigyōgaku no 2% Teido" [Bond Issues by FILP Organizations to Be about 2 Percent of Their Totals], *Nihon Keizai Shimbun*, September 1, 2000, p. 5.

31. "Tomadoi no Zaitō Kaikaku Shidō" [Uncertain Start to FILP Reform], *Asahi Shimbun*, August 22, 2000, p. 13.

32. "The Role of Government and Its Financial Resources," www.mof.go.jp/zaito/zaito99e.html (the same photo appears in the Japanese language version of this site—www.mof.go.jp/zaito/zaito99.html [March 21, 2001]).

33. For the origins of this project in 1959 and the political ups and downs of Tokyo Bay development plans in the 1960s and 1970s, see Richard J. Samuels, *The Politics of Regional Policy in Japan: Localities Incorporated* (Princeton University Press, 1983), pp. 161–237.

34. Douglas Ostrom, "Tokyo's Changing Role in Financial Markets: Taking a Step Backward?" *JEI Report*, no. 43A, November 12, 1999, p. 9.

35. Ibid., p. 8.

36. "Most Big Banks' Loans to Small Firms Exceed FY '99 Target," *Japan Digest*, vol. 11,

no. 102, June 9, 2000, p.2; "Dozen Recapitalized Banks Missed Their FY '98 Consumer Lending Goals," *Japan Digest*, July 23, 1999.

37. "Handōtai ōkoku o Saisei Seyo" [Let's Revive the Kingdom of Semiconductors], *Asahi Shimbun*, August 15, 2000, p. 9.

38. "IT Kokka Senryaku, Nennai ni: Senryaku Kaigi Kettei" [An IT-Nation Strategy within the Year: Strategy Meeting Decision], *Nihon Keizai Shimbun*, August 31, 2000, p. 5.

39. See "'Chūkaku Jigyō' Shūchū ga Jōken" [Measures to Concentrate on 'Core Business'], *Nihon Keizai Shimbun*, July 13, 1999, p. 5.

40. Maki Hishikawa, "'Big MITI' Looms in Tokyo Plan," *Journal of Commerce*, March 4, 1999, p. 5A; and "Bills Raise Fears of Bureaucratic Control," *Nikkei Weekly*, August 2, 1999, p. 2.

41. Ministry of International Trade and Industry, "Law for Facilitating Creation of New Business," February, 1999, at www.meti.go.jp/english/report/data/glp1102e.html [March 21, 2001].

42. "Jūden mēkā no Saihen Hitsuyo; Tsūsansho no kenkyūkai ga Hōkokusho" [Reorganization of Heavy Electrical Equipment Makers Necessary: Report by MITI Study Group], *Asahi Shimbun*, June 28, 1999.

43. "Japan Plans Biotech Strategy to Catch up with West, Create Jobs," *Japan Digest*, February 19, 1999, p. 5; and Science and Technology Agency, Ministry of Education, Ministry of Health and Welfare, Ministry of Agriculture, Forestry, and Fisheries, and Ministry of International Trade and Industry, *Biotekunoroji Sangyō no Sōzō ni Muketa Kihon Senryaku* [A Basic Strategy to Create a Biotechnology Industry], unpublished report released July 13, 1999. See especially pp. 4–5.

44. Ministry of International Trade and Industry, *Summary of the Report on the Vision of Japan's Textile Industry and Ideal Policies for the Industry*, December 1998.

45. "National Land Agency to Create New Industrial Zones in Tokyo, Osaka Areas," *Japan Digest*, January 7, 1999.

46. "MITI to Subsidize Development of Jetliner," *Daily Yomiuri*, August 20, 1998, p. 1.

47. "MITI, Private Sector to Develop Stronger Material for Aircraft," *Daily Yomiuri*, February 4, 2000, p. 14.

48. "Ministry to Help Satellite Business," *Asahi Shimbun*, September 16, 1998.

49. "ITS Kanmin de Kaihatsu" [Developing Intelligent Transportation Systems Through Government-Business Cooperation], *Nihon Keizai Shimbun*, July 8, 1999, p. 1.

50. "2001: Japan's Internet Odyssey," *Nikkei Weekly*, December 6, 1999, p. 4.

51. "Chūshō Kigyō no Jōhōka Suishin" [Promoting the Informationalization of Medium and Small Business], *Nihon Keizai Shimbun*, December 6, 1999, p. 1.

52. Ministry of Agriculture, Forestry, and Fisheries, *Annual Report on Japanese Agriculture FY 1998 (Summary)*, www.muff.go.jp/hakusyo/kaigai/ehakusyo.pdf [May 3, 2001]/

53. "Postal Ministry Will Try to Jump Start E-Commerce with Free Lines," *Japan Digest*, vol. 11, no. 18 (February 1, 2000).

54. "Kigyō no Saizensen: Kanmin Shien Taisei Hirogaru" [The Front Line of Business: Broadening the Government-Business Support System], *Nihon Keizai Shimbun*, June 1999, p. 15.

55. "Government to Set Up Online System to Improve Freight Services," *Daily Yomiuri*, February 1, 2000, http://www.yomiuri.co.jp/newse/o201ec17.htm.

56. "Keizai Kyōshitsu: Kanmingaku de Senryaku Suishin Kikan o" [Establishing a Government-Industry-Academic Strategic Promotion Institution], *Nihon Keizai Shimbun*, November 3, 1999, p. 27.

57. "Kōteki Shien, Zeisei·Yūshi de Oneigai!" [Requesting Public Support through Taxes and Financing!], *Asahi Shimbun*, November 9, 1999, p. 11.

58. "Gijutsu Kaihatsu Kanmin Kyōdō Purojekkuto: Dijitaru Jōhō Shakai Kōchiku" [Government-Business Cooperative Technology Development Projects: Building a Digital Information Society], *Nihon Keizai Shimbun*, June 28, 1999, p. 3.

59. "Kigyō Saizensen: Kanmin no Shien Taisei Hirogaru" [The Front Line of Business: Broadening the Government-Business Support System], *Nihon Keizai Shimbun*, June 15, 1999, p. 15.

60. For further discussion of *amakudari* and changes in the 1990s, see Edward J. Lincoln, *Troubled Times: U.S.-Japan Trade Relations in the 1990s* (Brookings, 1999), pp. 190–99.

61. "Bōeikanbu Amakudari: 756-nin" [756 Defense High-Level Bureaucrat Amakudari], *Asahi Shimbun*, February 21, 2000, p. 1.

62. Hiromi Ochiai, "Keisatsuchō Amakudari 165-nin Jitsumei Risuto" [A List of Actual Names of 165 National Police Agency Amakudari], *Bungei Shunju*, January 2000, pp. 94–109.

63. "New Law Lets Aging Bureaucrats Stay on Past 60, at Half Pay," *Japan Digest*, vol. 10, no. 21, July 15, 1999, p. 5.

64. Statistics Bureau, *Japan Statistical Yearbook 1998*, p. 80; internet version www.stat.go.jp/english/1431-03htm, downloadable table 3-1, "Population 15 Years Old and Over by Labor Force Status"; and Statistics Bureau, Labor Force Survey, www.stat.go.jp/english/154a.htm, "Latest Monthly Results" [March 21, 2001].

65. Statistics Bureau, *Japan Statistical Yearbook 1998*, p. 92. Fourteen percent is the average separation rate for the years 1993–95.

66. "NKK 4000-nin Sakugen e" [NKK toward a 4,000-person Reduction], *Asahi Shimbun*, February 4, 2000, p. 2.

67. "JT ga Risutora-saku Happyō, Kaigai de mo 3-nen de 2000-nin Sakugen" [JT Announces Restructuring Plan: Even Overseas Down 2000 People in Three Years], *Asahi Shimbun*, www.asahi.com/0201/news/business01024.htm.

68. "Ote 10-Kō, Risutora Kasoku" [Restructuring Accelerates at the Big Ten Banks], *Asahi Shimbun*, June 13, 2000, p. 8.

69. Douglas Ostrom, "Corporate Japan's Restructuring Efforts: A Progress Report," *JEI Report*, no. 20A, May 19, 2000, pp. 7–11.

70. Bank of Japan, www.boj.or.jp/en/siryo/siryo_f.htm [May 3, 2001].

71. Shoichi Sakuma, "Kabushiki Mochiai Kaishō ni Gensoku Kenen?" [Concern over a Slowdown in the Elimination of Share Cross-Holdings?], *Nikkei Business*, September 4, 2000, pp. 6–7.

72. "NKK, Kawasaki Steel Plan to Merge Themselves in a Holding Company," *Japan Digest*, vol. 11, no. 187, October 26, 2000, p. 5.

73. Tatsumi Yamada, "Status of Current Japanese Accounting Standards—Recent Developments in International Harmonization," unpublished paper, March 1999.

74. "M&A Kensu Saidai ni" [M&A Cases at a High], *Asahi Shimbun*, January 8, 2000, p. 11.

75. Calculated from data in Lincoln, *Troubled Times*, p. 97.

76. Bill Spindle, "Japanese Companies Speed Up Sales of Cross-Holdings," *Wall Street Journal*, March 7, 2000, p. A18.

77. For pessimistic analyses of this merger, see Calvin Sims, "Japan Bank Merger Carries Old Burdens," *New York Times*, September 7, 1999; and Yumiko Suzuki, "Mizuho Merger Losing Its Luster," *Nikkei Weekly*, September 25, 2000, p. 1.

78. See Lincoln, *Troubled Times*, pp. 79–103.

79. "Nationalism Allowed Softbank to Buy NCB for ¥60 Billion Less Than Cerebus Bid," *Japan Digest*, vol. 11, no. 34 (February 28, 2000), p. 2; and Stephanie Strom, "Group Led by Softbank Wins Right to Buy Nippon Credit," *New York Times*, February 25, 2000, p. C4, www.nytimes.com/00/02/25/news/financial/japan-bank.html.

80. "Sangyō Saisei: Bei Dake ga Temoto Jyanai" [Industrial Revival: The United States Is Not the Only Way], *Asahi Shimbun*, August 25, 1999, p. 12.

81. Hiroyuki Takahashi, "Corporate Governance in Japan: Reform of Top Corporate Management Structure," *JEI Report*, no. 28a, July 23, 1999, p. 3. This article lists twenty-three corporations that have reduced their boards from twenty to forty-five members to a range of nine to twenty-six.

82. Andrew Pollack, "Japanese Companies Take New Look at Western Management Ideas," *New York Times*, May 23, 1997, p. D1.

83. "Sony no Shinkeiei Taisei wa 'Raisu bāgā-gata,' Utswa wa Beikokufu da ga Nakami wa Junwafu, Torishimeyakukai Menbā no Kahansu ga Shikkō Gyōmu Kenin" [Sony's New Management Style Is a 'Rice Burger': The Vessel Is American-Style but the Contents Are Pure Japanese, with over Half of the Board of Directors Holding Simultaneous Managerial Positions], *Nikkei Business*, no. 1041, May 15, 2000, pp. 4–5.

84. "Hetta 'Igi Nashi' Taiwa Jūshi e Ippo" [Declining 'No Questions,' One Step toward Dialogue], *Nihon Keizai Shimbun*, June 30, 1999.

85. "Sokaiya Presence Dwindles," *Daily Yomiuri Online*, www.yomiuri.co.jp/newse/0329cr07.htm.

86. "ROE Jōi ni 'Shinsangumi'" [The "Collection of New Participants" in the Upper Ranks of the ROE], *Nihon Keizai Shimbun*, June 30, 1999, p. SB-1.

87. Arthur J. Alexander, "The Japanese Economy in Transition," *JEI Report*, no. 44, November 19, 1999, pp. 4–5.

88. Robert A. Feldman, "Japan RoA Whodunit (I)—Every Nook and Cranny," Morgan Stanley Dean Witter Global Economic Forum, May 31, 2000, www.morganstanley.com/gefdata/digests/20000531-wed.html#anchor1 [May 3, 2001].

Chapter Seven

1. Mikiko Miyakawa, "Economy Has Growth Potential of 2.3 Percent," *Daily Yomiuri Online,* January 27, 1999.

2. Industrial Structure Council, "Challenges and Prospects for Economic and Industrial Policy in the 21st Century—Building a Competitive, Participatory Society," March 16, 2000, p. 4, www.meti.go.jp/english/report/data/gpros21e.pdf [April 11, 2001].

3. Economic Council, Main Points of "Ideal Socieconomy and Policies for Economic Rebirth," July 5, 1999, pp. 1–2, www5.cao.go.jp/99/e/19990705e-keishin-e.html [March 15, 2001].

4. Statistics Bureau, *Japan Statistical Yearbook,* www.stat.go.jp/english/1431-02.htm [March 15, 2001], downloadable table 2-9, "Population by Age Group and Indexes of Age Structure." Data are based on 1998; the change for 2000–20 should be close to the 1998–2018 change.

5. U.S. Department of Commerce, *Statistical Abstract of the United States, 1999* (Government Printing Office), pp. 805–08.

6. Ibid., p. 797.

7. Bank of Japan, *Balance of Payments Monthly,* April 2000, p. 159.

8. Edward J. Lincoln, *Troubled Times: U.S.-Japan Trade Relations in the 1990s* (Brookings, 1999), pp. 87–88.

9. For an extensive discussion of gaiatsu, see Leonard Schoppa, *Bargaining with Japan: What American Pressure Can and Cannot Do* (Columbia University Press, 1997).

10. For a discussion of the changes in the 1980s underwriting this new confidence and some of the directions in which it could have been directed, see Edward J. Lincoln, *Japan's New Global Role* (Brookings, 1993).

11. See Eisuke Sakakibara, *Beyond Capitalism: The Japanese Model of Market Economics* (University Press of America, 1993); Eisuke Sakakibara, "Mr. Yen Looking Back / 'Cybercapitalism' World Needs Map," *Daily Yomiuri Online,* January 31, 2000.

Index